A HISTORY OF ORAL INTERPRETATION

by

EUGENE BAHN, Ph.D.
Department of Speech
Wayne State University

and

MARGARET L. BAHN, M.A.

Library of Congress Catalog Card Number 73-103404
Standard Book Number 8087-0260-2

Front Cover. *Rhapsode Reciting,* detail from an Attic red-figured amphora, about 480 B.C. Reproduced by courtesy of The British Museum, London.

Dedicated to
Our Parents
and to
Meg

FOREWORD

It has been said that the writing of the history of any subject indicates that that subject has attained a certain stage of maturity and has been able to look back in perspective over its accomplishments or lack of accomplishments. It is indeed strange that the history of the oral interpretation of literature has not attracted more attention than it has over its three thousand or more years of existence. Certainly, very brief portions are found in a few isolated passages in nineteenth century books, and less is found in eighteenth century writings. In the twentieth century, articles, theses and dissertations have been written on certain periods and persons. There has been, however, no attempt, so far as the writers know, to give a somewhat continuous picture through some twenty-five or more centuries. In the present study the authors have endeavored to establish a chain of events extending from early Greek days to twentieth century America. Such a chain necessitates omitting the activities in this field in many countries all of which, it is hoped, will be investigated in the future. This present undertaking has been a fascinating project in that it follows the cultural patterns of development that extend from the miracle of Greece to the continent of America.

As one looks at the vast historical background of the oral interpretation of literature there is much of which we can be justly proud. Like all activities of man there are times when its contributions leave something to be desired, but when it served a vital purpose in the culture and life of a people it reached memorable heights. We hope that, in our own age, its contributions will be worthy of recognition over the span of history.

We wish to thank Elizabeth G. Youngjohn, George V. Bohman, Jacob E. Nyenhuis, Diether Haenicke, Evelyn M. Sivier, George Masterton, Clyde M. Vinson, William A. Boyce, Julie Paulson, and Virginia Fredricks for their suggestions and assistance in more ways than one.

Eugene Bahn
Margaret Linton Bahn

Grosse Pointe Park, Michigan

TABLE OF CONTENTS

Boy Reciting Poetry for His Teacher. Copyright. Courtesy Staatliche Museen, Berlin.

Chapter I
CLASSICAL GREECE

The greatest of man's treasures is the tongue
Which wins most favor when it spares its words
And measured is of movement.
Hesiod

A blind man, sitting cross-legged in the sundrenched courtyard of the mosque of Omar, from his lips a monotonous outpouring of the words of the Koran; it was a sight as old as our civilization and awesome in its antiquity. Did this old man in the ragged tunic and dusty turban have any idea that by this verbal rendition of literature he was carrying on a tradition even older than the Koran itself? Probably not. He seemed a simple soul unversed in ancient history, yet seeing him and listening to his wailing chant, the mind slid back through the centuries and across the miles to his predecessors in this ancient art.

From Jerusalem in the atomic age to Athens in the age of Pericles is a mental journey of some magnitude. It gives one pause to think that, in the face of all that has changed in the world between these two milestones in the history of western man, this tradition of oral recitation has continued in unbroken continuity.

The story begins in Greece, with Homer and the great men who followed him. Their thoughts and words were to build a literary tradition so sure and strong that it was to provide a solid foundation for the culture of our western world. In going back to the days in Ancient Greece when gods and men were closely entwined in the human concept we find similar desires and passions voiced then that cry aloud out of man's deepest needs today.

"The Miracle of Greece" is a phrase used tritely and unthinkingly today, yet rightly comprehended it leaves the mind stunned by the wonder of it. A land about the size of Portugal with a total population no larger than many modern cities, poor in natural resources, with barren and rocky hills baking under a clear bright sun—this was Greece. If greatness be reckoned in material wealth, she had small hope of fame. Though barren, she was beautiful, and beauty was to be her gift to the world. The clear minds of her thinkers matched the clear sky above them and even today this clarity has not been dimmed; the Greek mind both collectively and individually is alert and bright. And Greece had another great advantage. She lay at the eastern end of the Mediterranean Sea at a time when "mediterranean" was an accurate description of that sea's location and when all that we think of as civilization still came from the east. She was virtually an island, and her very poverty drove her sons to the seas for sustenance and thence led them to adventuring in far-away places. The land of the Pharoah in the days of its glory lay within reach of Greek ships, and the riches of Egyptian culture contributed to the flowering of Greek arts.

The sudden rise of Greece as the intellectual center of the world is as spectacular and dramatic as the legend of the birth of Athena who emerged full-grown from the head of Zeus. Even so did the Greek mind suddenly burst upon the world to be revered, like Athena, for its wisdom and power. In a brief flowering man's thinking process, his ability to analyze and evaluate, was to reach levels hitherto unthought of in the field of human achievement. The Greek genius was to take human emotion, primitive and untamed, and wed it to intellect to bring forth great art. Whether this union was brought about by Athena or by Athens, who shall say? Or care! The offspring are still with us, and it is possible to trace their line of descent through the ages. The branch of the family to be considered here is the art of oral literature.

Literature, to the Greek, was essentially something to hear or to say rather than to read. Blessed with a language amazingly rich and flexible, having a keen sense of the possibilities of that language and a passion for using it, the Greek sought supremacy in vocal combat as eagerly as he sought victory by force of arms. And he respected it no less. He engaged in verbal tournaments with his family, with his friends, and with any cronies he chanced to meet when he sallied forth to take a stroll in the agora. Indeed nothing pleased him more than to find a likely opponent for an intellectual duel. With sharp words he could try a thrust, a parry, a retreat and again a thrust to catch his opponent off guard and win the applause of the crowd for a point well taken in debate. Socrates is the best known example, and his debates, as recorded by Plato, are a valued part of literature to this day. This game of discussion made a tremendous contribution to the development of Greek culture; these combats not only sharpened the wits of the participants but held and preserved their thoughts for the delectation of future generations as fathers told their sons what the great teachers had said. Such oral debates opened up a new realm of excellence in which the abstract and the symbolic could come to fruition and in which a man's mind could bring him a prestige as great as that which he could earn by physical prowess. It was a long step forward for civilization and in this verbal arena our culture took shape.

Orators have come and gone, but taken as a general type the average Greek is still fluent. No longer expatiating in the agora of old, Greek men gather regularly of an evening in towns and villages today to discuss politics, education, or the news of the day. In many villages there are two coffee shops—patronized by members of two opposing political parties—and the debaters lack nothing in vehemence and seriousness to make them full-blooded descendants of the men who walked and talked in the ancient agora.

Spoken Word

To the Greeks of the classical era few things were more important than the power of the spoken word. They set such store by it that they were loath to entrust their most sacred truths to any other form of communication so that writing had a hard time striking roots in that vocal soil. To Greeks the spoken word was a living thing and infinitely to be preferred to the dead symbols of a written language. One is reminded of Dr. Burton Sanderson's definition of life. Speaking before the British Association in 1899, he developed the idea that life is a state of ceaseless change. The Greeks would have accepted this definition with regard to the spoken word, holding to the idea that "that word is most vital which can best transform and transmute itself according to the needs of its surroundings, thereby maintaining with them the most intimate connection . . . . In biological language the best teacher is he who is in most vivid correspondence with his environment . . . ."[1] The written word, by contrast, is rigidly set and unchanging and cannot adapt to new circumstances. This, to the Greeks, looked like the rigidity of death and they wanted no part of it. The philosophers, always respected in their state, were particularly reluctant to give up the oral for the written word. Socrates complained that even the very best writing was but a recollection of what one knows. It left no room for growth and development.

Today man is so accustomed to putting his trust in what he can see "written in black and white" rather than in "a merely verbal agreement" that it is hard for him to conceive of a time when the opposite order was preferred. But let us remember that the ultimate aim of either speech or writing is communication. In the days when all literature was oral it was a matter of passing the living word from author to audience. If the hearer did not understand, he could question the author at once, and explanations could be offered to make the meaning clear. Or perhaps the hearer might not agree with the author. There and then, by argument and discussion, author and audience could clear up any misunderstanding and, if necessary, adjust the author's words to arrive at a mutually acceptable statement. In this situation where the author was the speaker two people could complete the circle of communication.

Today much of oral literature filters through written symbols on its journey from author to audience, and from the author's written symbols the speaker or actor communicates and interprets the author's thought to the audience. There are few television or radio shows without a script of some kind. The accuracy with which an oral interpreter can recreate the living thought which the author primarily tried to embody in dead symbols must depend greatly upon (a) the accuracy of the symbols used (the author's responsibility), and (b) thorough comprehension of the meaning attached to those symbols (the educator's responsibility), and (c) the sensitive response to those symbols (the interpreter's responsibility). When all three are adequate the result is a good reproduction of the original thought. All that is then needed to complete the circle of communication is a receptive hearer. In this case four people are needed to complete the circle.

Elements of Oral Communication

The Greeks made valiant efforts to eliminate the middle men and avoid the dead elements in all matters of deep concern to them. The oral tradition was no mere ornament on the temple of knowledge to be discerned occasionally in the maze of design. It was the very stuff of every pillar supporting that temple, for it was upon oral tradition that the temple was built. Law and religion, for instance, were far too vitally important to be subjected to the restraint of dead symbols.

Oral tradition

Recognizing that the most permanent often appeared to be the most impermanent, the Greeks were convinced that what was planted in the minds of men had the greatest hope of survival for it was etched not on tablets of crumbling clay but in the living consciousness of mankind. They had looked to the east and to the south and they saw that little of tangible significance remained of once great powers such as Assyria, Media, Babylonia, Lydia and Egypt. Only that which had become part of man's mind remained. Some of the best of this thought had been handed down orally from one age to another and had thereby become indestructible.

In this world of words what power the skillful speaker held on the tip of his tongue. The sons of Aesculapius were not slow to put this fact to use. Empedocles, renowned physician of his day, was ready to attest to the value of words in the treatment of disorders of the mind or of the body. Songs and incantations were part of his stock-in-trade and dramatic indeed were some of the cures attributed to their efficacy. He tells of one man so possessed by the furies that he was ready to murder his own father. He was brought back to a more normal frame of mind by Empedocles himself who chanted soothing words to the accompaniment of his lyre until the violent passions subsided and the patient's mental balance was restored.

As therapy

That the mind was the safest storehouse for matters of vital importance was so taken for granted that long after writing had been invented Aristotle said, evidently with approval, that the Greeks could more easily remember their laws by repeating them aloud. Even today, men are well aware of the power of an unwritten law. It was the Greek belief that the true meaning of the law could be ascertained through discussion and any alleged misunderstanding corrected on the spot. This had the advantage over written laws that it left less opportunity for the unscrupulous to find a loophole in the wording of a law and so free a culprit who offended against the spirit of the law. In his efforts to close every possible loophole modern man has largely proved the validity of the Greek contention; he has found it necessary to develop a legal language so cumbersome that it is usually incomprehensible to those who have most need to understand it. Just men knew what the law was trying to say, and by the flexibility of the living word they were able to interpret justice in the light of the case before them.

Laws recited

To the Greek of early days, a law was not so much a prohibition against doing evil as a piece of good advice on how to oil the machinery of society to assist in the smooth functioning of the community. Law helped man to live at peace with his neighbor, and it was not out of place, nor uncommon, at a social gathering to recite the laws of the land. Often these laws were in rhyme and sometimes set to music so that they were easily remembered, and no doubt they were as widely known as the folk songs of today.

The minstrel

The spoken word thus played its role in the spheres of religion, medicine, and law. Less unusual to modern thought is the Greek idea that oral delivery was necessary to poetry. While it is true that today more people read poetry silently than speak it aloud, few would deny that the symphonious use of sound is one of the most beloved aspects of poetry and that the beauty of poetry can be greatly enhanced by the human voice. "Lend to the rhyme of the poet the beauty of thy voice" was a request which Longfellow would not have had to make of an ancient Greek. How else could poetry be enjoyed? Since poetry was meant to be heard, one of the most respected professions in the ancient world was that of the minstrel. Long before there appeared on the scene any of the names generally accepted as historical, long before Homer (who is himself sometimes regarded as a legendary figure), this art was practiced.

Iliad and *Odyssey*

It is common to think of the works of Homer as being the starting point of Greek literature, but this can hardly have been the case. Rather, these Homeric poems must have been the fruits of long labor in the development of this art. The stories which were brought together to make up the *Iliad* and the *Odyssey* depicted life in the Mycenean civilization of about 1600 B.C., and already at that time the minstrel was recognized as a character of prime importance.

This reciter, this singer, this merchant of words, whose wares would influence every phase of the national character, was the key to unlock the emotions of men. With him lay the responsibility for preserving the annals of the city, for developing national pride, for—inspiring hero worship, for doing honor to the gods and for providing his hearers with pleasant entertainment in their leisure hours. No sinecure this. But if the responsibilities were great so, too, were the rewards. A place of honor at the royal court, the attention and respect of the highest in the land, were accorded the minstrel who perfected his craft.

The skill of these artists impressed men so deeply that they were ready to believe such talent must derive from other than human sources. They felt that the minstrels, more skilled than mortal man, must be taught, or inspired, by the muses or even by the god Apollo himself. Nor were some of the minstrels, at least, unwilling to accept this flattering theory. Phemios, for instance, who practiced his art in Ithaca, once told Odysseus, "I am self-taught; it was a deity that implanted poems of all kinds in my heart."

Demodocus

Of the many whose fame was great in their time only a few names have come down to this day. In the *Odyssey* one reads of Demodocus, a minstrel at the court of Alcinous. This man was treated with the respect and dignity befitting a disciple of Apollo. When the king and his councillors gathered to feast, a chair set with silver was placed for the minstrel who was further honored by being served a goblet of the royal wine. Not as a slave or vassal, but as a successful member of a profession, which even princes were not too proud to practice. Demodocus offered his songs and recitations to the assembled court. That his talents were great may be deduced from a description of his prowess. According to Homer, not once but twice during one recital, he so played upon the emotions of Odysseus that the latter had to cover his face with his cloak to hide his tears. Alcinous finally stopped the performance so that the mood of melancholy would not take such hold of the assembly that gaiety would be banished from the hall. In all probability Demodocus was reciting his own compositions. In any case, his performance so impressed Odysseus that when it was over he personally served food to this respected artist.

The minstrel did not confine his activities to the royal court, although acceptance there was certainly an achievement of which he could justly be proud. In Homeric days he wandered over the land and took part in contests. Thamyris, bard of Thrace, claimed that he had even dared to contest with the muses, a presumption for which those angered spirits struck him blind. However, most minstrels were content to test their skills against other minstrels, frequently starting by winning in small contests and gradually climbing the ladder of fame until they reached the more important festivals.

As time elapsed and the fame of Homer became more deeply rooted, the Greeks longed to hear more frequently the stories of their gods and of their ancestors. To satisfy this popular desire there arose another type of reciter known as a rhapsode. The rhapsode was an itinerant performer who wandered over Greece from city to city and from festival to festival. Rhapsodes originated in the Ionian district, which has been sometimes regarded as Homer's birthplace, and were variously known as rhapsodes, Homeridai, disciples of Homer, or "singers of stitched lays." Proud of their profession, they developed the art of recitative and in course of time banded themselves into guilds. The earliest reference to them occurs in the sixth century B.C. by which time they were evidently so well established that Cleisthenes (600-560 B.C.) feared the power which they wielded, especially since the theme of their lays was the glorification of what he most hated—Argos and the Argives. Rather than listen to enemy propaganda being declaimed in the grand manner by these influential speakers, Cleisthenes had them suppressed during his reign. This was probably good political strategy, for the rhapsodes were the history teachers and moulders of public opinion as well as the entertainers of their day. They were also the publishers in a society where knowledge was spread not by books but by spoken words. To this day it is difficult to draw a definite line between entertainer, commentator, and propagandist.

The rhapsode

Cleisthenes

Although the rhapsodes did not find favor with Cleisthenes, they did not lack for followers. Dressed in gorgeous robes and dramatic in their delivery, they had great popular appeal. Appearing before large audiences they usually performed in the open air. This perhaps explains the different methods of delivery which they seem to have developed. The minstrels had used a lyre while they recited, but the rhapsodes, if they used a lyre at all, probably did so only at the beginning of their performance to set the pitch of the voice. They are credited not only with replacing song with recitation, but also with divorcing narrative verse from music, a development which had widespread effects in freeing the spoken word; great clarity of thought apart from the emotional quality of music and musical poetry then developed. Instead of the lyre, the symbol of their profession came to be the myrtle or laurel staff which they perhaps used to emphasize the rhythm or to give grandeur to their gestures. The rhapsodes declaimed in a theatrical manner with gesture and varying inflections of the voice. We can imagine the scene; an exuberant audience and the chatter of voices rising to a pitch of intense emotion, then subsiding as the rhapsode stepped to the center of the platform. The spell he cast upon his listeners seemed to bring before their eyes Hector, Achilles, Priam and Helen as the characters of legend marched across the stage of memory and the glory of Greece filled their minds.

Rhapsodes' appearance

Lyre

Staff

The stories which the rhapsodes told were not new. They were the old Homeric tales familiar to almost every Greek, but at least in the early days of their craft, the rhapsodes were free to improvise

Use of Homer

and alter the tales at will. A set form of the Homeric poems was not established until the sixth century B.C.; at this time Cynaethus was in charge of a committee to undertake this task. Until then the rhapsodes had their own versions of the age-old legends; and giving more thought to poetic values than to historical accuracy, they would change them to suit their whims or the temper of a particular audience. One thing only the rhapsode was prohibited from doing—he dared not speak falsely. Exactly what this implied is difficult to say, but it may be that he could alter wording as he wished provided he respected the rhythm, metre, and subject matter.

Cynaethus

Apparently this flexibility left scope for creative rhapsodes, and upon the acceptability of the changes made, as well as upon the rhapsode's personality and ability as a reciter, his reputation was built. His appearance too was of great importance; in Plato's *Ion* Socrates says that a rhapsode must "look beautiful." As time went on and performances became more standardized, even the robes which the rhapsodes wore became more conventionalized. At a later time the rhapsodes recited the *Iliad* in a red and the *Odyssey* in a violet costume.

It can truly be said that the rhapsodes wove a web of wonder wherever they went, yet they were not without their critics. Plato did not have high regard for the logic of the rhapsode. Xenophon, in his *Memorabilia,* quoted Euthydemus as saying that rhapsodes were very foolish men even though they knew the poems of Homer extremely well. Xenophon came back to the same theme in his *Symposium* where he referred to the rhapsodes as stupid. This was on a par with the modern cynics who define an uneducated man as an expert away from his subject. While sharing a wry smile for the modicum of truth in this evaluation, few would deny that the expert is an exceedingly valuable member of society and a highly respected citizen. So it was with the rhapsode. He was respected for his skill in an art which men revered. Even if he knew nothing but Homer, it mattered little, so long as he knew his Homer well. Plato's *Ion* infers that it was a matter of some pride to have given one's whole soul to Homer. When Socrates was interviewing Ion, who had won first prize at the festival of Aesculapius at Epidaurus and was preparing to compete at the Panathenaea, he asked the rhapsode if he could recite from other poets such as Hesiod or Archilochus. Ion responded that he could not. He claimed only "to speak well on any part of Homer" and made it clear that that was enough for any one lifetime. No false modesty prevented him from saying he could interpret Homer better than anybody else who ever lived, not even excepting such celebrities as Metrodorus of Lampascus, Stesimbrotus of Thasos, or Glaucon, and he asked Socrates to explain why this was so.

Plato's *Ion*

Socrates said Ion's ability to speak excellently about Homer was not an art but an inspiration and that a divinity moved on Ion which was like a magnet. Since it is through divine power the poet sings, he can sing only that which the muse impels him to do; if the poet had learned to sing by rules of art, he would know how to speak on many themes and in many types of verse. The divinity takes possession of the minds of the poets and uses them "as his ministers, as he also uses diviners and holy prophets, in order that we who hear them may know that they speak not of themselves who utter these priceless words in a state of unconsciousness, but that God himself is the speaker, and that through them he is conversing with us."[2]

Art versus divine power

While Ion was willing to concede that he was inspired by a god, he was understandably less pleased with the idea that he was possessed by a god and performed in a state of unconsciousness. A good rhapsode reacted to divine inspiration through his own emotions, and Ion admitted that he was transported to tears when he told a piteous tale, and that he was frightened and excited when he related a tale of horror. In other words, he was no mere impersonal voice mechanically reproducing the words of the poet; while he did not say that he became or impersonated the characters, he did respond to their joys and sorrows.

Emotion

Plato touches upon another point of interest to the reciter, namely the knowledge a rhapsode should have of the topics on which he recited; for example, if he told a story of cowherds, charioteers, or physicians, must he know as much about these occupations as these men themselves know? Ion answered no; they would know better than he what to do in a given case. But when asked if the rhapsode should know what a general would say to exhort his soldiers, Ion answered yes. He went on to claim that with Homer as his master he, Ion, could be the most excellent general.

While one may deplore Ion's self-conceit, one cannot but admire his dedication or fail to see the profound influence of Homer upon the life and thought of the time. Illogical and vain as Plato deemed Ion to be, nevertheless the rhapsode's enthusiasm, his pride in his profession, and his reliance on the divine Muse made him a man to be reckoned with, and his skill and his value to the state were not questioned.

Plato did admire the company Ion kept, for his life was lived with the poets. Nor did Plato underrate the unique quality of Ion's skill, for not only did he learn the whole of Homer by rote, as many Greeks did, but by long association with the poet he had come to an understanding of him without which he could never have interpreted the poet's message. The fact that Plato devoted one of his dialogues to the rhapsodes attests to their importance in the social order.

The fame of a rhapsode was usually established through his participation in the great festivals and contests which were so much a part of the life of ancient Greece that they came to be held at regular intervals and at certain places in honor of the gods. To these

Religious festivals

festivals were brought offerings to Apollo, Athena, Demeter or some other favored god, but while the primary significance of these events was religious, the social and intellectual impact of them was no less important. Indeed, it is not too much to say that whatever degree of union was achieved in Greece was brought about by religion, art, and games rather than by politics, and the festivals were, of course, the focal points of these activities. Here men brought to the altar of the gods the best that they had to offer, whether physical prowess or mental acumen.

In a land where the intellect was particularly nurtured, it was natural that, although physical beauty was appreciated and physical prowess revered for the training and discipline which it represented, such temporal values could not be allowed to crowd out the homage due to gifts of more enduring greatness. The spoken word was the most trusted repository for the best of Greek thought, and inducements would be offered to men who set themselves the task of developing minds capable of retaining and voices capable of communicating the treasures of their culture. They were given a respected place in the festival program where, along with other events, music, philosophy, literature, and the oral arts had an opportunity to flourish. Such festivals were held all over Greece in villages, in famous cities, and wherever a holy shrine was found. Among the more renowned were those at Sicyon, Delphi, Olympia, Delos, and Epidaurus, but probably the most famous of all was the Panathenaea, held once only every four years in Athens.

Panathenaea

The Panathenaea! The Olympic games of today cause no more excitement than did the Panathenaea in its time. Every child had heard of it, had listened to tales of how his father or his grandfather had walked miles to worship at the shrine of Athena. How exciting had been the great procession, the colorful banners, the blowing of trumpets, the incense burners swinging forth their enchanting odors, the noble virgins carrying the sacred robe to their goddess, the maidens with garlands, the songs, the brilliant robes of the priests, acolytes, the young horsemen, the chariots, and the dignitaries whose names were household words. Yes—and the humble hawker selling onions, garlic, dates, figs, olives and thyme, sesame seeds, or wine to the hungry, thirsty crowds who would buy of his wares to add to the packet of cheese they had cannily tucked away in the folds of a chiton.

In this great throng attention focuses on the poets and the rhapsodes. In gorgeous robes, the rhapsode was an impressive sight, seemingly no mere mortal, but a being inspired by the gods to re-live the deeds of the great heroes. And his staff—long, slender and eloquent in its use—it, too, had a part to play in the recital. It had its own illustrious history, and who could say which rhapsode was justified in his claim that he possessed the very staff which Hesiod assured the world he had been given by the gods on Mt. Helicon? At the Panathenaea the rhapsodes were at the height of their glory. It was the custom at all such festivals for them to open their part of the events by reciting one of the Hymns or Preludes of Homer. These recitations were, as the name suggests, introductory poems and were addressed to the particular deity—Apollo, Aphrodite, Demeter or Zeus—whom the speaker wished to honor upon that occasion. By the time the Rhapsodists had finished their introductory recitation the audience had had time to settle down and was in the mood to hear the great epics.

Only Homer's poems recited

So great was the importance attached to the Panathenaea that special laws were drawn up regarding the procedure. One law stated that at this event Homer's poems only were to be recited by the rhapsodes. The orator Lycurgus (ca. 390-324 B.C.) says of Homer: "In your father's eyes he was a poet of such worth that they passed a law that every four years at the Panathenaea he alone of all the poets should have his works recited."[3] Originally these poems were probably recited in their entirety, but later it became the custom to break them up into episodes. There may have been several reasons for this. For one thing the poems themselves probably became longer as one rhapsode after another made his alterations and additions to the original and found popular acceptance for his embellishments; but, more specifically, the divisions probably became necessary to meet festival requirements. With the number of rhapsodes competing in these contests it would be physically impossible for an audience to sit through the whole poem several times. Thus it came about that each rhapsode was allotted a certain time to show what he could do. Under these circumstances even disciples of Apollo were no doubt human enough to be tempted to choose that section of the poem which would best display their personal talents and create a sensation by its emotional appeal to the audience. But if too many reciters chose the same section, as could easily have happened, this would become boring to the listeners and would moreover have offended against the Greek ideal of completeness which lies at the core of all their art. Consequently a law was drawn up by Solon (ca. 594 B.C.), or by Hipparchus (527-514 B.C.), which required that one rhapsode should take up the tale where the other left off.[4] Often the Homeric passages lent themselves to something akin to dramatic treatment in that one rhapsode gave the speech of one character and the next the speech of the character who replied. This gave cohesion and logic to the sequence of the recitation besides making it possible for the audience to hear a more varied program. Another law, which probably brought more pleasure to the Athenians than to their Ionian cousins, had to do with the language of the Homeric recitals. This law required that the poems be translated into the Attic tongue instead of remaining in the

Law for reciting

original Ionic speech which was provincial, and therefore, in Athenian eyes at least, quite unworthy to be the vehicle for anything as elevated and important as the *Iliad* and the *Odyssey*.

From the pinnacle of glory there is nowhere to go but down. It was a healthy thing for Greek literature that although Homer was not to be ousted from a place of honor, men realized that poetic creativity had not died with him. Other poets gradually began to steal some of the limelight. And so it was with the rhapsodes. Even as their master had to step aside to make room for other men, so did they in turn find their province being invaded by men who were not of their profession but with whom they would have to share the art of recitation. These newcomers were the poets who, in the manner of their day, were eager to publish their works by reciting them to any available audience. One after another they emerged as individual characters playing against a background of traditional art, and as they grew in numbers and in ability the glory of the rhapsodes gradually dimmed, at least for a time.

Thus far our concern has been with the recitation of the heroic epics. Inevitably Greek society continued its evolutionary changes socially and intellectually. Life became more complex; there were revolutions, there was more commerce, there was exploration and colonization. The ancient monarchy began to break, tyrants arose and fell, and democracy began to evolve. These many changes wrought their effects upon the people. There were personal decisions to make, and judgment and the analysis of individuals and issues became important. Man was concerned with his personal problems. There was less concern for fate and omens and more reliance on reason. These changes had some influence in extending the form of expression from epic grandeur to other types of poetry. The new forms did not supersede the old, but were gradually added to them to enhance man's life with an ever widening variety of aesthetic fulfillment.

As life became more complex, poetry became more personal. Moreover, the poet began to emerge as a man, and the poetry he composed was his own. Instead of poetry being thought of as general public property associated with traditional names, it became directly associated with the name of the poet. The seventh to the fifth centuries B.C., the second period of Greek literature, gave rise to new forms of poetry. Out of his pain and grief man evolved the elegy—or lament, which helped him express a sorrow which was beyond logical thinking. Such poems were recited at funerals and other sad or solemn occasions. For his joyful outpourings the poet found the lyric, probably composed to be sung, more suited to his mood. The very word "lyric," suggesting the relation of this type of poetry to the lyre, indicates that there was some kind of musical accompaniment. Some say that a flute was used as well. In Greece lyric poetry sprang from two schools, the Aeolic and the Doric. The former was recited by one person using some kind of lyre while the Doric was sung by a dancing chorus. This lyric form was at home in happy gatherings and was often used on the occasion of prize-giving to victors of the games. Satiric verses and those verses nearest to ordinary speech used the iambic meter, so well suited to sharp and bitter themes. According to legend only the maid Iambe could make Demeter smile after the loss of Persephone, hence her name was given to the verse frequently used in satire. This meter lent itself more easily to recitation than did the lyric forms.

Lyric poetry

It is of interest to trace the various poetic forms through some of the poets who developed them and the reciters who relayed them to the world at large. Particularly in the early days, reciter and poet were, of course, very often the same man. Such was Hesiod, one of the earliest poets after Homer.

Hesiod

The Greece which Hesiod knew was no longer the nomadic society described by Homer, but a society which had taken to the more settled life of a farmer. Hesiod's theme, in his *Works and Days,* was the world as he knew it; he described the labors of a Boeotian farmer, the seasons, and even lucky and unlucky days. Hesiod's realistic approach to literature forsook the loquacity of the rhapsode's Homer in favor of a greater economy of utterance, and he employed the simple language of the farmer. *Works and Days* is the earliest example we have of didactic poetry. It expressed clearly and concisely, and in a form easily memorized, much of the information which it was useful for a farmer to know; it was a new use for poetry but one which was to prove helpful and has continued to be so to this day. At a relatively recent date Cypriot farmers still received much of their informal elementary agricultural instruction in ancient rhymes which made the information easy for them to remember. When asked a question in school, Cretan boys and girls will, even today, respond in spontaneous verse. Such customs may well be as old as Hesiod.

Theogony

Hesiod, as a transition poet, did not entirely forsake gods for farmers; it would have been unreasonable in his era to do so, for he lived about 850-800 B.C. when men and deities often shared the same world. Hesiod himself claimed to have been in communication with the supernatural. In the opening lines of his *Theogony,* which deals with the birth of the gods and the evolution of Nature out of chaos, he tells of receiving his staff from the Muse on Mt. Helicon. This claim may explain why, from that time forth, the staff was to be the symbol of the reciter. Hesiod seems to have been worthy of his staff, for he relates how he won a prize for his poetry at the funeral games of Amphidamus at Chalcis, and tradition has it that he defeated even Homer at this contest. Be that as it may, he was, in any case, the chronological successor to Homer, and his poems, like Homer's, were published and long preserved orally.

Callinus

To Callinus, (circa 650 B.C.) goes the honor of being the first known elegiac poet. Undoubtedly, he first published his works by reciting them himself; later they may have been written and passed on to friends and admirers to reach a wider audience. The same may be said of his contemporary Tyrtaeus (ca. 640 B.C.) whose elegies so inspired the Spartans that a law was passed requiring the soldiers, on military campaigns, to hear the verses of this poet *en masse* in the king's tent, which so stirred their patriotism that they were ready to die for their country.[5] The soldiers also took turns reciting Tyrtaeus' poetry at meal times. Each man tried to outshine his fellows, and the one who was considered best was rewarded with an extra portion of meat.[6]

Tyrtaeus

Archilochus

Archilochus (ca. 650 B.C.), whom the Greeks ranked next to Homer himself, composed elegies which were chanted at funeral banquets. It is a mark of the high esteem in which he was held that one of his poems was often sung by the victor and his friends when, after the contest, they went to the temple to get the prize. The genius of Archilochus was also evident in his ability to use the vernacular speech as a poetic medium. As emphasis shifted from the heroic themes of the great epics to the more personal experiences of ordinary mortals, it was a natural corollary that the traditional stylized language of the epics should be replaced by the common language of the day. For poetry to remain a meaningful thing in the lives of average people, this was a necessary development. With the change in language came the need for a new metric pattern. Archilochus was probably the first to use the iambic meter, a vehicle, as noted above, well suited to his satires and invective. Sharp, bitter, and incisive, this form is still popular with the Greeks in those areas where folk traditions have not yet been lost in the onrush of sophistication. Even today shepherds, young folk, and people unspoiled by the bustle of great cities delight in composing and reciting such verses impromptu, quite unaware of their debt to Archilochus and his contemporaries.

Iambic

By developing this meter, better adapted to recitation than to song, Archilochus advanced the oral tradition. He may simultaneously have contributed to the growth of the written tradition as well; it is said that he not only recited his poems to small groups but also sent his verses to his friends. His poems were delivered in the theatre by the famous reciter Simonides the Zacynthian who, rather than standing to recite, sat in an armchair to deliver them.[7]

Solon

Solon, the law-maker, wise man, and civic leader, was destined to write an elegy which would affect the course of history. It happened that Salamis, the birthplace of Solon, was claimed by both Megara and Athens. In her attempt to win Salamis, Athens suffered so many defeats that a law was passed making death the penalty for anyone who provoked the renewal of the struggle. Convinced that Athens, and Athens alone, should be the possessor of Salamis, Solon went into action. Pretending to be mad, he rushed into the agora and read to the astonished and excited Athenians his *Elegy on Salamis,* which so aroused their fighting spirit that they not only renewed the struggle but emerged from it completely victorious.[8]

While other poets could not perhaps match Solon's feat of winning cities or colonies for their state, they did achieve literary victories which in many instances long outlived the fame of battle. The growth of lyrical forms was to add many famous names to the roster of Greek poets. The poetess Sappho, who "loved and sang" on the island of Lesbos, was to find this mode of expression much to her liking. According to Demetrius of Phalerus[9] many of her poems, though "lyrics," were better suited to recitation than to song and she, like Archilochus, employed popular language when that was more appropriate to the subject matter. Another lyric poet, Simonides of Ceos, said that poetry was vocal painting.

Sappho

Demetrius of Phalerus

There were poets of a later date, too, who recited what they had written and were able to find an audience among the great men of the day. One of the many to come to the court of Alexander the Great was Antiphanes who read his play to the king.[10] It was also at the court in Pella that Euripides is said to have lived in the days of Alexander's father, Philip of Macedon. Still later, we hear of a quarrel between the poet Callimachus (ca. 310-240 B.C.) and his pupil Apollonius, which arose because the latter managed to usurp his master's place and recite his own poem at a festival for Apollo. In revenge, Callimachus was successful in having his pupil's poem rejected by the judges. This so discouraged and humiliated Apollonius that he left Alexandria for Rhodes where he became a teacher of rhetoric; this gives some idea of the importance attached to a festival success.

Mention must also be made of the epic poet Antimachus who rendered his *Thebais* aloud although only one person remained in the audience. This audience of one, however, made up in quality what it lacked in quantity, for the lone listener was Plato, whom Antimachus estimated was worth a hundred thousand ordinary mortals.[11] Looked at in that way Antimachus had drawn a crowd which might satisfy the most ambitious of readers. As if to prove the value of an audience of one, Plato, in turn, was on another occasion to have the experience of offering his *On the Soul* to an apathetic audience which gradually dwindled until only Aristotle remained. But Aristotle was also in the one hundred thousand class, and Plato's masterpiece survived in spite of the indifference of his public.[12]

Antimachus

Plato

An interesting story is told of how Sophocles turned his own poetic ability to good advantage. Accused in his old age of neglecting his personal affairs, and charged by his sons with mental deterioration, Sophocles, in his defense, read to the court a work which he

Sophocles

had newly composed. This was his *Oedipus Rex.* So impressed was the court with his brilliance that its members burst into applause as if in a theatre. Sophocles, of course, won the verdict, but one wonders what might have become of this great dramatist and his timeless drama if he had not been given the opportunity to read it aloud on this exciting occasion.

There were never enough poets to satisfy the great throngs of would-be listeners; therefore, more and more men came forward, as the rhapsodes had done, to recite poetry which they had not themselves composed. They chose poems which they had enjoyed hearing and which they were eager to share with their fellowmen. In the fourth century B.C., Demetrius of Phalerus revived the art of the rhapsodes and broadened their material to include, in addition to Homer, the poetry of Hesiod, Archilochus, Mimnermus, and other poets. These works were presented in the theatres. Reference has been made to Simonides the Zacynthian, the rhapsode who recited the poems of Archilochus. There was also Hegesias, the comedian who presented the poems of Hesiod in the theatre at Alexandria, and Cleomenes, the rhapsode who recited the *Rites of Purification* of Empedocles. Other performers included the Ionicologi who recited the Ionic poems of Sotades; Alexander of Aetolian; Pyres of Miletus; and Alexus. Nor should one forget the hilarodists, those hilarious "joy-singers," dressed in white garments and topped with a golden crown, who made men laugh by parodying tragedy to the accompaniment of a harp; nor the magodists who wore feminine clothing and sought to spellbind an audience by reciting in a "magical" manner.[13]

Revival of rhapsodes

All of these men played their part in widening the scope of oral recitation and adapting this form of entertainment to suit an evergrowing variety of tastes and standards. That some of them appealed to lower tastes was inevitable as the circle widened, but they carried the seeds of a vital oral tradition which men have found valuable enough to preserve throughout history.

Reciting is an art in which all manner of men from kings to commoners have been eager to participate. From the king in the *Iliad* who sought to refresh his soul by singing of heroic deeds (while strumming on a looted lyre) to the many recordings of poetry today, the line leads through the famous, the infamous, and the unknown. Alexander the Great was an enthusiastic patron of this art. He admired Homer so much that he always carried a copy of the poet's works on campaign; at night he tucked this treasure under his pillow along with his dagger. When a precious box which had been taken from Darius was brought to him, he announced that he would use it to hold his copy of Homer.[14] He gave prizes to rhapsodes to encourage recitation and did all in his power to attract writers and scholars to his court at Pella. That this grew out of a desire for his personal aggrandisement rather than out of a desire to spread

Alexander the Great

education generally may be suspected from the fact that he also wrote a petulant letter to Aristotle expressing great displeasure when the latter published his books on his "oral teaching."[15] Such publication, by making available to the many, things which had hitherto been the privilege of the few, diminished Alexander's preeminence in knowledge and pleased him not at all.

To Alexander, a man of action, anxious to hold the limelight, it was not enough merely to watch others perform; he wanted to participate himself. Guests at his royal banquets were often to be regaled by the king reciting long passages from Euripides, who was another of his great favorites. Doubtless this entertainment was acceptable to all, for not only was Alexander a sincere and competent scholar able to acquit himself well as a reciter, but Euripides was a poet universally and deservedly popular.

Euripides

In an earlier age Euripides might well have found himself promoted to the status of a demi-god; the adoration which he inspired in all sections of the populace was as dramatic as anything he wrote. The wide range of his influence may be appreciated if one considers the story of the Athenians who were taken captive after the battle of Syracuse. It was well known that Athenians were devoted to the theater, and so eager were their captors to hear the works of Euripides that they offered food and drink to the men who could recite them. Some Athenians even won their freedom by teaching to their conquerors the lines of the beloved playwright.[16] Those lucky enough to return to Athens naturally paid homage to the benefactor whose genius had served them so well.

On another occasion a Caunian ship which was suspected of being a pirate ship was refused harbor until it was made known that its passengers could recite the verses of Euripides.[17] This, evidently, was more than could be expected of even a very superior pirate so, its good character being established, it was allowed to anchor.

Some audiences were willing to tolerate any kind of performer so long as he offered them Euripides. But not so Demetrius the Cynic who was once so disgusted by an uneducated reader's poor rendition of the *Bacchae* that when the reader came to the lines describing the awful deed of Agave and the fate of Pentheus, Demetrius, living up to his name, seized the book and tore it up, saying, "It is better for poor Pentheus to be murdered by me than by you"–a drastic remedy for poor reading and no doubt a lesson to all who were negligent in their art.[18]

Another group who could not afford to be bad readers were the booksellers, who often advertised their books by reading them aloud to the passersby. Having tempted the leisurely to stop and listen, a good Greek salesman could be trusted to do the rest. These instances are enough to show how many and varied were the uses of oral reading, but here it is enough to consider it only in its relation to literature.

So far this study has been primarily concerned with the frequency of reciting and oral reading. The next question concerns the methods of delivery. Through the years there has been much discussion among scholars as to the manner in which Greek oral literature was delivered in its early stages. Was it sung, spoken or chanted? There are, as might be expected, different answers to so ephemeral a question, for it immediately poses another—did "sing," "speak," and "chant" mean the same to the ancient Greek as they mean to us today? This is very difficult to ascertain, as descriptions of gestures, colors, or sounds can only approximate the originals. Yet this is a significant part of the subject, and the available evidence must be considered. First of all one needs to consider the nature of "speech" in ancient Greece. It was not so dependent, as is speech today, upon stress and emphasis. Inasmuch as it was intoned, it can rather be likened to the Chinese language; and it is entirely possible that if we heard it today, it would sound more like chanting than speaking in the present sense of the word. It was much more highly inflected than is English or modern Greek.

Method of delivery

Homer made it clear that the delivery of poetry differed from ordinary conversation by his use of two different words to describe them. He uses ϵπη to indicate ordinary conversation while he uses another word Αοιδή when he refers to the oral delivery of a poem. Other authorities have gone a step further by recording a difference between speaking and singing. The poet Theognis says at one point that he likes to chant aloud, to recite or to carol to the pipes or "the manly lyre," and again repeats

> To revel with the pipe, to chaunt and sing
> This likewise is a most delightful thing.[19]

As noted earlier, Demetrius of Phalerus observed that some of Sappho's poems were better suited to reciting than to singing, indicating that these were two distinct activities. Aristoxenus in his *Harmonics* noted that in singing and speaking the high and low of the voice are different. While the speaking voice moves without any seeming rest, the singing voice moves by intervals and rests on definite pitches. The more definite the pitches become, the more clearly does the rendition become music rather than speech. Another of the ancients, Aristides Quintilianus, described the reading or reciting of poetry as using both specific rests of pitch and slides of pitch. This would, it seems, suggest a combination of music and speaking which may describe a transitional stage and would support Gilbert Murray's belief that all Greek poetry had its origin in some form of song.[20] The theory has also been put forward that since Greek poetry was accompanied by the lyre it was probably recited in a monopitch. According to Muller the word "song" is simply a catch-all to cover "any high-pitched sonorous recitation" which had uncomplicated vocal modulations.[21] This seems a logical conclusion.

Aristoxenus

One may ask now whether, if poetry was recited or chanted, a lyre or any other musical instrument was required. That the lyre was used in early days is certain, for in the *Odyssey* there are frequent references to this instrument. In the story of Demodocus, already cited, the lyre was brought in, it was hung where the minstrel could reach it, but no mention is made of how he used it when he took it down and began his performance. Whether it provided an integral part of the melody or merely a musical background is not clear; it may have served only as an introduction to set the pitch of the voice, or as a prelude to oral recitation.

Hesiod at Delphi

Hesiod brings one still more definitely into the sphere of spoken poetry. He seems to have had no feeling that a lyre or any other musical instrument was a necessary part of his accoutrements, for he once went to take part in the contests at Delphi and was not allowed to compete because he did not have a lyre with him. The significant fact is not that the contest rules, probably following tradition, required a lyre, but the fact that Hesiod did not consider a lyre necessary. He had already dispensed with the musical instrument in favor of his famous myrtle bough, and since this practice was adopted by the rhapsodes, there seems little doubt that by the time they were performing at least Homer was being recited, not sung, to a musical accompaniment. Terpander, (676 B.C.) according to Plutarch, set Homer's verses, as well as his own, to music and sang them at public contests.[22] If Terpander had to set them to music, presumably they were not so offered in the first place, or, the practice had been discontinued.

Recitative or song

In considering the rhapsodes and poets of a later date more specific evidence is available. The poet Pindar used a flute while others favored a cithara, and Archilochus, Plutarch tells us, first showed how iambic verses could in part be recited and in part be sung to lyre accompaniment.[23] Plato again supplies information: in the *Phaedrus* Socrates says, "Go and tell Lysias that to the fountain and school of the Nymphs we went down and were bidden by them to convey a message to him and to other composers of speeches—to Homer and other writers of poems whether set to music or not . . . ."[24] This suggests that some poems were not sung but recited. In other places Plato distinguishes between singers-to-the-harp and rhapsodes, and Aristotle makes a distinction betweeen Sosistratus, who used too much action when he recited, and Mnasitheus who had the same fault in singing.[25] When Aristotle compared tragedy and the epic he noted that tragedy had all the elements of the epic **plus** spectacle and music. Probably, to quote Bowra, the epic was not "a song sung to a tune but a recitative intoned to a simple accompaniment."[26]

From music, to poetry, to prose was a natural progression, and with Herodotus a new field of oral literature came into being. The

Herodotus

events of his era were to awaken in this professional storyteller a desire to recite the facts of history to his listeners. Herodotus, the father of history, was born in 484 B.C., six years after the Battle of Marathon and four years before the Battle of Thermopylae. The Greek people, overjoyed at having successfully overcome their powerful enemies, were no doubt in a mood to find the tales of historical events as gripping as any myth-embroidered narrative. Not that Herodotus refrained from embroidering his tales. He undoubtedly did; indeed, Thucydides, his admirer and disciple, was to complain that Herodotus was more concerned with telling a dramatic tale than with strict adherence to the truth. This was no doubt a valid criticism, for Herodotus was first and foremost a storyteller. He competed in the great festivals as the rhapsodes did, and there he was competing as a reciter. His first such appearance was at the Olympic Festival in the fifth century B.C. at which time he evidently felt sufficiently competent in his art to match his skill against the outstanding narrators of his day. Composing, reciting, revising, and again reciting a story before public audiences, he learned to tell his tale effectively and dramatically. Like Homer he used dialogue; he divided his narrative into episodes, but whereas Homer found poetry a worthy vehicle for his tales of legendary heroes, Herodotus was to find prose a more natural mode of expressing what he had to say. Travelling far and wide, telling his tales in Athens, Thebes, Corinth, and other places, he developed style in both delivery and expression as he described places and people to bring them to life for his listeners. He earned his bread and butter by reciting his stories (logoi). On the road he collected fresh material to add to his collection. He tells of going to Tyre and of speaking to the priests at Memphis to verify certain facts. Although his stories may have lacked historical accuracy in some cases, they were nevertheless based upon actual events and dealt with historical characters in true geographical settings. All this, at first incidental to his storytelling, was to lay the foundation for his later fame as an historian.

When he was about forty years old, Herodotus went to Italy with a group of colonists and there, as the culmination of his travels, research, and reciting, he wrote his history. Herodotus, the first known person to give form and order to a collection of historical incidents, had as his purpose the recording of the deeds of Greek and Barbarian alike so that these events could be remembered. It is interesting to note that though he recited his works, he sought to preserve them in writing.

Himself a reciter, a "logopoios", Herodotus was thus a link in the chain of rhapsodes who carried on the tradition from poetic Homer into the area of relatively factual history and the person who made prose into an acceptable form of oral literature. Such a contribution well deserved to attract disciples who would develop the trend so well begun. After some of his chapters had been read in public in 446 B.C. the Athenian Assembly gave him an award for his achievement.

Herodotus was fortunate in his successors. Thucydides, born in Athens about 460 B.C., may well have heard Herodotus give a recital at the Olympian festival. If so, this may have influenced the boy so that he was determined that he, too, would become an historian. Not even his military career, and he was destined to become a military leader, was to prevent Thucydides from realizing this ambition and taking his place as the greatest of the ancient historians. Unlike Herodotus he based his history not on tradition, legend or hearsay, but upon facts alone, a point which he was at pains to make clear. With him accuracy took precedence over the story, and history came of age. He included speeches in his history which, to the best of his knowledge, were like those given by the actual historical characters. These speeches, dramatic in nature, take up a considerable portion of his works and show the influence of Homer. Influenced by Herodotus, who was influenced by Homer and the rhapsodes, Thucydides in his turn carried on the oral tradition.

Thucydides

Another adventurous soldier, Xenophon, was the third of the great historians. Born in Athens in 430 B.C. he was to continue in his *Hellenica* the work of Thucydides; his *Memorabilia* preserved for posterity precious memories of his teacher, Socrates, and the adventures of Cyrus the Younger were to provide the material for his *Anabasis.*

The form he used is significant. Following the custom of his day, Xenophon divided his story into chapters of suitable length for oral recitation–beginning each section with a summary of the preceding episode to refresh his hearers on the subject and to prepare them for the next adventure. This was still a useful form for a manuscript to take because, although the written word was gaining in importance, the spoken word was still preferred for both practical and psychological reasons. Copying manuscripts was a costly and tedious operation, and for this reason oral publication was the best hope of authors who wished to reach any considerable number of people; even more importantly, the education of young people could best be extended through the medium of the spoken word.

Xenophon

For generations the Greeks had trained themselves to retain what they heard, and it was not too uncommon, as Xenophon noted, for a youth to be able to recite much, or all, of Homer by heart. Other authors, among them Hesiod, Phocylides, and Theognis, were used in the "reading" lesson which often meant recitation by the teacher and subsequent memorization by the pupil. Reared in the oral tradition, Greek fathers and teachers regarded memorization as the backbone of education, and the ability to recite or speak well was the first requirement of an educated man. No matter how brilliant a man might be in other spheres, it was difficult to gain public recognition without this skill.

Probably no one better demonstrates the length to which men would go to acquire verbal facility than Demosthenes, that frail child with the weak voice and a speech defect, who seemed ill-equipped to make his mark in an oral culture. We are told that he practiced speeches with pebbles in his mouth to cure his speech defect; that he recited before a mirror; and that he strengthened his voice by repeating verses while going up a hill or when he was out of breath. Such diligence had its reward, for he became one of the famous orators of all times. He credited the actor Satyrus with opening his eyes to the possibilities of expression. Demosthenes had gone to Satyrus for help, and the actor, after listening to Demosthenes recite from Sophocles and Euripides, rendered the same verses with such beauty of tone, such effective inflection and gesture that the orator realized for the first time the potentialities of the human voice.

Demosthenes

Listening, imitating, memorizing, reciting, the Greeks learned from each other at every opportunity, and ultimately the idea became implanted in their minds that recitation was not merely a privilege or a pastime, but an important duty which the educated man owed to his fellows. Epicurus, in his discussion of the wise man, said that he must, among other things, be grateful for criticism, establish a school, and if he is asked to do so, read in public.

The Greek mind, then, as now, was analytical. Such a mind naturally turned to the dissecting of theories, to the criticism of ideas in politics, philosophy, religion, or literature. Whatever the topic it was fair game for analysis. Plato in his *Phaedrus* tells us that neither prose nor poetry, written or spoken, is of much value if it is only to be believed. It should be of more use than that: it should provide an opportunity for critical analysis. In Greece, reading aloud was the first step in literary criticism. Hearing a poem read, the listener should be able to penetrate into its meaning, its purpose, and its structure. This was true not only of short poems but also of tragedy. Aristotle found that a tragedy could be judged as well by hearing it read as by seeing it performed. He thought the critical evaluation of literature was a job for the mind and not for the eyes alone; the ear, the inner eye, and the critical faculties were all needful to lay bare the strengths and weaknesses of the composition.

Criticism and oral reading

Another of the great minds of Greece, Theophrastus, also appreciated the relation of oral reading to criticism. Theophrastus, the philosopher and scientist, was also a great lecturer in his day, and two thousand pupils flocked to hear him speak. Theophrastus commented that it was not easy to build up such an audience, and that having built it up his worries were just beginning. He had to try to keep it. With two thousand minds set free to analyze and criticize

Theophrastus

everything he said, the lecturer had difficulty in keeping abreast of the revisions he was expected to make; and that he was expected to make them Theophrastus states very clearly when he tells us that pupils of his day would not tolerate a person who failed to accept criticism.

The importance of this attitude is perhaps nowhere more appreciated than in the field of philosophy. The philosophers were not primarily interested in a piece of literature as a completed unit of instruction. Instruction it should give, beauty it should have, but to these should be added the opportunity for analysis, the chance to arrive at some facet of truth. Anything which failed to challenge their intellect failed to arouse their interest. It is significant that modern man has not yet abandoned the method of arriving at the truth developed so long ago by the loquacious Greeks. Lawyers, diagnosticians, and educators still depend heavily on the Socratic method of question and answer, then question-the-answer when they want to sift the true facts from the false impressions. It was by just such means in classical times that men kept alive and justified their traditional faith in the sensitivity, adaptability, reliability, and vitality of the spoken word.

The importance of the oral word and the oral recital of literature was not to die in Greece. As older civilizations became quiescent, new nations arose in the west to carry on their own adaptations of the traditions of ancient Greece.

References

1. S. H. Butcher, *Some Aspects of the Greek Genius* (London: Macmillan & Co., 1891), p. 181.

2. Plato, "Ion," *Dialogues of Plato,* tr. Benjamin Jowett (New York: Random House, 1937), Vol. I. p. 289.

3. Lycurgus, "Against Leocrates," *Minor Attic Orators,* tr. J. O. Burtt (Cambridge: Harvard University Press, 1954), Vol. II. 102. p. 91.

4. Diogenes Laertius, "Solon," *Lives of Eminent Philosophers,* tr. R. D. Hicks (London: Wm. Heinemann, Ltd., 1925), Vol. I. p. 57,59.

5. Lycurgus, *op. cit.,* Vol. II. 106-107. p. 95.

6. Athenaeus, *The Deipnosophists,* tr. C. B. Gulick (Cambridge: Harvard University Press, 1937), Vol. VI. XIV. 630f. p. 403.

7. *Ibid.,* Vol. VI. XIVc. p. 341.

8. Diogenes Laertius, "Solon," *op. cit.,* Bk. I. II. 46-47. pp. 47-49.

9. Demetrius, "On Style," *Aristotle The Poetics: Longinus on the Sublime and Demetrius on Style,* tr. Rhys Roberts (Cambridge: Harvard University Press, 1960), III. 167. p. 407.

10. Athenaeus, *op. cit.,* Vol. VI. Bk. XIII. 555. p. 3.

11. Cicero, "Brutus," *Brutus Orator,* tr. G. L. Hendrickson (Cambridge: Harvard University Press, 1952), II. 191. p. 163.

12. Diogenes Laertius, "Plato," *op. cit.,* Vol. I. III. 37, p. 311.

13. Athenaeus, *op. cit.,* Vol. VI. XIV. 620c, 621d, pp. 347-349.

14. *Ibid.,* "Alexander," *Plutarch's Lives,* tr. B. Perrin (Cambridge: Harvard University Press, 1958), Vol. VII. XXVI,1. p. 299.

15. *Ibid.,* "Alexander," Vol. VII. VII. 3. pp. 241-242.

16. *Ibid.,* "Nicias," Vol. III. XXIX. 3. p. 309.

17. *Ibid.,* "Nicias," Vol. III. XXIX. 3. p. 309.

18. Lucian, "An Illiterate Book Fancier," *The Works of Lucian,* tr. H. W. & F. G. Fowler (Oxford Clarendon Press, 1905), Vol. III. 19. p. 273.

19. Theognis, *The Works of John Hookham Frere* (New York: A. Denham & Co., 1874), Vol. III. p. 347.

20. Gilbert Murray, *A History of Ancient Greek Literature* (New York: D. Appleton & Co., 1927), pp. 76-77.

21. K. O. Muller, *A History of the Literature of Ancient Greece,* tr. J. W. Donaldson (London: John W. Parker & Son, 1858), Vol. I. p. 44.

22. Plutarch, "De Musica," *Plutarch's Moralia,* tr. B. Einarson & P. H. deLacey (Cambridge: Harvard University Press, 1967), Vol. XIV. 30. p. 359.

23. *Ibid.,* p. 417.

24. Plato, "Phaedrus," *Dialogues of Plato, op. cit.,* Vol. I. p. 281.

25. Aristotle, "Poetics," *Aristotle The Poetics: Longinus on the Sublime and Demetrius on Style,* tr. W. H. Fyfe (Cambridge: Harvard University Press, 1960), XXVI. 6. p. 115.

26. C. M. Bowra, *Greek Lyric Poetry* (Oxford: Clarendon Press, 1936), p. 3.

A Roman Poet Reciting. Courtesy Deutschen Archaelogischen Institute, Rome.

Chapter II
ANCIENT ROME

Although Roman literature was not to achieve world fame until long after the Age of Pericles, the seeds of its future greatness were already beginning to germinate by that time. When Roman hills were little more than pastures and the Eternal City had given no hint that it would aspire to such a proud title, the art of spoken verse was slowly but definitely evolving. Neither the date nor the circumstance of its birth can be ascertained, but some of its earliest forms have been preserved. Of these forms, that known as Saturnian verse is so old that legend, according to the poet Varro, credits it with being the verse form in which the fauns of nebulous days delivered their prophecies.[1]

Saturnian verse

The primitive beat of Saturnian verse which, like the ballad dance, may have had its origins in the rhythm of an ancient rustic dance, was used on widely differing occasions. Its versatility might be tested on anything from a festival honoring the gods to a charm for curing the gout. One of the ancient verses which has come down to us was an entreaty to the gods, used by a group of twelve priests, the *Fratres Arvales,* when they celebrated the agricultural festival in May. It went:

> Enos, Lases, iuvate!
> Neve lue rue, Marmar, sins incurrere in pleores!
> Satur fu, fere Mars! Limen sali! Sta! Berber!
> Semunis alternei advocapit conctos!
> Enos, Marmar, iuvato!
> Triumpe![2]*

An example of a remedial charm is "terra pestem teneto, salus hic maneto."[3]** Somewhere between these two extremes, this irregular trochaic meter might be employed to put an infant to sleep or ward off the evil eye. A very important function of spoken verse in

*"Help us, O Lares! And thou, Marmar, suffer not plague and ruin to attack our folk. Be satiate, O fierce Mars! Leap over the threshold. Halt! Now beat the ground. Call in alternate strain upon all the heroes. Help us, Marmar! Bound high in solemn measure." Each line was repeated three times, the last word five times.

**"Let the earth receive the ill, let health with me dwell."

ancient times was protection against the evil eye, and even in the present age there are countless jingles recited to prevent bad luck under certain circumstances.

Folklore was full of devices for appeasing the jealousy of the spirits which hold sway over the destinies of mortals, one of the most common being to decry the virtues or achievements of the person being honored so that the gods would not feel the human triumph a threat to their supremacy. To this end buffoonery and ridicule, often in verse form, were heaped upon the lucky man to curb his pride and make him safe from the charge of the aping or trying to rival the gods. When joyful celebration was the order of the day, the form of expression often found most suitable for the occasion was that known as Fescennine verse. Often coarse and boisterous, this form enjoyed a long popularity at harvest celebrations, wine festivals, and weddings, and victorious soldiers were often feted in these stanzas. What probably started as a protective measure against divine envy proved to be so much fun for the "protectors" that they gradually forgot the helpful aspect of the game and concentrated more and more on the humiliation of the hero. Originally a safeguard, the verses finally became a menace, and sometimes it took more courage to face the celebration than to win the victory which inspired it. Not content with reducing mortals below the level of the gods, ridicule was carried to extremes and brought the hero-victim to shame before his fellowmen. So sharp in its vindictiveness did this practice become that it was found necessary to pass a law prohibiting such scurrilous attacks upon individuals.

Fescennine verse

Probably from the town of Atella came another literary form known as the *Fabulae Atellanae.* These Fabulae had stock characters who often used riddles to make the audience laugh. They were a form of broad comedy and later developed a written plot. They enjoyed a long period of popularity during the years of Rome's growth to power, by which time amateurs of noble rank would sometimes act in them, and they continued to flourish until overshadowed by the greater popularity of other kinds of expression.

Fabulae Atellanae

Another early type of literature was the **satura.** This resembled the Fescennine verses in some ways, but it was slightly more developed. The satura began as impromptus having little or no plot, but with peasants harrying their fellows by word and action. Performed by one or more actors they presented a spirited and happy melange of subjects.

Satura

These were some of the native foundations on which the literature of Rome was to be built. They sufficed for many years, but Rome was to receive influences from the east far greater in the development of her life and literature than anything she produced on her own soil. A part of her good fortune lay in capturing a young Greek imbued with the culture of his native land. He was Livius Andronicus who was brought captive to Rome in 272 B.C. Like many of his countrymen, he filled the Romans with admiration for Greek civilization, culture, philosophy and literature and inspired some to build a Roman culture worthy of that mighty empire.

Livius Andronicus

In the tradition of the Hellenic world, this young man wrote his own compositions and won acclaim by reciting them as the poets of his homeland had done. He did this so frequently and with such hearty vigor that he lost his voice. For most reciters this would have been the end of his career, but it was not so for Livius Andronicus. He solved his problem by employing a chanter to stand by the flute-player's side and recite the verses for him, while he himself acted out the words in pantomime, an art which is occasionally revived even today. Livius Andronicus may be taken as a symbol of the state of affairs in the eastern Mediterranean, while Rome's tentacles were reaching even farther to bring new lands within her grasp. Rome conquered Greece by force of arms; inexorably, though, Greece put the stamp of her culture upon the literature of her conquerors so that culturally Greece conquered Rome. One major step was taken when Livius Andronicus translated the *Odyssey* into Latin, thereby influencing Latin and European literature for centuries to come. One need only compare the literary products before and after Greek culture seeped into Italy to realize the transformation that came to Latin literature with this penetration.

Ennius

Shortly after the First Punic War (264-241 B.C.) the poet Ennius, "noster Ennius," as Cicero called him, was born. This versatile man, the first great Latin poet, lived from 239-169(?)B.C. He wrote poems, comedies, and tragedies. A powerful influence in literature, his *Annals,* in verse, inspired Vergil; his satire affected Horace as well as others; and his style left its mark on the tragic dramatists. Ennius served his country by accompanying Scipio on all of that leader's military campaigns and entertained the soldiers after battle by reciting his verses to them.[4]

According to Horace, Ennius never came out to sing of arms unless he was drunk; nevertheless, his popularity was well deserved, and his poetic importance far outweighed his human failings. Two centuries later he was still to command the respect of such significant minds as Quintilian who said that Ennius, like the groves, should be revered not so much for beauty as for sacred associations. Even though he was to be surpassed in concept and execution by those who came later, Ennius was the first poet of stature in Latin literature whose name has come down to us; many of his successors were to owe their inspiration to this man who established the glory of Rome in verse, sang her heroes and cherished her ideals, and who, above all, passionately believed in her great destiny.

Informal reading and reciting

In the Roman world the oral presentation of literature, which was as important in the development of Latin literature as it had been in the Hellenic, took two paths. First there was the informal reading or reciting of poetry in the home or before small groups of friends. In itself this was a welcome social event, always a delight to the Roman spirit. The poet's purpose might have been to give his friends pleasure, or to receive critical comments, or, by noting the reaction of his hearers, to arrive himself at a sound evaluation of his verses. Whatever it was, he and his friends loved to dine together, to read aloud, to listen, and to comment on what was read.

While much of this literary activity was a source of pleasure and profit to reciter and critic alike, a popular and able critic might be so inundated with requests for his opinion that his appetite became dulled. When Terence (ca. 195-159 B.C.) offered his *Andria* to the Aediles in Rome, they told him to read it first to the poet Caecilius. Caecilius, at first, showed scant enthusiasm at the prospect of hearing another versifier, but after Terence finished reading his play, Caecilius recognized the genius in his presence and was warm in his praise of the unknown writer.

In another instance we find that the young Accius (170-87 B.C.), seeking the judgment of those far wiser than he, read his tragedy aloud to Pacuvius to get the older man's comments upon his work. Such informal reading and its subsequent criticism were more valuable in the development of literature than the elaborate public recitals which came later and which sometimes took on elements of theatrical display and vainglory to the detriment of both literature and reciter. These public events were started by Asinius Pollio (76 B.C. - 5 A.D.), who was the first to read his poems before an audience.

The practice of reading aloud to friends and small groups grew so steadily that by the time of Cicero (106-43 B.C.) it was an established part of Roman cultural life. Cicero took it so much as a matter of course that he wrote in his *To Atticus* (XVI,2), "I am sending you my *De Gloria.* Please keep it as usual but have select passages marked for Salvius to read when he has an appropriate party to dinner."

Cicero

With Cicero, Roman literature achieved real stature and strength, but the Ciceronian era, which was to usher in the Golden Age of Rome, was a period of great authors rather than of great reciters. Nevertheless, honest and intelligent criticism still had to do its work, and Cicero realized how useful this could be in raising the standards of literature. In his *De Officiis* he wrote that ". . . painters and sculptors and even poets, too, wish to have their works reviewed by the public, in order that, if any point is generally criticized, it may be improved . . . ."[5] The phrase "even poets too" suggests that the oral reading of poetry before a public audience was a new departure in Cicero's day.

Reminiscent of earlier developments in Greece, as the public thirst for entertainment was whetted, small Roman villas were no longer adequate to accommodate the throngs who wished to listen; thus, along with the familiar private reading parties, public recitals on a much grander scale came into being. An evergrowing interest in the arts followed in the train of Roman prosperity, power, and security. Mistress of the known world and no longer predominantly preoccupied with war and conquest, Rome began to give more of her energies to the cultivations of the arts.

Public recitals

The Augustan Age, which followed the death of Cicero in 43 B.C. and lasted until 14 A.D., was the most flourishing age of poetry in the history of Rome; at this time oral reading developed to an unprecedented degree. Poets read their own works and professional reciters presented the works of others to an ever larger host of listeners. There were many reasons why poetry flourished at this time. Hitherto, oral literature had been largely represented by the orators who sought to sway men's minds by their persuasive and impressive speeches, and so gained for themselves an office of state. Having reached its zenith in the time of Cicero, this art was now on the decline. In the Augustan era, ability as an administrator, rather than oratorical prowess, paved the way to success. The public, however, had enjoyed the lively speeches in the forum, and it was more than ready to accept some other form of oral entertainment. To fill the void left by the great orators, the poets came out of their small private gatherings and jostled each other for a place in the sun. Encouraged by the emperor, the cleavage which was apparent in early Rome between the practical and the poetic disappeared. Poets and reciters, to their surprise, found themselves important members of the community and their standing was recognized by the foundation of a poets' guild. Poets were no longer men apart from their fellows; their chief honor was to be a good citizen, and their great task and privilege was to enhance the glory of their beloved state. The climate of Rome at the beginning of her Golden Age was favorable to the further development of arts and letters.

Augustan Age

Vergil, Horace, and Ovid led the literary cavalcade in fame and excellence. Everyone was either writing and reciting poems or thronging to hear the great poets read their works. With such a burst of activity in creating and reciting poetry, the importance of criticism was intensified; it was necessary to sift the gems of worth from the general mass of material. Criticism had played a major role in private groups, and now it expanded to include in its sphere those large impressive gatherings, popular with many patricians and with some poets. The great authors of classical Rome readily acknowledged their debt to the criticisms of their friends or of the general public and were often willing to act upon the suggestions they received. Vergil preferred intimate groups to large gatherings. He

Vergil

would sometimes stop while reading his poems aloud, to make corrections, or to compose new lines according to the comments of his audience. Some poets, isolated from a critical audience, were denied such assistance.

Ovid

It was precisely the lack of this kind of help, which the exiled Ovid so bitterly deplored, when he found himself banished to a desolate town on the Black Sea, far from the intelligent appraisal of his reliable Roman friends. "There is nobody," he cried, "in this land, should I read my verse, of whose intelligent ear I might avail myself . . . ." Recalling happier days he said, "Ofttimes Propertius would declaim his flaming verse by right of the comradeship which joined him to me. Ponticus famed in epic, Bassus also, famed in iambics, were pleasant members of that friendly circle. And Horace of the many rhythms held in thrall our ears while he attuned his fine-wrought songs to the Ausonian lyre."[6]

Horace

The search for criticism was beset by certain dangers as the more serious writers were well aware. Horace, whose *Art of Poetry* is one of the world's valued treatises on criticism, knew the rewards of the critical discussion which had become traditional in the Rome of his day, but he was by no means blind to the rank abuses of this practice. Flatterers, cajolers, and parasites were eager to attach themselves to a would-be poet with a well-lined purse, and then, having found such a benefactor, they were ready with smiles, tears, and laughter to praise and extol his verses even though they themselves knew little and cared less about the principles of good criticism. Such sycophants had no other end in view than to keep the good will of their patrons and so earn for themselves ever larger gifts. That they must have been numerous may be deduced from the frequent references made to them by reputable Roman writers, and there can be little doubt that they played a large part in breaking down standards of criticism. Horace gives a word of warning in his *Art of Poetry* as he says,

Art of Poetry

> And you, if you have given or mean to give a present to anyone, do not bring him, in the fulness of his joy, to hear verses you have written. For he will call out "Fine! good! perfect!" He will change colour over them; he will even distil the dew from his friendly eyes, he will dance and thump the ground with his foot. As hired mourners at a funeral say and do almost more than those who grieve at heart, so the man who mocks is more moved than the true admirer . . . If you mean to fashion verses, never let the intent that lurks beneath the fox ensnare you.[7]

Another group which both Horace and Vergil abhorred was the swarm of over-zealous reciters who wearied their friends with unsolicited performances and attached themselves to their unwilling victims on every possible occasion. Horace made a conscious effort not to offend, for he said he did not recite to

> anyone save my friends, and then only when pressed–not anywhere or before any hearers. Many there are who recite their writings in the middle of the Forum, or in the baths. How pleasantly the vaulted space echoes the voice! That delights the frivolous, who never ask themselves this, whether what they do is in bad taste or out of season.[8]

When the Augustan Age began, though there had been much commendable work by numerous competent poets, Rome still did not have her *Iliad.* No Homer had given life to myth and legend, no Herodotus had arisen to eulogize the heroes of fact and fiction in words worthy of their deeds; no one, in short, had been able to produce poetry capable of inspiring the populace with the greatness of the Roman spirit. It fell to Vergil to remedy this lack. He was the ideal choice for such an undertaking, for he was not only a fine poet but was, in addition, the darling of Rome, famed for the beauty of his voice and assured of an eager audience any time he could be persuaded to read his poems aloud. So great was his popularity that when he entered the theatre the audience rose en masse to do him honor. At the emperor's request this gifted idol embarked upon the task of composing his *Aeneid.* That his genius was equal to the demands made upon it was fortunate, for the fame of the *Aeneid* nearly preceded its writing. No sooner did it become known that Vergil had begun work on his masterpiece than Sextus Propertius said, "Yield ye Roman writers; yield ye Greeks; A greater than the *Iliad* is born." With such extravagant advance publicity whetting the public interest it would have been easy for Vergil to dash off an inferior work and trust to his popularity to see it through. Instead he devoted twelve years to writing the *Aeneid* and justified his emperor's confidence in his worth. While he was writing this poem he read three books of it aloud to Augustus and Octavia. Octavia was so deeply affected by the verses about her son that she fainted as Vergil read them. Fortunately for posterity, Vergil's dying wish that his works should all be destroyed was not carried out, and at Augustus' command the *Aeneid* was published, and Roman literature rose in stature.

Vergil's *Aeneid*

In Augustus' reign another form of entertainment, the declamation, became popular. The love of hearing speeches did not die with the republic, and this new form captured the Roman fancy and drew large crowds. Often on imaginary and fantastic subjects, these declamations, according to Seneca, were of two kinds, the **controversia**, and the **suasoria.** In the latter the speaker might give counsel on matters of behavior to some historical character. The **controversia** might be based on an imaginary theme or case at law in which the

Declamation

narrator speaks not as himself but as one of the persons involved in a legal case; thus a dramatic element was present. Among those who achieved renown in declamation, the poet Asinius Pollio was outstanding. He declaimed on imaginary themes and became one of the chief declaimers of Rome. Another important declaimer and a teacher of this art was M. Porcius Latro who had an unusual approach to teaching. He did not have his pupils declaim and then criticize their efforts as was the usual custom, but did the declaiming himself and let the pupils listen while he performed in his best manner. Then he parodied the style of his chief rivals. Through comparison the pupil was supposed to see the better style. Devotees of this art flocked to hear the experts declaim in home or hall giving much thought to ways of arousing emotional reaction in writing or speaking. These declaimers also studied history, current events, and philosophy—tying everything into an inextricable mass of logic and emotion which often became tearful and intemperate. While declamation was a form unto itself, it had in it some of the elements of both reciting and the theatre.

Asinius Pollio

M. Porcius Latro

As the Golden Age of Latin literature gave place to the Silver Age, this craze for declamation encroached upon the domain of oral poetry but did not extinguish the older art. As in the previous age, poets still found recitation and reading aloud a valuable means of obtaining criticism and their best mode of publication. In the first century A.D. huge quantities of papyrus were brought from Alexandria to Rome, and readers dictated to hundreds of slaves, yet it was primarily by oral publication that a writer brought his creation before a sizeable number of people.

Silver Age

If the Silver Age of Latin literature did not produce poets of Golden Age stature, it atoned by giving overwhelming support to innumerable poetry recitals of various kinds. At Trimalchio's famous and extravagant feast, described by Petronius in his *Satyricon,* recitation by slave and elocutionist was part of the entertainment. One slave, exhibiting a silver skeleton, discoursed upon the transience of life, and another with piercing voice shouted Vergil's lines so vehemently that the narrator vowed it was the first time he had ever found Vergil's lines distasteful. The elocutionist's contribution to the program was a bombastic rendition of some Greek verses. Other reciters were finding audiences in humbler circumstances, but regardless of the environment the art flourished. These events became so popular that, with true Mediterranean exuberance, all Rome was caught up in the excitement of recitals given by poets and reciters both famed and obscure. Halls were crowded, large villas were packed, rich men and emperors built special recital halls to which the great, the fashionable, the literati, or those who aspired to be so described, came in throngs. Favored poets were privileged to use the houses of the rich, such as that of Titinius Capito,[9] for their

Petronius

Recitals popular

recitals, and so generous were some of these hosts that Juvenal tells us the plantations and columns of Julius Fronto echoed at all times with the tones of reciting poets.[10]

Certainly these patrons were important in the encouragement of the arts, but the poet was at their mercy and could rise or fall at the rich man's nod. Some poets basked in the favor of an emperor's smile and fared extremely well, as did Saleius Bassus who was given a large sum of money by Vespasian. But others were less fortunate. Hobnobbing with Nero, for example, eventually cost Lucan his life. Lucan, an adroit and able courtier, shrewdly advanced his career as a poet by reciting a eulogy in honor of Nero at the Quinquennial contests. This auspicious beginning won him the good graces of the Emperor and was followed by a public reading of his poem on the struggle between Pompey and Caesar. Things went well for a time and might have continued to do so indefinitely but for the fact that Lucan was a poet of considerable merit who became extremely popular with the public. Since the self-centered Nero had ambitions as a poet and could not countenance anyone but himself winning poetic honors, he set out deliberately to destroy this rival. While Lucan was engaged in a public recital, Nero ostentatiously walked out of the hall. This insult so infuriated the temperamental Lucan that he joined in a plot to murder Nero. The Emperor discovered the plot and decided Lucan had lived long enough. Nero graciously permitted his erstwhile friend to commit suicide, thereby robbing the Silver Age of Rome of an able poet and popular reciter who had made the mistake of turning on his mighty emperor.

Lucan

An even greater favorite with Roman audiences was Statius, whose beautiful voice and kindly manner added to the popularity of his famous *Thebais* so that the whole fashionable throng eagerly awaited the day when this much loved poet was to recite. As Juvenal points out, however, a poet cannot live on acclaim alone; and even after his verses have earned enough applause to bring down the house, he may starve if he does not sell his poems.[11] Statius did not starve. He had a wealthy patron named Pollius Felix, and on one occasion won a contest sponsored by Domitian at the latter's Alban residence. Although he never achieved his ambition to win one of the really great contests, he was regarded as a successful poet and performer.

Statius

The poet who could not acquire a patron had a harder time of it. Juvenal, Tacitus, and Pliny all describe his plight with warm sympathy. After he finished the labor of composing his poem, he had to hire a room, erect a stage, find benches, distribute programs and invitations, and trust that his many efforts would result in an audience for his recital. With all this successfully accomplished, he had achieved merely the publication of his work. He had to wait to see whether he had achieved lasting fame or had merely received a polite hearing. Even if he was well received, memories in Rome were as short as they are today; the next day's genius might easily erase him from men's minds, and all his work and hopes were in vain.

Such endeavor might be expected to have deterred all but the most stouthearted, yet recitals took place daily. For a poet to recite was as normal a procedure as for his poems to be printed today. Even dramas were often recited rather than acted; the tragedies of Seneca, for example, with their long static speeches could quite effectively be so presented. Indeed, as the prestige of poets grew, so also did the ranks of those who tried to be numbered among them. Not only were there too many versifiers in public recitals, but there were also too many in the small gatherings which, throughout the years, had done so much for recitation and the encouragement of literature. The situation became such that banquets and dinners were often given with no other object in view than that the host might inflict his latest doggerel upon his hapless guests. So long as the honest desire for criticism was the object, the host might inflict his latest doggerel upon his hapless guests. So long as the honest desire for criticism was the object in presenting verses, listeners and critics could enjoy their role and be of real value to a writer. Again, if the recital gave pleasure to the audience, it had performed a useful function. Many recitations, however, were given both in public and in private with neither of these worthy purposes as their aim. Applause and egotistical satisfaction were the goal, and some reciters even hired handclappers or instructed their slaves to see that they were cheered; thus while enthusiasm for reciting increased, the genius that should accompany it lost pace. With no sense of artistry and none of a real poet's creativity, poetasters, amateurs, and charlatans made their way to the reading platform to exhibit their shallow verses. Empty poets, empty poems, vacuity covered with bombast were all that could be discovered in the decadent entertainers who, combed, perfumed, and robed in white, stood poised on the platform smirking and rolling their eyes for the delectation of an equally decadent audience. Some performances were so poor that they were called not **recitationes** but **ostentationes.**

Martial

A picture of Roman life in the throes of a poetry epidemic was ably drawn by the poet Martial. In sharp satire, he held up to scorn some of the worst enemies of good literature—the conceited, incompetent poet, the insincere and self-seeking critic, and the plagiarist who, all too often, impaired the works of other men by a poor rendition of verses he quite probably did not even understand, but nevertheless tried to pass off as his own. Describing a parasite named Selius, Martial says he would applaud and praise ecstatically in ridiculous superlatives with no other end in view than to earn an invitation to dinner. Men of taste, on the other hand, were so jaded with reciting hosts that when Martial himself, whose verses had merit, invited a friend to dinner he promised his visitor an enticing menu of lettuce, leeks, tunny fish, broccoli, sausage, bacon, raisins, Syrian pears, chestnuts from Naples, wine, olives and parched peas. If this were not enough to tempt the most reluctant guest, he offered the further inducement that he would **not** read from a ponderous book.[12] On another occasion he went even further, promising Julius Cerialis that not only would he refrain from reading his own works, but he would even listen while Julius read to him all of his own epic and pastoral verses. Hospitality could go no farther.

Pliny and recitals

The fact that there were almost daily private or public recitals, which a man of importance was expected to attend, had turned what was once a pleasure into an almost intolerable duty. To rid themselves of this burden many Romans, so Pliny related, remained chatting in the lobby during the performance–merely sending in a servant from time to time to see how far along the reciter was in his program. When they were sure he was near the end, they dropped in briefly, just to be seen, but withdrew before he concluded. When so many poor exhibitions were repeated time after time, the intellectual class, losing interest, ceased to attend. Even the recitals of poetic geniuses, and there were some, had trouble in attracting a discerning audience. Pliny, with conscious virtue, tells in detail the efforts he made to rescue literature from this impasse. He well knew that letters and literature were closely related to the reciter and reader, and the failure of one meant, in many cases, the downfall of the other. With this in mind he conscientiously attended every recital and praised the worthy and determined poets who continued with their art in spite of dwindling public interest.

In common with writers of every age Pliny was easily convinced that while rivals' verses were often boring, his own were gems which no cultured Roman should miss, so he spared no pains to bring them before the public. Like Silius Italicus and Silius Proculus, he continued the custom of orally publishing a composition and then inviting criticism upon it.

Pliny and criticism

He believed that the poet who recited his poems became a sharper critic of his own work and could evaluate the comments made by his listeners and also their inarticulate reactions. Pliny would invite friends to his home and have his freedman read his master's works; Pliny himself, so he says, though he recited orations effectively, was a poor reader and quite unable to do justice to his poems. This should not have distressed him unduly, as he mentions elsewhere that one enemy of sound criticism is the too-expert use of the well-trained voice. He was wary of poets competent in reading and reciting and possessed of beautiful voices who could skilfully gloss over their literary defects with an emphasis, a tone, or a tempo to minimize any inherent flaws. Pleasant for the casual listener, this blunted the perceptive powers of the serious critic and thereby ill-served the cause of literature. The real champion of sound literature was the honest reader who tried to bring out of the poem the ideas and mood that the author had put into it. So while one is surprised that Pliny was not always content to read his own works, yet at the same time one is pleased that he did admit that there is an art of reading. As a result, he sought to insure the best possible production of his own works and worried about such details as how he, the author, should behave while the freedman read; should he be silent and relaxed or should he, as some poets do, follow with hands and eyes the words of the reader. Perhaps he was thinking of Livius Andronicus, who had employed a reciter long ago.

After Pliny became consul he composed a panegyric in honor of the emperor, and to publish it he sent out an informal invitation so worded, he reports, that any unwilling guest could easily find an excuse not to attend. To Pliny's delight his friends did come, in spite of bad weather, and he recited his masterpiece for two whole days; and, he says, "... when I thought it would be immodest to detain them any longer, they insisted upon my going through with it the next day. Shall I consider this as an honor paid to myself, or to polite literature? Rather let me suppose to the latter, which though well nigh extinct, seems to be now reviving amongst us."[13]

One may well wonder what impetus there was, besides the efforts of men such as Pliny, to keep the art of reciting at relatively high levels in spite of the abuses to which it was subjected. For one thing it was kept alive in the home. Quite apart from dinner parties, recitals, and ostentatious display, reciting was a pleasant family pastime, a basic factor in education, and a source of delight to men of learning. Everyone was accustomed to hearing reciters and readers. Favorinus, the philosopher, for instance, had a slave read from philosophical writings or other scholarly works while he dined. Others would have servants read to them while they enjoyed the relaxation of the baths. In the schools, Latin and Greek literature were taught, including the works of Ennius, Accius, Lucilius, Terence, Cicero, Vergil, Horace, Ovid, Lucan, Statius and eminent Greek authors.

It was customary for pupils first to read aloud, memorize, and then recite from memory. With this as a tradition deeply ingrained in childhood, it was a process not even to be questioned. Then, too, the schools or rhetoric, so popular in Rome, used oral expression. Teachers and pupils alike read and recited orations as part of the young orator's training. Teachers used both good and faulty orations to develop judgment and to give their students a sense of propriety and style. At this stage in his development the young orator was advised to use in his orations apt literary quotations drawn from his earlier education in memorized recitation.

Training the orator

Interest in oral reading, reciting, and the speech arts began before the child was ready for school. Attention to speech education started practically at birth, for cultured families insisted that the child's nurse must have good speech so that the child, by imitation, would learn to speak well. Speech defects were regarded as a social handicap; for example, no matter what qualifications a noble maiden might have, if her speech was defective she could never aspire to be a Vestal Virgin, the most sacred and coveted honor in Rome. The importance of vocal quality was appreciated in every walk of life, public or private. Ovid himself counselled the lover, when he went a-wooing, to read tender poems in a soft and gentle voice. And though Pliny might argue that a beautiful voice was a deterrent to good criticism, criticism itself was but a means to an end; it was the ultimate achievement of aesthetic satisfaction that really counted. Pleasing speech was therefore a prime necessity for good oral entertainment. Orators and poets, bent on making their words acceptable to the public, often went to great lengths to develop this desirable attribute. With this tool at their command, they were ready to study the added techniques put forward by their teachers as the means of achieving good delivery.

Good speech essential

A few basic principles have governed the philosophies of expression throughout the centuries. The imitative method, for example, which was to persist in some form for more than two thousand years, was well known in ancient Rome through the work of M. Porcius Latro. Latro achieved some renown with his imitative method, but fortunately more support was given to the more significant theories of Cicero and Quintilian.

Imitation

These two great Romans, separated by almost a century, had much in common, and one can better see their similarities and differences and can better understand their philosophies by studying them side by side. Both were convinced that the foundation of good delivery was the speaker's or reader's complete understanding of his material. This basic requirement, with the aid of such fundamentals as correct breathing, pausing, inflection, range of tempo, thought units, and changes in volume should enable one to read well. Quintilian believed that such techniques would follow more easily if the pupil first **understood** what he read.[14] Understanding was the golden rule. The development and perfection of certain elements of delivery such as voice, gesture, emotion, imagination, style, and propriety were regarded as essential whether in speaking, oral reading, or reciting. Comparing the voice to a stringed instrument Cicero found it to have high and low notes, variety in tempo and volume, and either a sustained or staccatto touch, all of which helped achieve variety and assisted in the more complete interpretation of emotions and ideas. To strengthen the voice he advised the young speaker to work on the middle pitch range.[15] Both Cicero and Quintilian recommended the use of literature as a means of freeing emotional expression in reading and speaking; both realized the

Under-standing

Voice

Emotion

Gesture

importance of vocal quality and gesture in helping a speaker express an emotion which he felt and sought to arouse in his audience. In this regard Cicero cautioned that the use of gesture should be restrained, that it should be suggested rather than exaggerated, and that under no circumstances should it ever be allowed to become theatrical. Quintilian's advice that a speaker's gesture and voice must be suited to each other was sound and has been re-echoed many times since his day.

Propriety

With the same end in view, namely a sincere interpretation of the material, Quintilian insisted that the feeling must first be experienced by an individual if it is to be convincingly reflected in his voice, the purpose of techniques being to convey the feeling, not to substitute for it.[16] To sum up the various factors involved in effective delivery Cicero used the word **propriety.**[17] This constituted an appreciation of what was correct and proper for the individual speaker using that particular material in a specific situation or, as Cicero defined it, a sense of the appropriate or fitting, that element which brings harmony between speaker, subject, and hearer and must be evident in the speaker's expression, gesture, voice, and gait. It was that which "leads to harmony with nature and the faithful observance of her laws."[18]

Cicero: Poetry and Oratory

Although both Quintilian and Cicero were primarily interested in the education of orators, all of these principles were applicable to both oratory and reading. In ancient Rome, where both poet and orator were important citizens, their arts were closely related and actually affected each other, the techniques employed by one often being helpful to the other. As Cicero remarked, the practice of arranging words effectively and modulating the voice was carried over from poetry to oratory; a study of the great poets could be of major importance to the orator by helping him develop facility and clarity of expression. Rhythm, too, was an asset to an orator whose style must not be without form, although he was less bound by it than was the poet. Cicero credited Isocrates with being the first person to realize that a rhythm was to be used, although it was not to be as set in form as poetry.

Study and reciting of poetry

Poetry, on the other hand, although more restricted by its rhythm, had greater choice in the arrangement of words, and Cicero observed, with seeming disapproval, that some poets were more concerned with sound than with sense. Quintilian taught that poetry should be read with a manly quality, with dignity and with sweetness, but without a careless sing-song or effeminate affectation which, apparently, he had sometimes observed in readers. He was in complete accord with Gaius Caesar who complained to a reader, "If you are singing you are singing badly; and if you are reading, you sing."[19] Quintilian further urged that the reader analyze a poem conscientiously line by line to arrive at an understanding of its meaning, metre, and structure, a method still acceptable in the twentieth century.[20] Close acquaintance with the great tragedies and comedies, and with some of the lyric poets including Ennius, Pacuvius, Lucilius, and Terence was recommended as the best means to develop desirable qualities of eloquence, mental maturity, and integrity.

Most of Quintilian's theories have stood the test of centuries and are as valid today as they were in his time because his basic tenets were the need for understanding and the ability to communicate without affectation or pretense. That there was a reason for such a plea not only in his day but in the century which followed may be surmised from the stories told by Aulus Gellius in his *Attic Nights.* In one instance, coming upon a braggart who claimed that he and he alone could interpret the satires of Marcus Varro, Aulus Gellius called the man's bluff by handing him a copy of the satires and asking him to recite. The boaster read badly and mispronounced so many words that he quite destroyed the thought. Aulus Gellius could hardly endure it, and even the man himself realized that his performance was not satisfactory, so he returned the book with the excuse that his eyes were weak.

Roman emperors

The development of literature and reciting throughout the history of the Roman Empire was affected by others besides the poets, rhetoricians, and educators. It was greatly influenced by the abilities and tastes of the various emperors who were powers in poetry as well as in politics. A long succession of them, ranging all the way from the great, such as Augustus, to the very stupid, such as Nero, exerted a strong influence upon their times. Although rulers in many countries have supported the arts, Rome was unusual in that many of her famous emperors actively participated in them. The Golden Age owed much of its glory to Augustus who was himself a diligent student of oratory and read and declaimed daily under the supervision of his teacher. Reciters and storytellers found a welcome at his court whether to entertain his guests or to help him pass a sleepless night, and two of Rome's great poets, Vergil and Horace, owed much to his support and encouragement. Ovid on the other hand, condemned by Augustus, ate out his heart in exile but achieved fame in spite of his emperor's displeasure.

Augustus

Claudius

In contrast to Augustus was the "deified Claudius" (41-54 A.D.), but one can hope that his undesirable traits are at least partially redeemed by his histories and his support of the oral arts. He constructed a new museum in Alexandria where his Etruscan and Carthaginian histories were to be read aloud in alternate years. Moreover, he both attended and gave recitals, although at times his lack of personal control made him a ludicrous character and an unreliable performer. At one of his recitals the weight of a very corpulent listener proved to be too much for the benches and they collapsed. This mishap so convulsed Claudius that long after the hilarity of the audience had subsided, he himself was still unable to control his laughter. He suffered from a stammer and, finally giving up reciting, he had a professional read aloud what his "divinity" had written. Whether he would have improved with age will never be known, for a gift of poisoned mushrooms from Nero's mother, Agrippina, removed Claudius from the scene, and Rome had a new master.

Nero

Nero (54-68 A.D.), whose lust for blood was equalled only by his thirst for acclaim, having thus acquired the coveted title of Emperor of Rome set out to add to his fame by making himself the foremost poet and reciter of his day. His methods were original and disconcertingly direct. His program for disposing of rival poets began with the wholesale removal of the statues which had been erected in their honor. These statues he defiled or destroyed according to his whim, and having thus disposed of his predecessors, he was ready to build up his own claim to a seat of glory. He instituted in honor of himself the Neronia contests in oratory and poetry, and through his deputies let it be known that he himself had better be awarded all the prizes at such contests. An expert at self-deception, Nero solemnly accepted these awards with as much satisfaction as if he had earned them. So great was his delight in winning contests that he not only "won" all those he did attend but gleefully accepted prizes from far distant places which he had not even graced with his presence. When, on one occasion, he did set out to do a round of all the contests which were doomed to award him prizes, some festivals had to be held out of season or even repeated twice in the same year in order to accommodate him. What effect this had on the celestial beings who found themselves being worshipped at the most unexpected seasons cannot be ascertained, but it did not bother Nero. While lesser men might have worried lest the earthquake which occurred during his debut in Naples was a sign that the gods were restive, Nero simply went on with his recital. Presumably he forgave the gods for their breach of good manners.

Many and varied have been the devices advocated by learned men for holding an audience, but few can have been more successful than Nero's simple habit of locking the gates after everybody was in. No one dared leave the hall while Nero was performing, not even women seized with the pangs of childbirth and, according to Suetonius, rather than risk Nero's displeasure by leaving, some women actually bore their children in the theatre.

Every performer hopes for applause, but while the impractical artist may be content to work on his material and leave it to the discretion of the audience to express its admiration, such tactics had no place in the schemes of the Emperor Nero. In the matter of applause he foreshadowed modern radio and brought his own. This not only ensured the quantity but also the quality of the applause. Nero had a preference for the rhythmic style of applauding in vogue in Alexandria; since this was not practiced in Rome, he hired five thousand youths and had them trained to applaud vigorously in this manner.

It is easy to ridicule Nero and almost impossible to respect him, but we must give him credit for taking his profession as a poet and reciter very seriously. He was diligent, conscientious, and painstaking in his efforts to perfect his art. Night after night he would listen to Terpinus, the lyre-player; to improve his voice he would forego fine foods,–not easy for a man who indulged himself in every way; and he would lie with a leaden plate on his chest, his teacher at his side, assidiously practicing vocal exercises. To save his voice he never addressed his soldiers in person. When he performed in contests, which he knew in advance he would win, he meticulously followed the rules, never clearing his throat, never wiping his brow with his arm no matter how hot the day. On one occasion, when he dropped his sceptre during his recital, he was in a fever of apprehension lest, in this case, the judges would give the coveted prize to someone else. No judge with a desire to reach old age would have dared to do any such thing. Such, in part, was Nero who was to exclaim on his deathbed, "What an artist the world is losing!"[21]

Later emperors

Later emperors, more able if less colorful than Nero, were to add their influence to the continuing development of recitation; Domitian (81-96 A.D.) gave public recitals himself and also included prose declamation in his quinquennial contests; Hadrian (117-138 A.D.) a sensitive man of sound judgment and wisdom, erected the Athenaeum for the exclusive use of recitals.

In the study of the oral arts in Rome in the forms of recitation, criticism and literature, the major emphasis has been on the reading and reciting of poetry. It is important to note, however, that in Rome as in Greece, the public also enjoyed hearing readings from great historians. From emperors to ordinary citizens the people of Rome enjoyed the inspiration of history as related by Livy, Timagenes, or Ammianus; and Pliny spoke of the "divine efficacy" in history.

Roman laws

In fields rather more remote from literature, and again repeating the Greek pattern, the ancient Roman laws, dating back to 451 B.C., were repeated orally and were the chief subject of a school boy's studies up to the time of Cicero. Here, too, the spoken word was the vehicle for the preservation and propagation of the group mores. The therapeutic values of spoken literature, well recognized in the Roman world as in the Greek, were expounded by Celsus, who made numerous references to them. In his *De Medicina* he suggested reading aloud for such diverse physical ailments as relief of stomach disorders, indigestion, and chronic cough, while in the field of

Spoken literature as therapy

mental health he recommended storytelling, memorized recitation, or reading for the treatment of insanity and nervous disturbances.[22] Exponents of such therapy have appeared from time to time through the centuries to the present day, but since these constitute a study in themselves, a passing reference to them must suffice. Although they were of real importance, such subjects were a by-product rather than the main purpose of oral literature.

The oral arts were to continue as long as the Empire itself, and even when the dismal end was in sight and the barbaric hordes were advancing on the gates of Rome, men still were reciting and concerning themselves with the latest entertainment. By the time of Claudianus, the last pagan figure of literary significance, even statesmen in their council chambers spent their time arguing about the circus or reciting tragedies instead of giving their attention to affairs of state and devising ways to avert the tragedy imminently threatening Rome. Indicative of the decadence of their age, they were a credit neither to the arts nor to their once great empire.

Claudianus

Oral reading and recitation have sometimes been accused of killing the art of poetry in Rome. While at first glance there might seem to be some truth in this view, a more careful study reveals that it was not the art of oral recitation, but rather the prostitution of this art by insincere reciting that was responsible for any such decline. Just as poor reading or recitation could in the course of time affect literature, so on the other hand could poor literature, filled with bombast, encourage poor reading. The art of the oral interpretation of literature thrived in classical Rome as long as it remained true to the poetry it represented and as long as that poetry had integrity. When these conditions ceased to exist, it died.

References

1. Varro, *On the Latin Language,* tr. R. G. Kent (London: Wm. Heinemann, 1958), Vol. I. 36. p. 303.

2. Charles Thomas Cruttwell, *A History of Roman Literature.* (New York: Charles Scribner's Sons, 1891), p. 14.

3. Theodore Mommsen, *The History of Rome.* tr. W. P. Dickson. (New York: Charles Scribner's Sons) Vol. I. p. 287, footnote.

4. *Claudian,* "On Stilicho's Consulship," tr. Maurice Platnauer (London: Wm. Heinemann, 1922), Vol. II, III, Preface, p. 39.

5. Cicero, *De Officiis,* tr. Walter Miller (Cambridge: Harvard University Press, 1961), Bk. I. XLI. 147. p. 151.

6. Ovid, *Tristia,* tr. A. L. Wheeler (London: Wm. Heinemann, 1924), Bk. IV. X. 45-50. p. 201.

7. Horace, "Art of Poetry," *Satires, Epistles & Ars Poetica,* tr. H. Rushton Fairclough (London: Wm. Heinemann, 1929), I. 430-437. p. 485-487.

8. Horace, "Satires," *op. cit.,* I. IV. 73-78. p. 55.

9. Pliny, *Letters,* tr. Wm. Melmoth (London: Wm. Heinemann, 1924), Vol. II. VIII. XII. p. 123.

10. Juvenal, "Satire I," *The Satires of Juvenal, Persius, Sulpicia, & Lucilius,* tr. Rev. Lewis Evans (London: Henry G. Bohn, 1852), pp. 1-2.

11. *Ibid,* "Satire VII," p. 70.

12. Martial, "A Country Menu," *The Twelve Books of Epigrams,* tr. J. A. Pott, F. A. Wright (London: George Routledge & Sons, Ltd., 1936), Bk. V. LXXVIII. pp. 161-162.

13. Pliny, *op. cit.,* Vol. I. III. XVIII. p. 255.

14. Quintilian, *The Institutio Oratoria Of.,* tr. H. E. Butler (Cambridge: Harvard University Press, 1953), Vol. I. Bk. I. VIII. 2. p. 147.

15. Cicero. *De Oratore,* tr. H. Rackham (Cambridge: Harvard University Press, 1942), Vol. II. Bk. III. LVII. 216-222. p. 173-177; Vol. II. III. LXI. 227. p. 181.

16. Quintilian, *op. cit.,* Vol. IV. Bk. XI. III. 62. p. 277.

17. Cicero, "Orator," *Brutus, Orator,* tr. H. M. Hubbell (Cambridge: Harvard University Press, 1952), XX. 70. p. 357.

18. Cicero, *De Officiis, op. cit.,* Bk. I. XXVIII. 100. p. 103.

19. Quintilian, *op. cit.,* Vol. I. Bk. I. VIII. 2. p. 147.

20. *Ibid.,* 13-17. pp. 153-155.

21. Suetonius, "Nero," tr. J. C. Rolfe (London: Wm. Heinemann, 1924), Vol. II. XLIX. 1. p. 177.

22. Celsus, *De Medicina,* tr. W. G. Spencer (Cambridge: Harvard University Press, 1935), Vol. I. Bk. I. 7. 8, p. 75; Bk. I. 8. 3, p. 75; Bk. III. 18, p. 301; Bk. III. 18. 21, p. 303; Bk. IV. 10. 1, p. 389.

The Canterbury Pilgrims Leave Southwark for Canterbury Cathedral. (*The Works of Geoffrey Chaucer*, ed. John Urry, London, Published for Bernard Lintot, 1721) p. 1.

Chapter III
MEDIEVAL PERIOD

Greece had her Zeus and Rome her Jupiter, but the figure which was to dominate Europe in the Middle Ages was Christ. The prototypes of this era were not the supernatural figures of the *Odyssey* nor yet the war-like heroes of the *Aeneid*, but simple human beings struggling to subdue all those traits in their own natures which were not in accord with the concepts of Christian perfection as portrayed in the Bible. From deeds of lust and war many turned to reading and expounding the Bible and to studying the lives of the saints.

A whole new world opened up for the men who could carry the Bible's message abroad for the edification and salvation of their fellow mortals. This was a rich field for those skilled in oral communication. Through all the mutations which took place between the days of the early apostles who went out into the world to proclaim the gospel of love and forgiveness, to the terror ridden times caused by religious dissension, the role of the interpreter was vital.

Much of the early influence of the Bible depended upon the spoken word. The men who carried its message were legion. Such men found their own personal salvation between its pages and were, in turn, the source of inspiration to countless thousands who heard them read from the holy books. By the fourth century the reader was already an important part of monastic life. At that time one of the early duties in the monastery was to care for the religious books and to read the Holy Scripture aloud in church. This service was performed by young men and boys who remained readers until they were adult. While many unknown, though gifted men, played an important role in the reading aloud of Holy Writ, it is the well-known names in church history who continue the story of this phase of oral literature through the medieval period.

Reading aloud in the Church

St. Anthony was one of the early saints who attested to the effect which a good reader could have upon a receptive listener. When Anthony was about eighteen years of age, his parents died, leaving him in the possession of considerable wealth but at a loss as to what he wanted to do with his life. Trying to come to some personal conclusions, he happened one day to enter a church just as the story of the rich young ruler was being read aloud. The young man was so

St. Anthony

impressed by what he heard that he felt as if the message was meant specifically for him, and he forthwith gave his riches to the people of the village and dedicated his own life to the service of God. Although he was to find that temptation would come to him many times, sometimes even as he recited the Scriptures or played the harp, the impact of his moment of conversion was strong, and he was able to continue steadfast in the faith, despite all the sacrifices imposed by the moral precepts of Christiantiy.

St. Basil

Another who commented on the added inspiration which came from hearing words spoken aloud was St. Basil (329-379 A.D.). St. Basil said that when he gave voice to the Hexaemeron, he came much nearer in spirit to the Creator than he could ever succeed in doing when he read silently. Voice, ear, and eye working together had a more telling effect upon his mind than he could achieve when relying on the eyes alone to bring understanding.

As the Roman Empire continued in its decline, Christianity continued to grow, and the church gradually became the unifying link among the peoples of Europe and the Near East. With this change the emphasis shifted from politics and the study of the physical world to preoccupation with the relationship which existed between a man and his God. Not the best way to rule a state, but the best way to know God became the concern of scholars and clergy. Consequently, the names of significance to civilization in the Middle Ages were essentially those of the church fathers. Among these St. Jerome occupied an exalted place.

St. Jerome

St. Jerome's great talents and wide interests ranged through religious, academic, and practical matters. Part of his contribution consisted of a new translation of the Bible known as the Vulgate. His concern with the spread of Christianity is seen in his listing of the many countries where the new religion was gaining a foothold and whence came "crowds of monks every hour." Even the Huns, he said, were learning the Psalter, and the Getae carried tent churches about with them. Many of the devout and gifted church fathers were competent readers, and St. Jerome tells of having himself been so impressed when he heard St. Hilarion recite the Scriptures from memory that it seemed to him as if the saint were in the very presence of God.[1] Sensitive to the power of the spoken word, St. Jerome tried to impress upon all who were responsible for the education of young people the importance of effective oral reading, and his suggestions on the subject of education are of interest. He noted that school children were in the habit of reciting biblical stories such as the parables. Discussing a young girl's education, he advised that this should include reciting the psalms and prayers as well as reading and learning verses in Latin and Greek. By rendering her lessons orally, he noted that she could improve her diction as well as her knowledge of literature.

While such men were emphasizing the effect which good reading could have upon a human soul, others were making their contribution by finding new means of expression in church literature and music. For instance, St. Athanasius (293-373 A.D.) is credited with initiating the recitation of the psalms; his vocal inflections were so subtle that he seemed to be saying the psalms rather than singing them. From such recitative the psalm chants probably developed. In another field, the first great Christian poet, Prudentius (384 A.D.), produced his famous collection of hymns, known as the Cathemerinon. These, because of their extenuated form, seem to have been intended for reading rather than reciting or singing.

St. Athanasius

Prudentius

Confused and frightened by events in the world, people turned the more willingly to men with a steadfast faith in constant and unchanging verities. The growing church, with its emphasis on celestial, as opposed to worldly wealth, was in a position to hold out hope of spiritual survival when Rome's eight hundred years of material security vanished before the onslaughts of Alaric the Goth. When, in 410 A.D., ransom could no longer appease this enemy, calamity overtook the once-indestructible Empire, and the coming of the barbarians seemed to prove to the pagan mind that the ancient gods were angry.[2] To counteract this belief and offer consolation to the Christians, St. Augustine was at hand with his book, *The City of God*, which proclaimed that earthly society is self-centered in contrast to a love of God; in the worldly city there is a passion for domination; in the City of God all men serve each other in charity.[3]

St. Augustine

St. Augustine (354-430 A.D.) was one of those strong characters so essential to mankind in a time of crisis, and his influence as a writer and spiritual leader was profound. Intelligent, conscientious, and observant, he was an excellent chronicler of his time. Among other things, he made some illuminating comments upon the practice of the oral arts, ranging from the simplest oral exercise to the most highly developed art of persuasion. He recalled that much of his early training consisted of repeating to his teacher, in prose, what he had heard or read in verse.[4] He also told of an interesting practice in the church in which it was the custom for those who had been blessed by miraculous cures to make a statement to that effect. The clergy then read this testimony. Augustine told of a brother and sister who suffered from some kind of shaking palsy. They prayed at the tomb of St. Stephen for relief from their infirmity, and this relief was granted. St. Augustine himself read the testimony affirming the cure. Undoubtedly, the more eloquently the testimony was read, the greater the emotional impact the event would have upon the listening congregation.

The church required the endorsement of the spoken word in many of its practices. Christians, on joining the church, were expected to make a verbal profession of their faith before being baptized and, as participants in the church services, they were also enjoined to commit the Apostles' Creed to memory so that they could recite it at the appropriate time. Such were some of the uses of speech which Augustine cited in the learning process. However, he did not stop there but went on to discuss the training required by those who would go on to become teachers and leaders and missionaries of the church.

Since the mission of the Christians was nothing less than to change man's whole way of life, they needed to know the arts of persuasion. To bring people to turn their backs on the known world, to forsake its customs and pleasures and, if necessary, to endure privations for the sake of a future existence which they could neither see nor envision was a task of no mean proportions. The Christian missionaries had to be skilled in the art of winning the hearts and minds of their listeners. The weak and panic-stricken might grasp at a future hope to assuage a present grief, but the Christian philosophy, if it was to live, must also be made acceptable to the thinkers, the potentates, and the wise men of the time. To meet this challenge in the church St. Augustine applied himself to the study of the speech arts. Good voices and clear diction were essential because religious edifices were large and acoustics often poor. Consequently, the speaker was given a great deal of attention and teachers formulated rules for his guidance; various theories were advanced on how the word of God could best be presented to a listening audience.

In his philosophy St. Augustine was akin to the ancient Greeks believing, as they did, that a word is not a word until it is spoken.[5] That it might be spoken effectively, he urged speakers to master the art of eloquence, the best way yet devised to hold a man's attention and influence his thinking. St. Augustine felt that such power should be at the command of good men using it for noble purposes.

He offered some advice on how eloquence could be developed. First the student should master the rules of classical rhetoric, and secondly he should read and listen to the speeches of eloquent men. Ideally, he should pursue both of these lines of study. However, if a choice had to be made then, by all means, he should choose to learn from the speeches of the great orators. For, said St. Augustine, there were many who, without any knowledge of rhetorical rules, could speak more eloquently than many who had learned them; but no one achieved eloquence unless he read and listened to the speeches of eloquent men. For the Christian teacher, of course, eloquence alone was not enough. He had a primary responsibility to bring forth truth since his duty was not to persuade for the sake of persuasion but to teach what was right and refute what was wrong. St. Augustine was supremely conscious of the heavy responsibility which men assumed when they undertook to interpret the Scriptures.[6] First, he said, they must diligently seek to understand the proper meaning of the text, and then they must be equally careful in finding a mode of communicating that meaning to their hearers. He warned readers that they should never read or expound the Scriptures without praying for guidance in the performance of this responsible task. To this end, they must speak clearly and pay attention to good phrasing, proper vocal usage, and above all they must choose a style in keeping with the subject matter, all of which advice applies to reading aloud today.

Three Biblical styles

Augustine described three styles used in the Bible and cited examples of them from the works of St. Paul. These styles were (1) the subdued style as used by St. Paul in Galatians 4:21-26, (2) the temperate style in Timothy I, 5:1, Romans 12:1, 12:6-16, and (3) the majestic style as in II Corinthians 6:2-10 and Galatians 4:10-20. Quoting Cicero he said, "He then, will be an eloquent speaker .... who can discuss trivial matters in a plain style, matters of moderate significance in the tempered style, and weighty affairs in the grand manner." But here he added a word of caution, pointing out that though the Christian teacher would be speaking of great things, he must not use the majestic tone overmuch lest the hearer grow weary of it. Rather must the various styles be skillfully mingled, so that by lending variety to the discourse they may better hold the attention of the hearers. His *De Doctrina Christiana* did much to discredit the practice of declamation which had been popular since the Silver Age of Latin literature. St. Augustine placed the emphasis on clarity, simplicity, persuasiveness, beauty of diction, and honesty. The truth must always be more important than fine style. In his *Confessions* he lamented that a man was often more severely censured for an awkward phrase and an ill-spoken word than he was for an evil act. Greater glory sometimes came to one who could relate his misdemeanors in a pleasant and correct style than to some good man protesting his innocence in halting accents and misplaced stresses. Augustine says, ". . . men were set before me as models, who, if in relating some action of theirs, in itself not ill, they committed some barbarism or solecism, being censured, were abashed; but when in rich and adorned and well-ordered discourse they related their own disordered life, being praised, they gloried." (I. XVIII. 28)

De Doctrina Christiana

Confessions

Having the spread of truth as his aim, St. Augustine saw nothing to condemn in a man's taking material written by another, memorizing it, and then delivering it to an audience. This seemed to him to be beneficial to both speaker and hearer since there are many excellent speakers who have difficulty in writing or expressing what they have in mind. In his day the practice of reading and discussion at mealtimes was prevalent, and he encouraged this as long as the subject under consideration was suitable and the reader adequate.

Always deeply moved by the psalms, Augustine wished he could recite them throughout the world to counteract man's pride.

Isidore of Seville

Almost like an echo of St. Augustine's remarks on style, Isidore of Seville (560-636 A.D.) in his *De la Retorica y Dialectica* described three types of elocution. Here he said that less significant things should be spoken lightly, average subjects with moderation, and great topics with grandeur.[7] A low sonorous tone should not be used for small matters, but magnificence and splendor must be shown in speaking of God. Isidore also divided poetic forms into three categories; one in which the poet speaks; another in which the poet speaks through his characters; and a third where both the poet and his characters speak as, for example, in the *Aeneid.*[8]

Benediot of Nursia

Isidore has been mentioned immediately following St. Augustine to show the similarities in their teachings, but chronologically they were separated by one of the great figures in church history. This was Benedict of Nursia (480-554? A.D.) whose famous Benedictine Rule was to prevail in monasteries for centuries to come. This important treatise was intended for those who wished to lead the Christian life. It covers many facets of religious practice and makes numerous and explicit references to reading aloud as used in the church services and at mealtimes in the monasteries.

St. Benedict dealt with the readings at matins and at the night office which were either from the Bible itself or from commentaries on it by the best known church fathers. There was also to be reading at meal times.[9] He decreed that the brothers who were competent readers should take turns in performing this service and, to insure that standards in reading would be maintained at a high level, they were to make careful and prayerful preparation for this role. Anyone guilty of irreverence or negligence in this matter was to be punished. In the monastery, the monk who was assigned to be the reader at meals for the ensuing week was given a special blessing on the Sunday before he entered on his duties. His brethren were asked to pray for him lest the importance of his assignment should make him guilty of undue pride. While the reading was in progress, the monks were forbidden to speak even in a whisper; if they required anything at the table they must so indicate by visible signs, but not by speech, for only the voice of the reader was to be heard. After leaving the table, the monks were advised to rest in silence or to read alone. If they did read, they were not to disturb others, an injunction which would imply that even when reading alone, they read aloud.

Benedictine Rule: its importance

The Benedictine Rule found wide acceptance, and its influence upon the oral reading of later centuries was extensive. It not only pointed up the importance of this practice, but also emphasized that it required great skill to be effective. Since the monasteries were the great centers of learning in which were retained the cultural inheritance from the past, their influence, when the Renaissance brought a wider diffusion of knowledge, was enormous. One of their most ingrained traditions was the Benedictine Rule and its insistence on good oral reading.

Also of note is the constant struggle which the church waged to keep the Bible and writings of the saints in the forefront of literature. St. Gregory the Great (590-604 A.D.) in his position as Pope once wrote a letter of correction to the Bishop of Vienna because that gentleman had seen fit to give lectures and recite poetry on secular topics. It was Gregory's opinion that one could not praise both Jupiter and Christ, and that it was inconceivably wicked for a bishop to recite poetry from pagan literature. The Bishop was severely reprimanded.

St. Gregory the Great

To Cassiodorus (480-575 A.D.) mankind is indebted for carrying much of classical learning into the Middle Ages. From decaying and despoiled libraries he collected many famous manuscripts and took them to his monastery. He taught monks to read and directed them in copying manuscripts; he is considered the founder of the system of copying and collecting materials which was prominent in medieval monasteries. By such means, the thread of oral reading was carried on from the great days of the Roman Empire into the early Christian period. Its emphasis, however, changed. In Roman days it was a means of publishing literature and of obtaining criticism for the perfection of that literature and for entertainment. In the early Christian period its chief aim was to further the spread of Christianity.

Cassiodorus

By the sixth century the missionary zeal of the Christian church had borne its message as far as England, and there the philosophies and practices already noted in Europe were continued and adapted to meet the needs of a different culture. To understand the conditions in England it is necessary to cast a brief glance at the history of that land before the coming of Christianity. In pre-Roman days the custodians of the island's culture were the ancient Druids, and some idea of the scope of their learning can be gleaned from Julius Caesar's assertion that when he came to Britain in 54 B.C., a youth had to be with his Druid teacher for twenty years before he could learn all that his master had to teach. This culture gave way to the Roman and, for four hundred years, Britain was in touch with the continent through its ties with the rest of the Roman Empire. After the withdrawal of the Roman armies, successive invasions from the continent disrupted the island's education and brought it to a low ebb. When Pope Gregory the Great sent St. Augustine and a group of missionaries to England in 597 A.D., little remained of the culture which England had known in Druid and Roman days.

Roman Britain

St. Augustine arrives

These missionaries came to a land with no political unity, and where literacy was at a low level even for that day.[10] It was to be their task, and that of their successors, to ameliorate some of the educational deficiencies, to convert the natives to Christianity, and to strengthen the church. While St. Augustine was establishing the Roman church in Southern England, the influence of Irish and Scottish missionaries was spreading the new religion from the north. The differences between these two branches of the church were resolved, and in the year 664 the Synod of Whitby established throughout England the practices of the Roman church.

Theodore and Hadrian

In 668, the pope sent Archbishop Theodore and Abbot Hadrian to Canterbury. These men from Italy knew Latin and Greek. They gave a new impetus to learning, and this was not limited to churchmen. Soon after their arrival, Theodore and Hadrian travelled over England to instruct the people in astronomy, arithmetic, and ecclesiastical poetry. The historian Bede was greatly impressed with their contribution. He said that that age was a very happy one for the Britons since there were teachers to instruct anyone who wished to be taught to read the Holy Scriptures.[11]

Abbot John

Theodore and Hadrian were followed by the Abbot John who came from Rome in 680 A.D. Abbot John taught both singing and reading aloud to the churchmen, for with the establishment of the Roman church came its traditions of chanting and oral reading. To learn these arts monks came from many parts of Britain to hear John and to urge him to visit their monasteries.

England had progressed in many ways from the land which St. Augustine had known nearly a century ago. However, conversion of the populace to Christianity was not acomplished overnight, and while churchmen studied the oral arts for the purpose of spreading the gospel of Christ, other groups, the scops and gleemen, were still finding a ready audience for pagan literature. The Church did not look with favor upon these secular entertainers, yet they were respected members of society and were popular with a large section of the community. To them must go the credit for preserving the little that did survive from the pre-Christian culture. The scop and the gleeman, both of whom were reciters, were frequently poets as well. The scop was usually attached to a court on a relatively permanent basis. He received rich gifts for his performance and often fared very well. Part of his duties was to compose poems eulogizing his master, but he also entertained the court with the old pagan legends of the Germanic tribes. While it is true that some scops, either out of wanderlust or to better their lot, moved from court to court, they were less nomadic and held positions of greater security than did the gleemen.

Scop and Gleeman

The gleeman, like the scop, performed to the accompaniment of the harp or "glee wood." Occasionally he attached himself to one particular court, but he was most often a wandering entertainer, and he was less likely than the scop to compose his own poems. He relied more on the work of others for his material.

Widsith, regarded as the earliest known poem in the English language, was written by one of these early poets. It dates back to the 7th century and paints a very happy picture of the scop's or gleeman's life. It opens with the lines:

Widsith

> Widsith spake; unlocked his word-hoard; he who, of all men, had journeyed most among the tribes and peoples of the earth . . .

Because of his travels, Widsith says he "can **sing** and **tell** a tale," recount in the mead hall how men of high rank gave rich gifts to him; altogether he leaves the impression that he found his way of life both happy and exciting.

But there was another side to the coin. Coveted positions in rich courts gave rise to bitter rivalry among the entertainers, and *Deor's Lament* tells the unhappy tale of an aged minstrel who had been ousted from his master's favor. A pitiful outcast, the poor fellow chants his dole. Although he had been good and faithful to his lord, a mightier gleeman came along and separated him from his master.

Deor's Lament

It is difficult to prove whether the poet or gleeman sang his songs, as described in *Beowulf*, or whether he recited them, for the verbs sing and say have the same concept. For as Koegel says, the phrase, "mit singender, d. h. pathetisch gehobener Stimme erzählen" suggests a raised tone.[12]

One of the most famous of ancient tales is *Beowulf*. The composer of this poem may well have been a scop or gleeman, for in this tale the gleeman plays an important role. The poet tells in dramatic style how King Hrothgar built a huge hall "for the drinking of mead." The completion of this hall was celebrated with a wonderful feast at which Hrothgar presented his guests with gems and rings and all manner of costly gifts. For days the revelry continued, with the strings of the harp and the voice of the gleeman an important part of the entertainment. Another feast, celebrating Beowulf's victory over the monster Grendel is another part of the story. Again the poet gives details of the lavish gifts showered upon the hero, and again he makes it clear that amid all this splendor the bard of Hrothgar was an important figure. Seated on a bench, he entertained the company with his recital of the fight between Finn and Hengest. Sometimes, instead of recounting the deeds of brave men, the poet would tell of the creation of the earth, the beautiful land, and the waters; how the whole earth was covered with leaves and branches and how life was given to all creatures that move and breathe.

Beowulf

While eulogies on pagan themes and earthly heroes remained popular, the religious themes of Christian literature made their appearance. In fact, old English Christian poetry contains many references to the gleeman or scop. They are frequently mentioned in

Cynewulf

the works of Cynewulf. In the eighty-ninth riddle, attributed to Cynewulf, the speaker is presumed to be a gleeman. At the conclusion of *Elene* Cynewulf mentioned that he was a weaver of words and had received rich gifts in the mead halls. Not only did Cynewulf recite his poems himself, but he took for granted that others would use them too. In the conclusion of his poem *Juliana* he begged that every man who recited that poem would remember the author and pray to God on his behalf.

Caedmon

In England, the earliest Christian poet known by name is Caedmon (ca. 670). At a social gathering in his day, not only professional minstrels performed. Each man in turn took the harp and entertained the company with a song or recitation which he either composed on the spot or repeated from memory. Caedmon was a very shy man, and rather than face the ordeal of performing before an audience, he would slip away from the company as his turn drew near. One night he hid in a stable and there he fell asleep. According to legend someone came to him in a dream and urged him to sing. Caedmon pleaded lack of ability, but the voice insisted until Caedmon consented. When he awoke, he was able to repeat before an audience everything he had sung in his dream. This seemed so miraculous that he was taken to the nearby Abbey at Whitby. There, to test his ability, monks explained a part of Holy Scripture to him, and Caedmon's task was to put into verse what he had heard. This he did by the next morning, which so impressed the abbess that she persuaded him to become a monk.[13]

From then on Caedmon learned as much as he could by religious instruction, and then put the knowledge he had acquired into the most beautiful verse. So skillful was he that his teachers became his audience. Among his important Christian poems are the "Creation" and the "Exodus from Egypt"; others dealt with parts of the New Testament and other religious subjects. Since his memory was as exceptional as his ability to versify, the church gained a valuable helper when Caedmon learned to use the art of gleeman and scop to tell the Christian message.

Aldhelm

Aldhelm (650-709), a contemporary of Caedmon, a great scholar in the church, and one of the most important English writers of Latin, was to take the same art and adapt it to a different use. He composed poetry in English which he could either sing or recite ("vel canere vel dicere"), and he put his talents to use. His semi-barbaric congregation departed from the church after mass was said and did not wait to hear the sermon. Aldhelm conceived the idea of standing on a bridge which his congregation had to cross and, in the manner of a minstrel, he chanted popular verses to them. Then, when he had their attention he recited verses from the Scriptures.

Perhaps the greatest scholar of the age was the Venerable Bede.

Bede

Bede's whole life was devoted to the monastery. He entered it at an early age, and straightway he began to memorize the psalms, hymns, chants, and responses used in the services. He and his companions had to apply themselves, since making mistakes in reading and reciting was a serious offense and punishment was severe. Bede wrote on many subjects, and his written works contain many references to reading aloud. In the preface of his most famous work, *Ecclesiastical History of the English Nation*, where he addressed King Ceolwulf, he referred to the pious reader or hearer.[14] Elsewhere he requested that all who heard or read his history would pray for him, the author. This indicates that he expected the book to be read aloud. This important historian provided most of the available information about the early church fathers and their works. Many of the sources from which he compiled his history were oral. His primary authorities, he said, were noted churchmen, chief of whom was the Abbot Albinus. Albinus collected material from written and oral sources and sent it to Bede by the priest Nothelm. Nothelm, in turn, relayed the information sometimes in writing and sometimes by word of mouth.[15]

Ceolwulf

Bede was not only a great historian but a great teacher as well. To the last day of his life he continued to teach and is said to have dictated the final chapter of St. John as he lay dying. It is reported that he died with the words of the *Gloria* on his lips. His Ecclesiastical History had established him as the most outstanding scholar of the western world. The influence of this outstanding historian and teacher did not end with his death.

Alcuin

Many of the ideals of the Venerable Bede were carried on by Alcuin of York (735-804), who became well known as an educator. The skillful reading of the Bible had been continuously fostered by the church, and the Council of Cloves in 747 had decreed that abbots, abbesses and bishops should ensure good reading of the Scriptures. Alcuin gave much thought to methods of training good readers. The Rule of St. Benedict, with its emphasis on oral reading, was still of importance. In 793 Alcuin wrote to the monks at Wearmouth, and Jarrow asking that this rule be read more frequently and that it be explained to the hearers in their own language instead of in Latin.

Alcuin's *Rhetoric*

In 794 Alcuin wrote his *Rhetoric.* Though basically concerned with rhetoric, he made some pertinent remarks on delivery. Training in voice and diction, he said, should be continuous from an early age to achieve flexibility in voice and body. Adaptation of the voice to the sense as well as control of the body are both essential to good delivery. He warned against errors, such as inhaling when speaking, inadequate control of voice and breath, poor diction, and too much or too little volume.[16] In a letter reminiscent of Pope Gregory's reprimand to the Bishop of Vienna he said that a skill so carefully nurtured should not be wasted on unworthy matters. In 797 he wrote to Hygebald, Bishop of Lindisfarne, protesting the reading of heathen poems. In it Alcuin said that religious literature was to be read aloud at meals, rather than listening to stories and music of pagans.

Alcuin's influence on education was extensive. As a youth he studied under Aelbert with whom the young scholars learned grammar, rhetoric, and jurisprudence while others recited verse. His fame as an educator spread to the court of Charlemagne. Since Charlemagne enjoyed hearing histories and tales of noble deeds, he had introduced into his court the monastic practice of reading or singing at mealtimes. He demanded a high standard of reading and set up strict rules which readers must follow.

Charlemagne

Charlemagne, himself, never read aloud publicly, but he took reading seriously. The custom at that time seems to have been to assign to various readers the portions of the book which they were to read aloud. This gave them a chance to rehearse their part so that they could give a polished performance. Charlemagne, however, had other ideas on how to obtain good reading. He made it necessary for everyone to be perfectly acquainted with all the material at all times, for he reserved the right to ask anyone to read any part of the manuscript. The state of constant preparedness which this demanded built up a large corps of excellent readers at the palace. Charlemagne simply pointed his staff at an individual who then began to read and continued to do so until he heard the signal to stop, a guttural sound, uttered by the Emperor. It was to this influential court that Alcuin came as an honored scholar, bringing with him his own theories as well as the principles of the Venerable Bede.

While churchmen thus linked England to the continent intellectually and, at the same time, gave her religious unity at home, they had little interest in helping her to achieve political unity. The country was still broken up into small kingdoms and warring factions and was, in short, ripe once more for invasion. Near the end of the eighth century the Scandinavians invaded England, and by the middle of the ninth century they came in large numbers. The Norsemen, like the Anglo-Saxons before them, came first to plunder and then to stay. Once more the culture of the people was to suffer. Buildings were destroyed, monasteries were ruined, books were burned and almost the last vestiges of Roman civilization disappeared. The plight of the islanders was desperate when Alfred (849-899?) became their king.

Invasions

Alfred's mother had fostered in her sons a love of learning, and Alfred was one of the first English kings who was able to read. As a boy he had often heard Saxon poems recited, and since he had a good memory he was able to keep many of them in mind and could memorize and recite with ease. If legend speaks truly, the gleeman's

King Alfred

art played no small role in establishing Alfred's supremacy in his kingdom. Relying on the desire of the invaders for entertainment, the king, by disguising himself as a gleeman, gained admittance to the Danish camp and learned the plans of battle. Successful spying by this royal scop enabled him to plan a surprise attack and overcome his enemies.[17]

Alfred was interested in learning and gave it every support he could. He had a strong desire to learn the liberal arts, but he was frustrated in this at first because, he said, "there were no good readers at that time in all the kingdom of the West Saxons."[18] According to his biographer, Asser, this did not discourage the king. Not only did he himself continue to recite the Saxon books and memorize the Saxon poems, but he made others learn them too. He welcomed scholars to his court and had them read to him at every possible opportunity. Asser himself lived at the court for eight months and had to be available day or night to read any books which the king requested. When a quotation particularly appealed to Alfred, it was copied into a book which he carried in his bosom. The king also read many books himself and enjoyed discussing them and studying topics of general interest so that he became a scholar in his own right.

When he became king, he said he doubted that there was one man south of the Thames who could translate a letter from Latin into English. Before he died, he himself was to translate not only the works of the Venerable Bede but was also to give his countrymen a translation of Boethius, which was so well done that Ethelwerd in his *Chronicle* said it seemed to bring that remarkable man's book to life again for those who heard it.[19]

The oral reader played an important role in Alfred's plans to acquire and spread education. When Alfred came to power, little remained of the former culture except what the storyteller had stored in his memory. Upon the narrator's skill and integrity as an interpreter rested much of the responsibility for transmitting and elucidating what he knew and for shaping the minds and attitudes of his fellowman.

Gleemen, chant or recite

Of necessity the nature of the storyteller's performance changed with time and circumstance, and in the early centuries of the Christian era it is hard to tell just how he did perform. Authorities differ on whether the gleeman chanted in a clear, rather monotonous recitative or whether he recited. When Widsith says he "can sing and tell a tale," it would seem to indicate that he made some distinction between the two. It is difficult to say whether the gleeman sang his songs as described in *Beowulf*, or whether he recited them. In Middle High German "sagen" means to say, narrate or recite poetry, and the "sager" is the individual who recites or reads poems aloud. At a later date Martin Luther used the phrase "ich singan und sagen will" in a well-known Christmas carol. It may be taken literally, or it may be used for emphasis.[20] (See reference no. 12)

It is also difficult to ascertain how gesture and music were used in telling the ancient poems, and about the only thing we can be sure of is that they were rendered orally. Apart from the fact that very few people could read, this premise seems borne out by the frequent references to recital by scop and gleeman and by the verse form and the structure of the poems themselves.

Evidence of oral recitation

In poem after poem, *Beowulf, Andreas, Juliana,* and *The Nativity*, to name a few, the expression "Lo" or "Hwaet" was used. This was a form of address to a hearer, and the gleeman may have uttered it after striking a chord on his harp to command the attention of his audience. Another clue to oral recitation is found in the frequent use of dialogue in early English literature as, for example, in *Beowulf, Elene,* and *The Battle of Malden. Christ* with its dialogue between Mary and Joseph would be a delight to a reciter because of its dramatic range. Dialogue would probably be easier to convey through some kind of recitation, declamation, or chanting than through song, and this may give an additional clue to the mode of presentation at this time. The use of the speaking or chanting voice would also have been more suitable for the dramatic monologues found in old English literature. The form of such works as "The Banished Wife's Complaint," "The Husband's Message," "The Wanderer," "The Seafarer" and others, dramatic in nature, suggest speech rather than song. In any case singing and recitative are related, as are recitative and reciting, for there comes a point at which they are practically indistinguishable. In this period it seems probable that the minstrel did not confine himself to any one method, but used song, chant, recitative, or recitation according to the nature of his material, the situation, the audience, and his own particular skill or preference. This was undoubtedly true in early Anglo-Saxon days as well as in the time of King Alfred.

Alfred's descendants carried on his policies, strengthening churches, abbeys, and schools in order to spread education among both churchmen and the laity. That little now remains of their culture is not the fault of the men who followed Alfred, but the inevitable result of England's history. Two more invasions were to sweep over the land before it would be able to settle down to a long period of development and progress. The period 979-1016 saw the second Danish conquest, and no sooner had the Danes been assimilated than an even greater change was to be brought to England by the coming of the Normans in 1066.

Danish conquest

In Norman England the diseur or declaimer probably chanted his early compositions in metre to a musical accompaniment, and he may have relied on gesture and pantomine to make vivid his story. The lower types of performers entertained the ordinary people with coarse jokes, acrobatics, trained animals, and story telling. These, as well as the much higher types of performers, were variously known as minstrels, jougleurs, joglars, jestours, and joculatores. From this time on a much clearer picture of the island's culture can be obtained, and the path of oral literature can be more easily followed.

Taillefer

The story begins on the day William of Normandy invaded England. As his soldiers waded ashore, a romantic and dramatic figure pranced at the head of the conquering army. This was Taillefer, the trouvere or minstrel of the Norman court. He came juggling a sword and chanting the Lay of Ronceval. Wace says of him:

> Taillefer, Ki mult bien cantout,
> Sor un cheval Ki tost alout,
> Devant li dus alout cantant
> De Karlemaine e de Rollant
> E, d'Oliver e des vassals
> Ki morurent en Renchevals.[21]

Ritson translates this:

> Telfur, who well could sing a strain,
> Upon a horse that went amain,
> Before the duke rode singing loud,
> Of Charlemagne & Roland good.
> Of Oliver and those vassals,
> Who lost their lives at Roncevals.

These Normans were proud, gay, and fearless. They came from a land of fine courts, chivalrous deeds, and romantic ideals, and listened eagerly to the tales of the minstrels wherein both the life of the court and the world of adventure were vividly depicted. It seems probable that minstrels had been taken into France by Rollo and the Norsemen when they settled in Normandy, so that, by the time these people were again on the march, the minstrel came with them as a matter of course. The Norman minstrel, with his new language, ideas, and stories was a contrast to the Anglo-Saxon scop. He was a colorful creature whose Nordic sombreness (for part of.his tradition came from the far north) had been tempered during his stay in France by other influences from the south of Europe, especially Provence. In the south the traditions of ancient Rome had been passed on to the reciter-poet. He was thus a descendant of the reciting poets of Rome or of the **mimi** and **histriones**, and in all probability he combined the arts of both.

In England the minstrel's art had often been highly regarded in Saxon times, but it rose to new heights of popularity under the Normans, and for a long time, enjoyed high standing. In France there were schools for minstrels at Beauvais, Cambrai, and Lyons,

Successful minstrels

and there were also guilds. With luck and diligence a minstrel could aspire to an enviable position in Norman-English society. Berdic, under the title of **joculator regis**, or king's minstrel, owned a large area of land. Later, under William's son, Henry I, Rahere, who had previously been minstrel to the king, became the founder of St. Bartholomew's Priory at Smithfield. Master Henry of Avranches, as the King's poet, served in the court of Henry III, and was presented with a number of gifts by the king, and had won the favor of both court and church. Other minstrels were so highly esteemed that they not only performed in monasteries and priories but were probably permanent members of the staffs of such institutions. They might be specially invited to a castle or religious house, where, as guests, they were given special courtesies as well as pay.

The French **trobaires**, or **trouveres**, as they came to be called, were creative poets and composers of music, and were frequently of noble or even royal birth. In addition to them there were men of lesser skill and lower rank. Many of these lived the life of a wandering minstrel traveling throughout the land to find an audience for their performances. They recited tales and sang songs which may, or may not, have been of their own composition.

Minstrels in castles

Few minstrels could aspire to a permanent position in a royal court, but there were many plums to be had in the halls of the nobility. Many of the medieval romances paint the backdrop for the minstrel's act. The lord and his lady sat on a dais, surrounded by their entire household, since it was usual for everyone in the castle, from the lord to his simplest servant, to eat in the same hall. The diners sat in couples; lovers, husband and wife, or parent and child shared the same plate. A dinner at court was seldom a dull affair, and fist fights often occurred. The diners threw cheese, bread, or pieces of meat; if they were sufficiently angry they threw knives. After these temperamental outbursts were over, the meal proceeded. At its conclusion the tables were cleared, and the great event of the evening, the minstrel's performance, began. This probably brought quiet to the room, for the minstrel presented to his audience a great variety of imaginative adventures such as might be covered today by theatre, cinema, radio, television and reading. Nevertheless, if we are to accept the story of the Saxon hero, Hereward the Wake, the minstrel could not always command the full attention of his audience. After the Norman Conquest, Hereward returned by stealth to his former castle. He saw its new owner, a Norman lord, surrounded by his drunken knights and their women; a minstrel was trying, not too successfully, to entertain them by telling rude tales and by making fun of the Saxons.

Hereward the Wake

The Norman Conquest ushered in a new era when Norman-French was the language of the aristocracy, Latin the language of the church, and Anglo-Saxon the language of the servants' hall. In this period the new minstrel flourished and was never absent from a feast, wedding, tournament, or other happy occasion. It was his duty not only to recite to the guests, but to set into verse the events of such important days.

While some of the best minstrels were able to maintain the purity of their profession and devote themselves to composing stories in verse and songs, many found that, if they wanted to make an acceptable living, they must combine a number of skills. Audiences varied in background and in intelligence, and performers began to combine the arts of the various levels of minstrelsy ranging from the art of the able reciter to the juggling tricks of the vaudevillian.

Skills of the minstrel

In the fabliau "Des Deux Bordeors Ribauz" two minstrels engage in a dialogue, each contending that he has more skills than the other. One boasts he can sing songs and tell stories in Romance or in Latin, at court or at a feast. His repertoire includes stories of Vivien de Bourgogne, Bernart de Saisogne and romances of adventure such as those of the Round Table. The other minstrel replies that he knows many stories, dits, and fabliaux, and besides this can play with batons (sticks), knives, cords and slings. In addition he knows how to play the trumpet and how to cut a cape.[22]

During this period when the only audience for Anglo-Saxon poems was a conquered people, it was natural that Anglo-Saxon literature should suffer. However, the adjustments which it had to make to meet the challenge brought it to a greater flowering when it did come into its own again in later centuries. Not only did it broaden its scope in form and language, but it also developed new fields in subject matter.

The Crusades

The impact of the First Crusade (1095-99) was felt throughout Europe, for it opened a door through which men glimpsed the culture of the Orient. In the Near East and in India the story teller had long been a dominant figure. He was found in the market square, the cafe, and in almost every place where people congregated. He had a rich hoard of stories, many from the famous Arabian Nights' tales, and his stock never seemed to diminish. The public eagerly sought him out, for he was their great storybook, their endless fountain of imaginative literature. His tales had such a magical quality that physicians, as in classical Greece and Rome, advised the hearing of tales for nervous or sleepless persons or to assuage the pain of sufferers. The dreamy, somnolent voice of the story teller had a soothing effect on the hearer, as a palliative or as a gentle opiate. Gradually, through wars, crusades, adventures, and commerce the oriental tales were brought to the western world and became a part of the literature and of the minstrel's art in the Middle Ages.

In the twelfth and thirteenth centuries French literature held pride of place in Europe. French stories were so popular that they

French literature

were taken to other lands. In turn, foreign stories were taken to France and given a new style and treatment. The old poems, often epic or dramatic in nature, began to give way to a more intimate form—the romance. The romance had often more finesse and delicacy than the early poems and was generally better suited to entertaining a smaller circle. Usually in verse, its subject matter was concerned with three major areas. These were referred to as (a) "Matter of France," which dealt with stories such as those of Roland and Charlemagne; (b) "Matter of Britain," which told of British heroes and history; and (c) "Matter of Rome," which was concerned with people and events in the ancient world. In addition, there were tales from the north, tales from the east, and supernatural stories.[23]

The metrical romance

These romances, translated into English in the twelfth and early thirteenth centuries, became very popular and offered a wide variety of entertainment ranging from the delicate and the dramatic to the humorous and the coarse. They included tales of chivalry and adventure, tender love stories, and tales of miracles and marvels, as well as stories and legends of the world of make-believe such as were found in the Celtic romances. They told of battles between Christian and pagan and brought historical events before the very eyes of the people.

Subject-matter of romances

Many of the incidents related in the metrical romances were basically true or at least had elements of truth in them, but others were so preposterous that they lost their appeal when people became better educated.

In *Kyng Alisaunder* the author tells of India where, in the river Ganges, there are fish three hundred feet in length. He tells of people who have only one eye and one foot—but the foot is big enough to cover the body and is used for protection against rain and sun. Another group of people have ears so long that they wrap themselves in their ears to keep out snow, rain, or sun. The nature of the romances was summed up thus in *Sir Orfeo*:

Sir Orfeo

The layes that ben of harpyng
Ben yfound of frely thing
Sum ben of wele and sum of wo,
And sum of joy, and merthe also
Sum of bourdys, and sum of rybaudry,
And sum ther ben of the feyre;
Sum of trechery, and sum of gyle,
And sum of happes that fallen by while.[24]

Romances continued in popularity well into the fourteenth century, and in *Cursor Mundi* we read:

Cursor Mundi

Men lyekn jestis for to here
And romans rede in divers manere
Of Alexander the Conqueroure,

Of Julius Caesar the emperoure,
Of Grece and Troy the strong stryf,
There many a man lost his lyf,
Of Brute that baron bold of hond.[25]

Some of the metrical romances were very long and were probably divided into parts, one portion being presented at one sitting. No doubt the minstrel, like the serial story writer of today, deliberately interrupted his tale at the moment of greatest suspense to draw his audience back the following day to hear more. Sometimes, too, as a minstrel neared the end of a tale, he would try to whet the curiosity of his hearers so that they would want him to tell another. Near the end of the long story of *Gawain and the Green Knight* the poet or minstrel mentions Gawain's adventures, but says he will not tell about them at that time. Other long romances such as *Le Bone Florence de Rome* and the *Erle of Toulouse* were probably serialized too. Shorter romances like *Sir Orfeo* with its twenty-one pages of couplets may well have been given in a single performance.

Other literary forms

Shorter literary forms known as fabliaux, lais, and dits were also introduced into England by the French. The fabliaux were action-packed stories with fast moving plots which usually set out to make people laugh. Full of fun, with mischief, adventure, and infidelity as frequent components, they were the seed from which was to spring much of the literature of Europe, such as the *Canterbury Tales*, Boccaccio's *Decameron*, and other important works. Fabliaux probably originated in France, but they may well have been written in both France and England. These tales did not remain the property of the authors, but were passed on to others much as jokes are shared today. Though not always in the best taste, these stories were sometimes composed to illustrate a moral principle, and were frequently told for the amusement of the "best" people. For instance, it was not unusual for an anchoress, living in a pious retreat from the world, to have someone come to her window to give her the news and entertain her with fabliaux. As she listened, she was often convulsed with laughter, since the stories, though perhaps strange fare for an anchoress, were hilarious.

Lais were usually shorter than the fabliaux. Marie of France wrote lais in narrative form and memorized many stories which had been turned into lais by the Bretons, who were known for their skill in using this genre. The "Breton lay" was a short romance which could easily be read at a single sitting. Chaucer's Franklin describes the lai as he begins to tell one to the Canterbury pilgrims:

These olde gentil Britouns in hir dayes
Of diverse adventures maden layes,
Rymeyed in hir firste Briton tonge;
Which layes with hir instrumentz they song,
Or elles redden hem for hir pleasaunce.

The debats and dits dialogues, as the name implies, were forms suitable for more than one performer. While one minstrel, by using gestures and varying vocal tones, often impersonated several characters, the dit dialogue was a question-and-answer type of entertainment in which several persons could take part although they could also be given by one person. The theme was usually love, and the answers given to the questions posed were sometimes crude.

The form and language of medieval literature was influenced by the fact that it was still largely an oral literature. Although the number of people who could read was growing steadily throughout this period, the human voice was still the medium through which an author could reach the largest public. Illustrations of the speaker-listener relationship are manifold in the literature of the period. In the metrical romances, for example, the minstrel spoke directly to his hearers as "lordings," "lordys," "gode men," "mi leve frende dere," "lords . . . beurnes or bacheleres," and he frequently used "hear ye" or "hear," or their equivalent, in introducing his story. In *The Gestes of Alisaunder of Macedoine,* he varied this with, "Tend ye tytely to me and take goode heede." In *Havelok the Dane* there are many instances of "now herkneth," or "s'il vous plaist, escoutez," (Please listen); in *Horn Childe and Maiden Rimnild,* the minstrel says "Herken, and ye may here," asking his audience to listen while he tells his story as he heard it in the city.

Speaker-hearer relationship

Familiar or well-worn phrases such as "still as a stone," "lili-white," "blac so ever eny cole," "rose red," "whyte as snow," "red as any cherry," "wele and wo," "farre and nere" are common. Many of these are similes which can tersely present a picture. Frequent repetitions were very popular—both with the minstrel and his hearers. They served to simplify the problem of memorization for the minstrel, and they both refreshed the memory of the hearer and intensified the emotional effect. In *Emare* "she was driven" or "she was so driven" occurs four times in twenty-three lines, and a vigorous passage from *Havelok the Dane* owes much of its impact to the use of repetition:

Familiar phrases

Repetition

> He broken armis, he broken knes,
> He broken shankes, he broken thes[26]

In *Launfal* the phrases "Launfal took his leve" and "Launfal tok leve" are repeated within twelve lines, while the word "fifty" is used six times in nine lines.

In medieval romances changes of scene and character, or transitions, are very clear and definite so that the hearer is never in doubt as to where the story is taking place or which characters are involved. These transitions have a child-like directness and simplicity. In *The Squyr of Lowe Degre* the minstrel says "But leve we of the stewarde here, and speke we more of that squyer." and later,

Change of scene and character

"leve we hear of this squyr wight, and speke we of that lady bryght." In the *Erle of Tolous* we find "leve we now thys lady in care, and to hur lorde wyll we fare." Striving for verisimilitude the minstrel used such words as "as the romans trewly told," or similar phrases to substantiate his authority.

Singing and reciting

In the Anglo-Saxon period evidence was studied as to whether the entertainer sang, chanted, or recited. In Norman times the signs again suggest that he probably did all three—depending on his material, his preference, or his audience. Sometimes he combined singing and recitation in a single selection. *Aucassin et Nicolette* gives an unusually clear picture as to how this was done. It opens with a short section, which was apparently sung. Throughout this romance the phrases "now is sung" and "now they say and tell and relate" are frequently interpolated, showing how song and recitation were combined.

In *King Horn* the dialogue is in stanza form, which may indicate that the dialogue was sung, and narrative parts of the poem recited.[27] A combination of singing and reciting with alternating prose and rhyme also characterized some of the Scottish ballads such as "Young Beichan and Susy Pye." In many of these poems the minstrel recited the story while the audience joined in the chorus.

French poets of the twelfth century, according to Ritson, composed the music to their romances. He claimed that the "songs" of the minstrels had no definite melody but were chanted in a "monotonous stile to the harp or other instrument." It was Ritson's opinion that the minstrel always strummed on his musical instrument. From the evidence in the romances themselves it is clear that minstrels varied in their practices. In *Sir Orfeo* harp playing is extolled. In "Thomas the Rhymer" the poet says he does not care for harping for "tonge is chefe of mynstralcye."

Dialogue

There were others who had theories as to how the minstrel recited. Warton, too, in *The History of English Poetry*, suggests that each line was recited in a monotonous manner with a pause in the middle of the line. A translation of the Psalms in this period followed the same pattern. Gautier says "Le jongleur ne **lit** pas, il ne **dit** pas, il **chante**."[28] "The minstrel does not read, he does not speak, he sings." It seems clear that both fabliaux and lays had in the beginning some musical accompaniment. The early fabliaux were in verse, but as they developed, they began to be in prose, and the harp was abandoned and chanting began to make way for more ordinary speech. There are many instances of conversation where reciting would be more effective than singing. Changes in voice and characterization could be more easily achieved in recitation than in chanting. Even in the shorter lays the musical instrument was eventually omitted, and the minstrel became strictly a storyteller.

Whether minstrels read their stories or repeated them from memory has been a topic much discussed by some authorities. Those who would prove that minstrels were illiterate point to the fact that not a single metrical romance exists in English which shows evidence of having been written by a minstrel. Another argument sometimes offered is that frequent changes in names or spelling from one manuscript to another suggest that the writer who recorded the selection acquired his material from hearing it recited rather than from having seen it written. Neither argument seems very convincing. Neither proves that the writer did not hear the minstrel read, nor that the minstrel could not have read if that had been desirable. It is much more plausible that some minstrels could read, that they sometimes read and sometimes recited. There were also many who could not read and depended entirely on memory or on their powers of composition for their repertoires.

References to reading

References to books and reading are common, and such phrases as "we fyndeth ywryte," "als sayes the buke," "in romance as we rede," "in story as we rede" and "in boke as we rede" can readily be found. In *The Mabinogion*, a collection of Welsh tales, there is one entitled "The Dream of Rhonabwy." In this story the narrator says that a book was necessary, for there were so many colors on the horses, the arms, the equipment, the rich scarfs and precious stones that no one, not even a bard or a seer, could remember such descriptions without a book.[29] Again, the statement from *Sir Orfeo* seems to stress not only reading, but the frequency of reading when he says:

> We reden ofte, and fynde ywryte,
> As clerkes don us to wyte.[30]

Of course, it is quite possible that some of the minstrels may have pretended to a reading ability which they did not have, a pretense which would have been ludicrous if literate minstrels were unknown. Education and, of course, ability varied greatly. One minstrel said that he could tell tales in French and Latin, and that he knew a vast number of lays, chansons de gestes, and romantic adventures. If his memory was good enough, he had no need of books. Conversely, if he could read, he could put less stress on his memory. As already noted, the use of stock phrases reduced the problem of memorization.

Yvain

Whether or not the minstrel could read, he was faced with a problem when reading became more widespread among the people. In rich families it became the custom to read or tell tales as the company sat around the fire. Chretien de Troyes, in his romance *Yvain*, told of a family party at which the daughter of the house read aloud to the assembled group. The professional minstrel was to become far less important than he had been in the past because the task of entertainment was gradually being taken over by members of the family. They had heard the old romances repeated so often that they could recite them with ease, or if literate, could read aloud for the delight of the gathered assemblage. In the castles of kings reciting and reading aloud continued to be popular. Haakon, king of the Norsemen, who captured the western part of Scotland in the thirteenth century, enjoyed hearing the Norse tales and songs in the castles he occupied. And, as he lay dying on his way back to Norway, he listened to the chronicles of the Norwegian rulers. Bruce, King of Scotland, read to his men to keep up their spirits while they awaited their turn to be rowed across Loch Lomond. Story telling and reading aloud were also popular in halls of learning. At King's College in Cambridge, on Holy days, recreation often consisted of reciting poems and chronicles and telling tales of wonder. To keep such entertainment within the limits of acceptability the statutes of University Hall discreetly forbade the telling of love stories, the singing of vulgar songs, improper conversations and fighting.

Geoffrey of Vinsauf: *Poetria Nova*

With an ever-widening circle of people engaging in story telling and reading aloud it is worth considering what guidance was available to help them perfect these arts. In 1210 A.D. Geoffrey of Vinsauf wrote his *Poetria Nova*, and in the section entitled "L'Action" is found some pertinent information on the art of recitation.[31] The speaker, Geoffrey says, can communicate with his hearers through the use of his voice, his countenance, and his gestures. The voice has its own laws and should observe them as follows: Let the spoken sentence maintain its natural pauses and let the diction maintain its accent. Let those words which are separated by meaning be separated, and join those words which are joined by meaning. Delivery should be consistent with the subject matter and should be an image of the idea. Facial expression and gestures can aid the voice in communicating the idea, and are most effective when used with restraint. Many of his principles are consistent with theories of oral interpretation today.

Poetria Nova: **Emotion**

As to the part played by emotion in effective recitation, Geoffrey says that the emotion should not be as deeply experienced as in real life. In anger one is not to be overcome by that emotion, but should be moved to some extent and should indicate some of the outward signs of anger. Whatever the fanciful situation may be, the reciter should enter into it in a becoming manner, then employ an easy flow of speech, sophisticated transitions, and a firm reserve to achieve the desired effect. A charming reserve, he says, is like a touch of gold.

Poetria Nova was probably intended for the amateur as well as for the professional entertainer, and it is certain that many non-professional performers gave much thought to their delivery in this age of manners and form. Meanwhile, as the educated gradually began to read more and more for themselves, all but the ablest minstrels had to move down the social scale. The fortunate few who could find a position in a nobleman's hall continued to enjoy fine patronage, but even they had to seek new ways to please their masters. The others were thrown upon the simple villagers who were as keen as ever to hear stories in their homes, in taverns, and at fairs.

While this lowered the prestige of the wandering minstrel, he continued to fulfill the traditional functions of his calling. As in earlier and more prosperous days, he was often historian, newspaper, gossip-monger, and cultural custodian. It is thought, for instance, that the *Historia Regum Britanniae* by Geoffrey of Monmouth (c. 1136) was based upon tales recited by a minstrel. The events were probably first orally described by the minstrel and later collected by a writer or another minstrel and then recorded by Geoffrey of Monmouth.

Geoffrey of Monmouth

There were times when the minstrels not only recorded history but helped to make it. They were potentially the propagandists of their day. By presenting the news from a particular point of view, whether their own or that of a patron, they could often sway public opinion and influence the course of events. On occasion, some of the romances the minstrels told were revised to carry the ideas of rebellion and stir up the desire for equality where no equality existed. In the wars in the stormy reign of Henry III (1216-1272) the minstrels sided with the people, and as late as the fifteenth century the Welsh minstrels were accused of stirring up rebellion. There were even instances of the minstrels being involved in church controversies, as when Hugh, bishop of Coventry, accused the bishop of Ely of gaining popular support by paying minstrels to sing his praises to the public. On another occasion a poem in praise of his own country was written by Michael of Cornwall in reply to a critical comment by Henry of Avranches. It is this poem which Michael himself presented orally to leading church officials and at Cambridge. Such examples are enough to show that though the general prosperity of the minstrels suffered many ups and downs through the years, their influence as a class was never negligible and was sometimes formidable.

Minstrels: Political aspects

The oral work of the church continued to be of significance in the period following the Norman Conquest. In *The Monastic Constitutions of Lanfranc*,[32] the author, who was Archbishop of Canterbury in the days of William the Conqueror, had much to say about the training of readers. This training often began at an early age, and Lanfranc included comments on the training of children. Recalling his own early days in the monastery, he relates that on one occasion, when he was reading in the refectory, a prior wrongly "corrected" his use of stress. Instead of correcting the prior in turn, Lanfranc repeated the word as instructed, realizing that an error in reading was by no means as important as obedience. The fact that the question came up at all shows the value placed upon stress and

Lanfranc

emphasis and the sensitivity of master and pupil to rhythm in reading. In later days, when Lanfranc drew up the above-mentioned Constitution, the subject of oral reading received much consideration.

Keeping up the standards of oral reading was the cantor's responsibility, and the fact that the cantor ranked second in the church, as far as reading the lesson or chanting were concerned, is an indication that this was regarded as an important assignment. The cantor must ensure that no errors would occur in the reading or chanting of the church service. He must rehearse those who were to undertake these tasks, and in an emergency he must immediately be ready to take the place of anyone unable to carry out these duties. The cantor must also train someone to read to the workers when their labors were over for the day. He might do this himself, or he might coach a child to do it.

Children were important members of the monastic community, so it is not surprising that Lanfranc gave much thought to their training. He stipulated that they were to read aloud and practice their chanting in the cloister. Sitting apart from each other, they were to read in a loud tone. Novices in the monastery were not permitted to read in public, nor to sing anything alone, and they were instructed to listen in silence to the reading during meals and after vespers.

There was a great deal of ceremony to emphasize the importance of oral reading. At Christmas time, before the gospel of the day was read aloud, the reader had to prostrate himself before the lectern while prayers were said. When an abbot was elected, the entire membership of the monastery arose when he went to read and when he returned from reading. Even the cellarer felt the influence of oral reading. His duties were read aloud and explained to him, whereupon he had to fall prostrate and admit any shortcoming of which he had been guilty. The ceremony over, he provided an appropriate feast in the refectory during which reading was again heard. These are but some of the numerous references which Lanfranc makes to the practice and frequency of reading aloud in the monastery.

John of Salisbury

John of Salisbury was another educator and philosopher who had much to say about reading aloud. Born about 1115, he was educated in France, and later returned to England to be secretary to Thomas A. Becket, Archbishop of Canterbury. In the *Metalogicon* his defense of the Trivium is regarded as a masterpiece in pedagogical thinking. He defended the Trivium* and discussed grammar and logic. Grammar, he said, includes the study of letters, words, syllables, metre, accent, and punctuation. His comment that some use a colon where one is to inhale or pause, clearly indicates that he had oral reading in

* Trivium - grammar, logic, rhetoric.

mind.[33] He also mentioned a system of notation which he considered helpful for memorization and understanding and regretted that such a scheme was not in use. He spoke of grammar as related to accent and as regulating the voice so that it would be fitting for all persons and all topics.

Bernard of Chartres

His material shows his familiarity with Isidore and Quintilian. He said that poetry ought to be recited in one way and prose in another. He mentioned Bernard of Chartre's custom of requiring pupils to recite what they had heard in the lecture of the previous day, using encouragement, or flogging, as he deemed best. Their evening lesson, he reported, included training in speaking and writing, and at the conclusion of this session the "Penitential Psalm" and the Lord's Prayer were recited. Bernard also taught his students to read stories and poems with care and required each one to memorize something each day.

Convents

The education of women received some attention in the Middle Ages, and since the church was the pivot around which life revolved, many women took Holy Orders. Their convents and nunneries followed many of the same rules that governed the monasteries. Reading at meals was an accepted custom. Not all the sisters, at least in the early days, could read, but those who could were expected to do so. At the end of a meal there was responsive recitation. This allowed even non-readers to participate orally. Recitation was given further recognition in the twelfth century when Gilbert of Sempringham decreed that the hundreds of nuns in his order should recite rather than sing the psalms and hymns. By the fourteenth century literacy was sufficiently widespread that Thomas de la More, abbot of St. Albans, was able to request it as a condition of admission to the convent. He also required all who entered the nunnery to agree in writing that they would follow the Rules of St. Benedict. This, too, was tantamount to at least preferring, if not requiring, some degree of literacy in the applicant. In the following century reading aloud was also a part of *The Rewle of Sustris Menouresses.*

Gilbert of Sempringham

Such measures were aimed at keeping reading and learning on a high level within the church itself, but the ultimate aim of the church was to reach out and bring all men to God. Means had to be sought to interest the populace in what the church had to offer. One problem was to make the church service meaningful not only to churchmen and scholars but to the simple folk as well. The universal desire to hear stories offered an obvious means of arousing interest in religion, and various types of sacred stories and poems were introduced. As early as the twelfth century Wace had written legends in verse which were recited on the appropriate saints' days. With the unlearned listener in mind, Orm composed his famous *Ormulum* about 1200 A.D. This was a paraphrase of the gospels together with a homiletic exposition of the paraphrase. The lives of the saints

Saints' legends

provided another rich source of material, and legends of the saints were written in English verse in the thirteenth century. These legends were collected into anthologies and used on various occasions. One such anthology, the *South-English Legendary*, was written in couplets and was concerned with the lives of holy men and holy days. It was so designed that the life of a particular saint could be read in church on his holy day.

Homilies

The *North English Collection of Homilies* gives indications of having been prepared for reading in convents and possibly in church, with references being made to guide the reader. This collection was also written in English for, says the prologue, not all men can understand French or Latin, although they long to hear the gospel. About 1400 another significant collection appeared, the *Scottish Legendary*, attributed to John Barbour. A little later came the *Festial* prepared by John Mirk to help the priests in instructing the people. Following the calendar, it consisted of short sermons, legends, and religious stories for certain festival days.

Cursor Mundi, largely in couplets, describes Biblical history and provided English verses for the priests to read to the people. *Handlyng of Synne* by Robert Manning of Brunne and adapted from *Manuel des Peches* included incidents, stories, and examples. The *Ayenbite of Inwyt* by Dan Michel made, as the author says, for "lewd" (unlearned) people is a moralistic treatise based on a French work *Le Somme des Vices et des Vertus. Speculum Vitae* by William of Nassyngton (ca. 1380) is obviously directed to a hearer, as the author states his plan for a moral life:

> "Bot to my wordes only takes kepe,
> And whyl I speke, kepe you fro slepe . . .
> . . . . . .
> Lysten to me and ye may here,
> Whow ye schal reule yowre lyf."[34]

These and other materials were used by priests who recognized writers more talented than themselves. Some of these selections were read in part, while others were short enough to be read in their entirety. Such works gradually came into the homes of the people as literacy became more widespread. As time went on, there were more books on the virtues and vices than one could read in a lifetime.

Exempla

The clergy, then, as now, used incidents and stories to illustrate their sermons, and these were called "exempla" or examples. These examples ranged from expositions of high ideals to broad anecdotes. There were many collections of exempla from which the speaker could draw, such as the *Alphabetum Narrationum*, the *Gesta Romanorum*, the *Summa Predicantium* of John Bromyard, and the writings of Jacques de Vitry, Etienne de Bourbon, and Thomas de Chantimpre. These, along with the religious lyric or hymn recited in the church, constituted the main types of literature used by the clergy.

Fabliaux

The church also found a use for fabliaux. These often dealt with moral or social problems in a humorous way and were the stock-in-trade of many a wandering minstrel. Seeing how eagerly people hung upon every word of these popular entertainers, religious men began to compete with the ordinary minstrel in order to bring worthy thoughts rather than ribaldry to a story-hungry world. St. Francis (1182-1226) went so far as to call his followers *joculatores Dei*, "minstrels of God." Some of the stories recited by these men offered strong competition to the minstrels, especially among educated and religious people; this fact, coupled with the steady growth of the reading public, further seriously undermined the minstrel's position. Slowly he sank to the point where he was considered to be a minister of the devil and was classified with harlots and malefactors.

St. Francis

Wandering friars thrived, preaching in village squares, churchyards, and in some churches. The friars began as spiritual leaders using stories and legends to stress Christian virtues and conduct, but it was not long before some of them started to rely too much on the humor in the fabliau rather than on the moral. As early as the twelfth century friars were being accused of gross exaggeration in order to amuse their hearers. The church disapproved of this and began to interfere with their activity. In Italy Dante was objecting that people were being fed on jokes and clowning. In England many influential people, including Wycliffe, were complaining that the friars went too far in following the methods of the minstrels. Nevertheless, it was still felt that much good could come of the church's adapting the storyteller's art to its own purposes, provided the right material was presented in the proper manner.

God's minstrels

In *Cursor Mundi* the author says that since people are eager to hear verses and read romances about Alexander, Caesar, Brutus, and King Arthur, they will be just as anxious to hear Bible stories and legends of the saints if these are well told. Langland, in *Piers Plowman*, makes a similar observation when he says that rich people keep minstrels to entertain them and reward these entertainers with fine gifts. God's minstrels and jesters, he says, should be welcomed in like fashion. Piers claims that he will have no contact with undesirable characters like Robyn the Rybaudoure who tell rough stories. Another poem which consciously avoided the usual themes of the minstrels' repertoire was *Speculum Vitae*, in which the poet says he will not make "veyn speakyng"

> Of dedes of armes ne of Amours,
> Os don mynstreles and other gestours.[35]

But though the subject matter was different, many of the new poems echoed the same forms that the minstrels had made familiar.

Close speaker-hearer relationship was still common, as for instance:

Religious stories

> Listeneth lordynges leof and dere,
> Ye that wolen of the Sonday here;
> The Sonday a day hit is
> That angeles and archayngeles joyn I wis,
> More in that ilke day
> Then eny other, as I the say.[36]

or again:

> Sayn Mark byginnes his godspel
> Wit wordes that I wil you tel,
> And tas witnes of Ysaye,
> That spekes of Crist in prophecye . . .[37]

Such examples indicate that though the tale might change from a secular to a religious theme, the form often reminded the hearers of the worldly minstrels who had preceded the minstrels of God.

. . . .

The Middle Ages was an era of pilgrimages. Men and women alike sought to strengthen their souls by going, in person, to the holy places associated with the saints, there to find forgiveness for their sins or comfort for their sorrows. Story telling and reading were part of the pilgrimage from earliest Christian times. One person, probably St. Sylvia, visited many of the holy places mentioned in the Bible, at each place hearing the appropriate scriptural passage read aloud.

Canterbury Tales

Examples could be multiplied throughout ensuing ages, but of all the Medieval pilgrimages few are so well known as the fictional one described by Geoffrey Chaucer in his *Canterbury Tales*. This remarkable author has drawn characters as life-like and credible as any flesh and blood pilgrim who ever existed. His masterpiece is a gold mine of information about life in fourteenth century England and abounds in references to oral literature. This whole poem is built upon and carries on the traditions of the romances and fabliaux of earlier days. Chaucer's storytellers speak in the first person; they address their hearers directly; they use dialogue frequently. Their tales show Chaucer's marvelous sense of tempo and rhythm, precision in word choice, and remarkable clarity and depth in characterization. Chaucer often uses abrupt transitions from one scene to another in the manner of earlier medieval tales, and condenses whole scenes and episodes into a short verse. His stories end with an invocation to the Deity. Most of these elements are common in oral recitation, and Chaucer was writing stories which his characters had "told." By Chaucer's time many people could read, and he knew that he was writing for both readers and hearers; consequently, such phrases as "as men may rede," "yet preye I yow that reden that I wryte" are common.

Chaucer could tell as rollicking a tale as any minstrel, but he had been a page at court and had associated with educated and cultured people, so he knew when he was slipping beyond the limits of good taste. But, he says, anyone who tells a tale he has heard is obliged to repeat it as exactly as he can; otherwise "he moote telle his tale untrewe, or feyne thing, or finde wordes newe." In these few phrases he dissociates himself from anything which may be offensive in the tale and states his view of the duties and obligations of the storyteller.

His characters

The characters in the *Canterbury Tales* come from all walks of life. There is the gracious and dainty nun and the Miller with a mouth "as greet as was a Greek forneys." Chaucer carefully delineates each character and then ascribes to each one a tale in keeping with that person's nature and station in life. In Chaucer's day, telling tales to relieve the tedium of a journey was as common as the modern traveller's practice of providing himself with reading material for the same purpose. The landlord of the Tabard Inn took it for granted, saying:

> . . . And well I woot, as ye goon by the weye,
> Ye shapen yow to talen and to pleye.[38]

All that the host needs to do, as master of ceremonies, is to decide how many stories each pilgrim shall tell, the order in which they shall take their turn, and the prize to be given to the one who shall tell "tales of best sentence and most solas."

The knight tells the first tale, and tells it well. He is aware of attention values, pointing out to his hearers that "it were al to long for to devyse the grete clamour." He includes dialogue, changes scenes abruptly as when he says, "Now wol I stinte of Palamon a lyte, and lete him in his prison stille dwelle, And of Arcite forth, I wol yow telle"; he addresses his hearers directly in phrases like "you lovers, axe I now this question . . ."; and at the end asks for divine blessing on the company, thus providing the traditional marks of oral recitation.

In different vein is the Miller's tale. The Miller admits, "I am dronke, I knowe it by my soun," and Chaucer warns the reader that this story may be offensive. If so, "Turne over the leef, and chese another tale."[39] The drunken Miller, the Pardoner with his sermon, the lusty Wife of Bath, and the learned Oxford Scholar; Chaucer knew them all. Thanks to his skill it is still possible to journey in their company from Southwark to Canterbury and to know each pilgrim as a distinct individual.

But not everyone in the group was willing to contribute a story. The Parson, citing St. Paul's letter to Timothy as his authority, disapproved of the custom, saying:

> Thou getest fable noon y-told for me;
> For Paul, that wryteth unto Timothee,
> Repreveth hem that weyven soothfastnesse
> And tellen fables and swich wrecchednesse.[40]

But, with or without St. Paul's approval, the evidence is overwhelming that story telling and reading aloud lost none of their charms and that stories were successfully used as examples, or exempla, by the churchmen. The pardoner, for instance, tells how he used them to prove his theme in sermons:

> I stonde lyk a clerk in my pulpet,
> And whan the lewed peple is doun y-set,
> I preche, so as ye han herd bifore,
> And telle an hundred false japes more . . .
>
> . . . .
>
> Thanne telle I hem ensamples many oon
> Of olde stories longe tyme agoon,–
> For lewed peple loven tales olde,–
> Swiche thynges kan they well reporte and holde.[41]

Other excerpts contribute Chaucer's more serious thoughts on what constituted good oral delivery. In the *Maunciple's Tale* the speaker says:

> The wyse Plato seeth, as ye may rede,
> The word mot nede accorde with the dede.
> If men shal telle proprely a thing,
> The word mot cosin be to the werking.[42]

That is, the words should be appropriate to the subject matter. For a concise and exact picture of the nature of good speech at that time we need only turn to the *Squire's Tale* where the stranger knight stands before the king in his banquet hall and gives his message:

Art of speech

> With a manly voys . . .
> After the firme used in his language,
> With-outen vyce of sillable or of lettre;
> And, for his tale sholde seme the bettre,
> Accordant to his wordes was his chere,
> As techeth art of spech hem that it lere.[43]

This well established theory of the art of oral delivery which Chaucer approved in the fourteenth century is equally valid today.

In England the Middle Ages was a period of growth in both literature and the speech arts. In spite of the chaos caused by successive invasions, a thin thread of continuity could be found in the oft-told tales of the storytellers. These men helped to bridge the gap between the divers races struggling to live together on the same island. The pagan literature of the scop and the gleeman was carried into the Christian era; though it was often obscured by the biblical tales with which the Church of Rome tried to replace it, it was never quite obliterated. Instead, the churchmen learned the gleeman's art, and the gleeman learned some Bible stories. When the Normans came, they added romantic tales of chivalry and exotic descriptions of faraway places. As man's horizon expanded to take in more of the world, literature was enriched and preserved and made ready for the coming Renaissance. In large measure, the men who preserved it were the tellers of tales.

References

1. St. Jerome, "Life of St. Hilarion," *Early Christian Biographies,* tr. Sister Marie L. Ewald (New York: Fathers of the Church, 1952), Vol. 15, 10. p. 251.

2. St. Augustine, *The City of God I-VII,* tr. D. B. Zema and J. J. Walsh (New York: Fathers of the Church, 1950), Vol. VIII. Bk. I. Ch. 1. p. 19.

3. *Ibid.*, tr. J. J. Walsh and G. Monahan, Vol. VII. Bk. XIV. Ch. 28. p. 410.

4. St. Augustine, *Confessions* (New York: Grosset & Dunlap), Bk. I. XVII. p. 18.

5. St. Augustine, "The Teacher," *The Teacher, The Free Choice of the Will, Grace and Free Will,* tr. Robert P. Russell (New York: Fathers of the Church, 1968), Vol. 59. Ch. IV. p. 16.

6. St. Augustine, *Christian Instruction,* tr. J. J. Gavigan (New York: CIMA Pub. Co., 1947), Vol. IV. Bk. IV. Ch. 5. 7. p. 174.

7. Isidore, "De la Retorica y Dialectica," *Etimilogias,* tr. Luis Cortes y Gongora (Madrid: Biblioteca de Autores Cristiano, 1951), Bk. II. Ch. XVII. 1. p. 53.

8. *Ibid.*, "De la Iglesia y Sectas Diversas," Bk. VIII. Ch. VII. 11. p. 199.

9. *The Rule of St. Benedict,* tr. Cardinal Gasquet (London: Chatto & Windus, 1925), Chapter IX. pp. 71-72.

10. St. Augustine of Canterbury, 1st Archbishop of Canterbury, died ca. 605.

11. The Venerable Bede, *Ecclesiastical History of the English Nation,* tr. J. E. King (Cambridge: Harvard University Press, 1962), Vol. II. Chapter II. p. 11.

12. R. Kogel, *Geschichte der Deutschen Litteratur bis zum Aufgange des Mittelalters* (Strassburg, Verlag: K. J. Trubner, 1894), Vol. I, 1, p. 143.

    In Middle High German "sagen" means "to tell" to speak as to narrate, praise, or recite poetry. The "sager" is the person who narrates, recites poems or reads them aloud. The phrase "sing and tell" was also used for emphasis, and it appears in a hymn by Martin Luther, one part of which goes:

    Of good tidings I bring so much,
    About it I want to sing and speak.
    (Courtesy of Professor Diether Haenicke)

13. Baedae, "Story of Caedmon," *Opera Historica,* tr. J. E. King (Cambridge: Harvard University Press, 1963), Vol. II. Ch. XXIV. p. 145.

14. The Venerable Bede, *op. cit.,* Preface p. 11.

15. *Ibid.,* p. 5.

16. W. S. Howell, *The Rhetoric of Alcuin & Charlemagne,* tr. W. S. Howell (New York: Russell & Russell, Inc., 1965), 40. p. 139.

17. William of Malmesbury, *Chronicle of the Kings of England,* tr. J. A. Giles (London: Bell & Daldy, 1866), Bk. II. Ch. 4. p. 114.

18. Asser, "Life of Alfred," *Six Old English Chronicles,* ed. J. A. Giles (London: Henry G. Bohn, 1848), p. 52.

19. "The Chronicle of Fabius Ethelwerd," *Six Old English Chronicles,* ed. J. A. Giles (London: Henry G. Bohn, 1848), Ch. III. p. 37.

20. "Widsith," *The Exeter Book,* ed. W. S. Mackie, EETS (London: Oxford University Press, 1934), Part II. p. 18, line 54. "ic maeg singan and secgan spell."

21. Robert Wace, *Le Roman de Rou,* ed. Edouard Frére (Rouen: Libraire de la Bibliothèque Publique, 1827), Vol. II. pp. 214-215.

22. M. Anatole de Montaiglon, *Recueil Général* (Paris: Librairie des Bibliophiles, 1872), Vol. I. p. 1, 3, 4, 11, 12.

23. *Cursor Mundi,* ed. R. Morris, EETS (London: Kegan Paul, Trench Trubner & Co., 1877-78-92), Vol. III. p. 1651.

24. J. Ritson, "Sir Orpheo," *Ancient English Metrical Romances* (Edinburgh: E. & G. Goldschmid, 1885), Vol. III. p. 4.

25. *Cursor Mundi, op. cit.,* p. 1651.

26. *Havelok the Dane,* ed. W. W. Skeat, EETS (London: Kegan Paul, Trench Trubner & Co., 1868), p. 52, lines 1902-1903.

27. F. B. Gummere, *Old English Ballads* (Boston: Ginn & Co., 1894), p. lxxiv.

28. Leon Gautier, *Les Épopées Francaises,* ed. Welter (Paris: Libraire Universitaire, 1892), 2nd ed., Vol. II. p. 115.

29. "The Dream of Rhonabwy," *The Mabinogion,* tr. Lady Charlotte Guest (London: Longman et al, 1843), Part V. p. 418. Suggested by Evelyn M. Sivier.

30. J. Ritson, *op. cit.,* lines 1 and 2.

31. Geoffrey of Vinsauf, "Poetria Nova," ed. Edmond Faral, *Les Arts Poétiques du XII et du XIII Siécle* (Paris: Librairie Ancienne, Honore Champion, 1924), p. 259.

32. *The Monastic Constitutions of Lanfranc,* tr. David Knowles (London, New York: Thomas Nelson and Sons, Ltd., 1951).

33. John of Salisbury, *Metalogicon,* tr. Daniel D. McGarry (Berkley: University of California, 1962), Bk. I. Ch. 20. p. 58.

34. "Speculum Vitae," *Englische Studien,* ed. Dr. Eugene Kolbing (New York: B. Westermann and Co., 1884), Vol. 7. p. 469, lines 30-32, 54-55.

35. *Ibid.,* lines 36-38.

36. *The Minor Poems of the Vernon Mss,* ed. Carl Harstmann, EETS (London: Kegan Paul, Trench Trubner & Co., 1892), Part I. Vol. I. XXXIII, p. 251.

37. *English Metrical Homilies,* ed. John Small (Edinburgh: Wm. Paterson, 1862) p. 9.

38. Chaucer, *The Canterbury Tales,* "Prologue," lines 771-72.

39. *Ibid.*, "The Miller's Tale, Prologue," line 3177.

40. *Ibid.*, "The Parson's Tale, Prologue," lines 29-34.

41. *Ibid.*, "The Pardoner's Tale, Prologue," lines 391-394, 435-438.

42. *Ibid.*, "The Maunciple's Tale," lines 207-210.

43. *Ibid.*, "The Squire's Tale," lines 99-104.

The Chained Bible – First Reading of the Bible in the Crypt of Old St. Paul's, 1540. John Porter reading.
Painting by Sir George Harvey. Copyright. Courtesy Radio Times Hulton Picture Library, London.

Chapter IV
THE RENAISSANCE AND THE SEVENTEENTH CENTURY

It is a great part of happiness, and the greatest part of gratitude, if a man recognizes the blessings which he enjoys. We are bound accordingly to congratulate our own age, and to thank the Powers above, to whose goodness it is due, – that noble studies, for so many ages almost buried, are again in blossom over the whole world, and are propagated with the greatest success.[1]

Erasmus

These ecstatic words of Erasmus reflect the spirit of the Renaissance. They express the exultation of thinking men who contemplated the new discoveries of their age with full consciousness that what they were witnessing was nothing less than a renaissance of human dignity. The darkness which had come upon Europe with the barbarian invasions had been repulsed slowly, painfully, patiently. By flickering church candles and guttering lamps, lonely scholars had preserved some of the splendors of classical learning against the day when men could again appreciate it.

Renaissance in Italy

In Italy the Renaissance as a new movement in literature began about the end of the fourteenth century. Dante had a great respect for the classical writers. Petrarch, happening upon some of Cicero's letters, found himself so stirred by the intellectual honesty of this pagan thinker that Petrarch realized his own lack of sympathy with the reasoning of his day. He learned from the ancients to look at life as it really was and earned a place in history as one of the first humanist authors. His colorful contemporary, Giovanni Boccaccio, was another who looked upon the world and liked what he saw. Far from seeking to "reform" his fellowmen, he accepted human frailty as a part of human life, and with fearless realism dealt a shattering blow to the superstitions of his day. With the publication of his *Decameron,* humanism added another masterpiece to its list.

Humanism

Humanist writers were in harmony with classical thought, and since Latin was widely known, the works of Roman authors were the first to revive. The search for the wellspring of Roman wisdom led inevitably to the ancient Greeks, so side by side with the struggle for scholastic freedom went a renaissance of classical learning which was to stimulate the intellectual world for centuries to come.

England, nestling in her northern seas, lent a ready ear to scholars returning from the continent with the new learning. To freedom-loving people there was a strong appeal in humanism. Chaucer, on a visit to Italy, had come under its spell, and his work reflects its philosophy. His contemporary, William Langland, had shown similar responses in his *Piers Plowman* which reflects the age as the main body of the English people saw it; and in the first half of the fifteenth century, Humphrey, Duke of Gloucester, who had developed an important library at Oxford, encouraged humanistic ideas. However, it was not until the sixteenth century that a well-defined revival of learning could be discovered in England. By that time curiosity was beginning to replace traditional acceptance in the intellectual and scientific world, and the arts were striving towards new forms of expression. Painting and architecture reached new heights. Stiff two-dimensional paintings began to give way to more realistic likenesses, and gaunt medieval castles were forsaken for spacious, beautifully designed mansions whose great windows seem to be symbolic of the light pouring into the dark places of the mind. Literature changed from the charming naivete of the medieval minstrel to the full-blown grandeur of Marlowe and Shakespeare. At the same time came a deeper awareness of the beauty as well as the strength of the language, and a reappraisal of how literature could best be interpreted.

Castles

With such strong leanings toward classicism it was natural that the oral techniques of the ancients would again be studied in their original freshness rather than in the adaptations used to meet the needs of the Middle Ages. To this end scholars set themselves to the mastery of Greek as well as Latin. Sixteenth century England seethed with new movements in education to bring the schools into harmony with the times. In oral, as in written literature, the return to classical sources had its beginning in Italy; before studying the further development of oral literature in sixteenth century England, it would be well to consider some of the men who gave it its early impetus.

Italian influences

Educators had never lost sight of the need for good oral delivery, and every land had its famous teachers. In Italy, where beautiful voices were always cherished, the names of Guarino da Verona (1374-1460) and Vittorino da Feltre (1378-1446) stand out. Guarino stressed the need for distinct and sustained speech and strove for natural utterance purged of all affectation and exaggeration. He recommended that, after the elements of prosody had been mastered, poetry should be read daily. To attune the ear and develop a fine taste he suggested memorizing and reciting Vergil, while to improve facility and directness, and to develop purity of style, the same should be done with the epistles of Cicero. In reading poets, he said, one should concentrate on the basic concepts which the poets seek to communicate, rather than upon the imaginative situations through which they seek to illustrate them. Since, to be effective at all, oral reading must make the author's meaning apparent "in every tone of the reader,"[2] skillful inflections and the proper use of pauses were needed. Moreover, observed Guarino, despite fine diction and polished delivery, no reading could succeed unless expression be allied to understanding, since fine sounds without thought could never please a scholar. Vittorino da Feltre shared many of Guarino's views, especially the need for understanding. He, too, was at pains to develop good voices with clear enunciation and well-modulated tones. He trained his pupils to open their mouths, to breathe correctly, and to speak with fine rhythm, correct accent, and proper inflection.

Aeneas Silvius

Before leaving the Italian scene, mention should be made of Aeneas Silvius (1405-1464) who became Pope Pius II. His treatise, *De Liberorum Educatione,* cites many of the speech requirements just discussed. Like his contemporaries, he relied heavily on memorization, recommending the memorization of poetry or words of wisdom daily. To improve diction he suggested practice in pronouncing difficult phrases and verses. Expressive speech required active lips and tongue, and he urged that particular care be taken to enunciate clearly the final sounds which were so often slurred or dropped.[3] This problem still troubles teachers of speech.

Juan Vives

As the Renaissance spread to Spain, Juan Vives (1492-1540) became prominent, and his works were translated into English. He plied his pupils with readings from Aesop, Isocrates, Plato and other classical writers, much of which was read aloud. He hoped in this way to strengthen the pupil's grammar as well as his understanding. He also carried on the long tradition of Bible reading. The education of women, he said, should include much reading from the Bible and other holy writings. Women should also study the classical authors so that they would be prepared to educate their children in both the wise and Holy books. He also recommended that mothers read to their children "pleasant histories and honest tales."[4]

Johann Sturm

In the sixteenth century one of the most famous Latin schools in Europe was that of Johann Sturm (1507-1589) in Strassburg. Sturm based his philosophy of education on piety, knowledge, and the art of expression. The oral work in this school was extensive. At the age of seven the pupils began to read and speak in Latin, and to memorize the catechism in German. In succeeding classes they studied the classical authors and began to write verses. By the time they were fourteen years of age they were studying rhetoric, using Greek and Latin orations, and acting the comedies of Terence and Plautus. After this, they learned the connection between oratorical and poetic usage, read from Homer, and acted many Greek classical plays in frequent dramatic productions. In addition, they learned to expound the Epistles of St. Paul after the manner of the old rhetoricians. All this, together with declamation, made up Sturm's comprehensive program of oral work.

English influences

In England schools dedicated to the new learning were set up under the influence of scholars John Colet, Erasmus of Rotterdam, Sir Thomas More, Sir John Cheke, and others. To uncover the wisdom of the ancients and pass it on to England's youth, these men learned, and taught, the Greek language which had been sadly neglected in the Middle Ages. Scholars were no longer sure how ancient Greek should be pronounced, and in 1535 Sir Thomas Smith and Sir John Cheke conferred earnestly on this subject. Eventually, a way of pronouncing Greek was accepted, and Cheke held his ground that this newer method "was profitable for learning, sweet for speech, and clear in utterance."[5] In a few years this way of reading Greek prevailed throughout Cambridge University.

Not only the language but also the oral arts of the Greeks and Romans had fallen on evil days since the classical era had ended. Erasmus protested that ". . . Grammar herself, the mistress of correct utterance, and Rhetoric, the guide of copious and splendid diction, were heard only in mean and wretched stutterings, and those arts, which had formerly found expression in so many tongues, spoke only in Latin, and that of the worst."[6]

Stephen Hawes

With the coming of the Renaissance many books were written to guide student, gentleman, and educator. One of the earliest theories of reading aloud, in English, was written by Stephen Hawes, a groom at the court of Henry VII, who was also a poet. In *Pastime of Pleasure,* first published in London in 1509, Hawes presented a number of basic tenets of oral reading or reciting which were to be re-stated, with variations, well into the twentieth century. When he advised the speaker to moderate his delivery "adcordynge as by hym is audience,"[7] he touched upon a question which is still the subject of controversy and to which there will be occasion to refer again.

Teaching practices in different schools varied greatly in the Renaissance, for many educators were establishing their own philosophies of education. The development of writing had been slow in England, one reason being that paper was not manufactured there until the sixteenth century, and imported paper was costly. The early textbooks were "hornbooks," oblong boards, with the alphabet and usually a prayer on them. The board was covered with a thin sheet of horn which gave the books their name. However, hornbooks were used for learning only the simplest principles of reading. Beyond this elementary stage there were few textbooks as such, and it was manifestly impossible for the schoolmaster to depend on his pupils owning books. Since many a master did not himself own all the books from which he wished to instruct his pupils, it was not unusual for him to recite from memory the works being studied. More fortunate masters did read aloud from their books. It was then the pupil's responsibility to remember what he had heard.

Later, when paper was more readily available, lessons were copied either from dictation or from existing texts. In copying what they heard the pupils were writing their own books, and these they would treasure for the rest of their lives. A conscientious master would read to his pupils with great care to give them the meaning as well as the accurate wording of great poets and orators. A teacher's voice, his diction, and understanding were of major importance in conveying the majesty and beauty of the literature he read. People at that time had difficulty in separating the oral aspects of delivery from the written elements of style. As a result, a fine poem might go unrecognized if it were badly recited or read.

Learning methods

Among the most influential figures of the English Renaissance was Erasmus. As a boy Erasmus had studied at Deventer in Holland, his native land, and like many a boy before and since his time, took a poor view of his master's methods. Looking back, he deplored the time he had spent in studying, and memorizing and reciting the "silly" verses of John of Garland. This, however, was a complaint against the material rather than against the practice of reciting. In his *Familiar Colloquies,* he advised students to memorize what they had learned either by reciting to themselves or to another person, and this should be followed by meditation which assists "both wit and memory." In words which re-echo Plato, he says, ". . . menne (if they had heard anything, worthie to be knowen) thei wrote and graved the same, not in bokes, but in the harte and mind." However, after writing came into use every man ". . . knew still lesse and lesse."[8]

Erasmus

He was firmly convinced that children should learn by heart the best of the poets and other writers. He favored telling Aesop's fables and tales, such as that of Ulysses, to small children;[9] if such stories were beyond the child's comprehension, at least he would absorb some idea of the truths embodied in the story. Erasmus did not live to see a time when books would be plentiful enough to obviate the need for extensive memorization.

As to methods for achieving good oral delivery, Erasmus was far from satisfied with prevailing practices. For example, in "The Schoolmaster's Admonitions" Erasmus advised the pupil not to "speak fast, stammer, or speak in your Throat, but use yourself to pronounce your Words distinctly and clearly."[10] Such advice, of course, has been given to young scholars both centuries before and centuries after Erasmus. He was in favor of using declamations to promote facility and felt that if declamation were practiced from boyhood, as in Roman days, oratory would be improved. Erasmus himself declaimed in Greek.

The Praise of Folly

Erasmus considered that some of the schools of eloquence made themselves ridiculous by their exaggerated, false, and absurd forms of expression and gesture. In *The Praise of Folly* he satirized, among other things, the posturings of the grammarians, and also criticized the monks and friars saying of them:

> And now tell me, what Jugler or Mountebank you had rather behold than hear them rhetorically play the fool in their Preachments, and yet most sweetly imitating what Rhetoricians have written touching the Art of good speaking? Good god! What several postures they have! How they shift their voice, sing out their words, skip up and down, and are ever and anon making such new faces, that they confound all things with noise! . . . . And first they invoke what ever they have scrapt from the Poets . . . .

And further describing their speaking, Erasmus said:

> But they have heard from somebody, I know not whom, that the beginning of a Speech should be Sober and Grave, and least given to noise. And therefore they begin theirs at that rate they can scarce hear themselves . . . . They have learnt somewhere that to move the affections a lowder voice is requisite. Whereupon they that otherwise would speak like a Mouse in a Cheese, start out of a suddain, into a downright fury, even there too. . . . Again, because they have heard that as a Speech comes up to something, a man should press it more earnestly, they, how ever they begin, use a strange contention of voice in every part, though the Matter it self be never so flat, and end in that manner as if they'd run themselves out of breath.[11]

All in all, he was not pleased with the oral delivery of these men whom he could compare only to "mountebanks and stage players," so extreme was their use of voice and gesture.

The study of classical authors in the Renaissance was not always pursued in order to enjoy them primarily from an artistic point of view. Rather, the classics provided the pupil with an endless source of legends, fables, and philosophy expressed in a fitting style. Quintilian's ideal of a good orator was an accepted standard. This attitude was understandable since England, in this period, was changing from a feudal land to a land where a statesman with an eloquent tongue could aspire to a position of leadership. Young boys with ambitions for a career in government benefited particularly from a study of rhetoric, and probably nothing had a greater influence on their intellectual outlook in later life than did this study.

"Let Quintilian be your guide" was the unequivocal advice of Richard Mulcaster, who was an influential educator of the mid-sixteenth century. Mulcaster's book, *Elementarie,* (1582) was regarded as the authority on elementary education for several centuries, and his enthusiasm for Quintilian was shared by many. It has been said that every humanist treatise on education, including those of Aeneas Silvius and Erasmus, mirrored Quintilian. Quintilian had been interested in the whole of education, but he gave the speech arts a very important place in his educational program. This emphasis was readily accepted by Renaissance Englishmen, and as a result, their oral expression often followed not only a classical ideal but a classical pattern as well.

Influence of Quintilian

Clergymen, orators, statesmen, educators, and gentlemen all realized the need for acceptable diction, effective rhetorical expression, and reading skill, whether they sought to advance the church, the state, or the general cultural standards of the people. In *The Boke Named the Governour* (1531) Sir Thomas Elyot was concerned with the requirements of public life. He recommended a classical and literary education with the teacher reading Aesop's fables to his pupil to introduce the study of Greek. Parents, Elyot said, should follow the example of the Emperor Octavius Augustus and read to their children from the works of Cicero and Vergil. Further reading from the classics, with emphasis on poetry, should take the student through his fourteenth year, by which time he would be ready to tackle oratory, history, and cosmography. Quintilian and the Greek rhetorician Hermogenes should then be studied to train the youth in eloquence and oratory.

Sir Thomas Elyot

Rhetoric was given pre-eminence as a subject which an educated man must study, and as the century advanced the learned writings on rhetoric multiplied. Thomas Wilson, in *The Arte of Rhetorique* (1553) presented what Warton described as the first treatise or system of criticism in the English language. This work seemingly brought Wilson more fame than fortune, for in the prologue to the 1560 edition of it he says ruefully, "If others never get more by bookes than I have don: It were better to be a Carter than a Scholer, for worldly profite." Wilson's main preoccupation was with rhetoric, but his work has many useful comments on education and oral literature in general. Fables and words of the poets, he believed, were of value in enlightening man. Poets, being concerned with manners, nature, understanding, and the knowledge of truth, could be used to support a speaker's argument and persuade a hearer. Thus he used literature and oral recitation to train the orator and the gentleman.[12]

Thomas Wilson

In 1563 Richard Rainolde wrote *The Foundacion of Rhetorike.* Like Wilson he favored the use of the fable as "the first ground." A fable he defined as "a forged tale, containing in it by the colour of a lie, a matter of truth" and said the first exercise should consist of reciting the fable, praising the author, establishing the moral,

Richard Rainolde

discussing the "character's" contribution in bringing out the meaning, making a comparison, establishing an example, and presenting a conclusion.[13] The steps which Rainolde outlined show how thorough was the effort to ensure complete understanding of the material.

In a discussion of the parts of rhetoric and oratory, Rainolde discussed the three types of imitation. "Ethopoeia" he described as "a certaine talkying to of anyone, or an imitation of talke refferred to the maners, aptly of any certaine knowen persons," or "a certain oration made by voice and lamentable imitation, upon the state of anyone." "Eidolopoeia" he described as a dead person speaking, as when the dead "Polidarus" speaks to Aeneas (Book 11, *Aeneid*). "Prosopopeia" he defined as "when to anyone againste Nature, speache is feigned to be given."

Aphthonius

Rainolde was greatly impressed by Aphthonius' *Progymnasmata.* He listed the fourteen elementary exercises of Aphthonius, several of which are really projects in the oral interpretation of literature. The re-telling of a myth, the short narrative, the imaginary speech of a person or personified abstraction, and the lively or elaborate description, all have strong interpretative elements. Karl Wallace says that such exercises seem to indicate that the Tudor schoolboy had training in the use of voice, gesture, basic principles of interpretation, and acting, and even some knowledge of dramatic composition.[14]

Rhetoric

Rhetoric was important for its own sake and also because it lead to the oral study and appreciation of literature. With the great masters as models of style, vocabulary, and expression, the young scholar was helped to develop a good style of his own. Some of the literature studied was prose, but much of it was poetry. After studying the poetry of classical writers, pupils tried to compose their own verses in imitation of their famous models. These amateur verses and the models on which they were based, were both read aloud, and the young poet could avail himself of his hearers' criticism, as had his prototypes in ancient Athens. Many books on rhetoric included passages from poetry illustrative of rhetorical principles. These passages were explained by the master, then studied and memorized by the pupils in the hope that the precepts or rules which they exemplified would ultimately become a subconscious reservoir of high ideals and correct utterance. Since the main purpose of this study was competence in oral expression, it was fitting that oral practice should be the means of reaching that goal.

Poetry memorized and recited

Poetry was read aloud, memorized, and recited in great quantities. Though Erasmus had complained that, as books became more available, memories dulled, the amount which people memorized in that epoch would astonish a modern student.

Although by 1557 some six thousand books had been printed in England, this number was still far short of the growing demand.

These books supplemented, but could not supplant, the old tradition of learning by hearing since many a would-be scholar did not own a book and had to rely on ear and memory as his forebears had done.

Declamations and themes were important, and students were required to write themes and then to present them orally to the class or to the teacher. Wallace describes the theme as "any composition, oral or written, whose subject matter pertains to moral or to political matters, and whose aim is to inculcate, without entering the realms of controversy, love of virtue and hatred of vice." If this was read orally or memorized, and then recited, it could be a form of oral interpretation.[15]

Alexander Silvayn

The Orator, written in French by Alexander Silvayn, was translated into English and printed in London in 1596. This was a collection of declamations, some based upon ancient writers, others composed by the author himself, and designed to help train the lawyer or divine in pleading or persuasion. There are no directions for the use of this book, but if the selections were read aloud or memorized and recited, this too would have elements of oral interpretation.

Roger Ascham

In the early sixteenth century Renaissance schoolmasters were not content to limit their teaching to the Bible, some history, and Arthurian legends; they enthusiastically offered an impressive parade of Greek and Latin authors. As early as 1521, when Henry VIII re-established Canterbury School, the curriculum included the works of Horace and Cicero as well as the contemporary writings of Erasmus. Many English educators advocated reading aloud to develop a better grasp of style. Roger Ascham recommended that teachers read aloud to their pupils the letters of Cicero to promote fluency and ease of expression, and told of the benefit he himself had derived from listening to "Master Cheke" reading aloud all of Homer and other great classical authors. Later, as tutor to the future Queen Elizabeth I, Ascham read with his royal charge "that noble oration of Demosthenes against Aeschines."[16] He said that if a student read first the Bible, then Cicero in Latin, Plato, Aristotle, Xenophon, Isocrates, and Demosthenes in Greek, he will "prove an excellent man."

Range of literature studied

In many schools the literary fare included Homer, Aesop, Hesiod, Aristotle, Plato, Hermogenes, Aristophanes, Pindar, Sophocles, Euripides, Herodotus, Thucydides, Xenophon, Isocrates, and Demosthenes, while Rome was represented by Virgil, Ovid, Terence, Caesar, Cicero, Juvenal, Sallust, Lucian, Quintilian, Persius, Martial, and Plautus. Few modern students, with the books to be had for the asking, would care to tackle much more.

Along with the study of this literature went theories as to how it should be spoken. The works of Quintilian and Cicero were the foundation of practically every treatise on this subject in the

Understanding

sixteenth century. In accord with their teachings, understanding of the subject matter was of prime importance. "Legere et non intellegere negligere est" was also the favorite phrase of Renaissance educators like Wolsey, Ascham, Mulcaster, Coote, and others. Not until the interpreter had himself assimilated the meaning was he ready to consider the ways in which he could convey it to his audience.

Voice and Diction

The importance of good voice and diction was obvious, and many ways were suggested to achieve them. Roger Ascham regarded singing as beneficial to speech. Others recommended the use of certain poets to meet specific needs; for instance, reciting the works of Cato and Lily was recommended to develop good accent. Thomas Wilson made some useful comments on voice. He advised the orator to "file his tongue" to a lute-like sweetness, and in a manner both instructive and amusing, gave a pithy description of some of the more common vocal faults:

> One pipes out his woordes so small through default of his wynde pype, that ye would think he whistled .... an other speakes, as though he had Plummes in his mouthe ... An other speakes, as though his wordes had neede to be heaved out with leavers ... An other gapes to fetche wynde at every third woorde ... Some blowes at their noistrelles ... Some gruntes lyke a hogge. Some cackels lyke a henne ... Some speakes as thoughe they shoulde tel a tale in their sleeve ... Some spittes fier, they talke so hotely ....[17]

Wilson's contemporary Abraham Fraunce included in the second part of *The Arcadian Rhetorike* (1588) instructions in "utterance and pronunciation" which were applicable to oral reading or recitation, and Edmund Coote in *The Englishe Scholemaister* was concerned with teaching "distinct reading." He was concerned with adequate oral reading as well as adequate and pleasing voice, and he recommended various types of prose as well as verse, including the psalms.[18]

John Brinsley, whose *Ludus Literarius* appeared in 1612, spoke for many when he advised the pupil to "pronounce every thing audibly, leasurely, distinctly, and naturally; sounding out specially the last syllable, that each word may be fully understood."[19] Charles Hoole wanted teachers to note any defective sounds and to prescribe corrective exercises where necessary. The mechanics of voice production were treated by Gerbier (1650) who pointed out that "well speaking doth depend on the lungs, and the channell which receives and issues forth the Ayre, it depends of the Tongue and of the Teeth."[20] Such brief illustrations show the concern of educators to develop sweet and pleasing voices and to achieve clear pronunciation.

The well-bred youth of the Renaissance was expected to have a good physical bearing and the posture of a gentleman. Whether or not he was performing, he was expected to move with a certain grace and dignity that befitted his station in life; therefore it was natural that educators and rhetoricians should give some attention to this requirement. Action, or gesture, should not be random or undisciplined but should be related to the subject under discussion and reflect the action of the mind. Stephen Hawes said that a tale should be told "with ryght good manner, countenance and intent." Wilson gave an early statement of total bodily response, or "pronunciation," when he pointed out the need for "an apte orderings bothe of the voyce, countenaunce, and all the whole bodye, accordynge to the worthines of such woordes and mater as by speache are declared."[21] He agreed with Cicero that gesture is the speech of the body and must reflect the mind. He heartily disliked those amazing characters who nod "their head at every sentence. An other winckes with one ey, and some with both . . . Some cannot speake, but thei must go up and downe . . . An other will plaie with his cappe in his hande, and so tel his tale."[22] Wilson tells, too, of a teacher, who always looked at the same spot when he read to his students. One youth painted the devil with horns at this particular place, which evidently cured the reader of this mannerism and must surely have delighted the young artist. Even in those days of relatively severe discipline it seems the pupils sometimes taught the pedagogues.

Hawes

Wilson

Further evidence that bodily action was not regarded as separate from voice is provided by Abraham Fraunce, who considered gesture as a response of the entire body and taught that action must follow the change and variety of the voice. One can see growing indications of interest in mechanical systems of gesture which were generally attempts to standardize emotional expression through certain set and predetermined bodily action. Fraunce, for example, said that "the middle finger meeting with the thumb and the other three stretched out is an urgent and instant gesture,"[23] while the right arm extended went with continued and flowing sentences. "There is no gesture of the left hand alone," he said, "and the clapping of hands is fitter for the stage than the court."[24] He gave many other detailed directions for the use of head, arm, hand and finger movements to express specific emotions.

Fraunce

Trends in educational philosophies span the centuries, and in the seventeenth century Obadiah Walker and John Bulwer were to contribute further mechanical elements. The latter's imprint on the future through his *Chirologia* and *Chironomia* was so great that his influence lasted directly or indirectly into the twentieth century. Bulwer's *Chirologia* (1644) is an impressive study of the psychological significance of the various gestures and positions of the hand, describing "the speaking Motions and Discoursing gestures there-

John Bulwer

of."[25] He uses innumerable classical, Biblical, and contemporary sources to illustrate the various gestures of the hand in history, literature, and religion. While this book is not directly concerned with reading, it so greatly influenced later writings that it must be recognized. Bulwer's charts illustrating the positions of the hands are very graphic and clear and anticipated similar illustrations used in the nineteenth and even in the twentieth century. In *Chironomia* he explains the ancients' use of the fingers or hands in making the intervals and beats as they recited verse. Bulwer asserts that speech without gestures is unsound. As an illustration of this fact he mentions a sermon preached to Queen Elizabeth. This sermon impressed the queen when she heard it, and a copy of it was presented to her to read. However, when the speaker's voice and gestures were lacking, the sermon was ineffective. Elizabeth said it was one of the "best sermons she ever heard and the worst she ever read."[26] In Bulwer's book the emphasis on gesture was strong and there are again elements of the mechanical approach.

Renaissance educators were aware that there was more involved in the arts of reading and recitation than merely the correct use of voice and body. The relationship between the performer and his audience evoked much discussion. Not everybody agreed with the statement quoted earlier from Stephen Hawes that a reader should adapt his performance to suit his audience. Some felt that a work of art had a life and integrity of its own which no interpreter had the right to modify. This group believed that if a certain selection did not suit a certain audience, some other passage should be chosen. Such was the advice, for example, that Chaucer gave his readers and listeners in the Prologue to "The Milleres Tale." Others were equally convinced that since art is the embodiment of truth, the performer should make whatever adjustments were necessary to make the author's message intelligible and acceptable to the audience.

Emotion

Emotion was recognized as an important factor in interpretation, and theorists debated about the role which it should play. Should the reciter actually experience the emotions which the author sought to present, or should he merely simulate their outward manifestations? Should he attempt to convey emotion to the hearer? Should the hearer be emotionally affected by the reciter and, if so, how much? These questions were asked and answered pro and con at that time and down into the twentieth century.

In general, the Renaissance reciter was expected first to experience within himself the emotions he encountered in literature and then to transmit them to his audience. Stephen Hawes summed it up when he said that a performer should tell his story as its emotions dictate, carefully avoiding a rude and barbarous manner, and preserving a sense of perspective so that he could keep his emotions under control and not be overpowered by them. By so doing, the speaker could achieve moderation and preserve the dignity of his delivery.

The power of the voice to convey emotions was quite clear to many of the sixteenth century rhetoricians. Fraunce's *Arcadian Rhetorike,* for instance, gave detailed instructions for reciting some passages from classical and even contemporary literature. In pity and lamentation, said Fraunce, the voice must be "full, sobbing, flexible, interrupted." Citing an excerpt from the *Aeneid* he said, "in the last verses everie thing must be dilated and produced, the mouth opened, the vowels drawn out, that the Troyan calamitie may there especially appeare." He quotes other passages from the *Iliad* and the *Aeneid* where the voice must be "shrill, sharp, quicke and short" in anger. Fear and bashfulness can be simulated in a voice "contracted, stammering, trembling"; such, he said, "was Tullyes voyce in most of his beginnings." In order to portray "anguish and griefe of mind without compassion, a hollow voyce fetcht from the bottome of the throate, groaning" is effective. And, in happier vein, a "tender, mild and sweetlie flowing" voice bespeaks joy and gladness, while a voice smooth and submissive is an aid to flattery and conciliation. With many examples from literature to exemplify the manifestations of different emotions, Fraunce closed his chapter advising a pupil to learn a speech wherein were found as many varieties of voice as possible.

Emotion and voice

Obadiah Walker, almost a century later, was firmly convinced that emotion was the dominant factor in delivery, and that it was, in truth, the basis upon which good expression was founded. Only when the emotions were aroused could delivery "be exactly performed; which is as it were the hand to this instrument of the voice by which it is tuned several wayes, to the begetting like emotions, in the minds of others to those with which ourselves are first affected."[27]

Obadiah Walker

The art of story telling required not only the skillful fusion of vocal and bodily expression, but also their adaptation to the idea and nature of the story. Therefore, argued Renaissance experts the narrator had to determine in his own mind the purpose of his story. Was it to be mildly amusing, or to raise hearty laughter? Was it to excite, to sadden, or to make the audience thoughtful? Voice and movement must be adapted to play upon the emotions of the audience to evoke the proper mood and make clear the characters, events, and ideas. To do this it was essential to establish the right balance between the idea and the act. Here again one can trace a parallel between Italian and English thought. Works by Castiglione and de la Casa were translated into English in the sixteenth century. The storyteller, said Castiglione, should use voice and gesture so effectively that the spectator can imagine "muche more than he seeth and heareth."[28] His countryman, de la Casa, demanded such a

Voice, body and idea

realistic picture from the storyteller that the audience could see the events which were described just as if they were presented on a stage.

John Brinsley gave similar advice in the seventeenth century when he told his pupils "to pronounce every matter according to the nature of it as much as you can." The speaker, Brinsley believed, should give his impression of the essential characteristics of his story and convey his reaction to it which should, with honest thinking, get at the author's purpose. This led Brinsley to discuss another topic, the problem of characterization. Here he recommended that the performer grasp and portray as nearly as possible the nature of the character he presents. The interpreter should go so far in impersonating the characters in a dialogue that he seems to be the persons who are speaking. While there seems to be little subtlety in this concept of characterization, and little restraint, one must remember that a distinction was made between the art of the actor and that of the speaker or reciter, and there was disagreement as to how far a reciter was justified in using the breadth and sweep of action used by an actor. Many thought the actor's freedom of action quite inappropriate to a reader or reciter. Indeed, the actions of stage players were regarded as so extreme that speakers were often warned not to imitate them but rather to use only those actions which were "gravely and decently executed," as Fraunce had said.

Characterization

While poetry was easily the major form of literary expression in the sixteenth century, there was a steadily growing art of prose which was sufficiently significant to command attention. Again the question arose as to how prose should be read aloud. Should it be spoken exactly the same as poetry, even though it did not rhyme and its rhythm was less discernible? Or should it be read without regard to rhythm? Should it be read in a simple manner or in an "inflated" style? Such were the questions puzzling the authors, reciters, educators, and rhetoricians of the day. The answers varied. James Cleland advised that after the scholar is "perfect in the knowledge of the single letters, teach him to spel and read with a sweet accent, not pronouncing verse as prose or prose as verse."[29] Others, however, believed that prose and poetry should be read much the same. This group found a champion in John Brinsley, who contributed so much to the study of oral reading. Brinsley said that "in all Poetry, for the pronunciation, it is to be uttered as prose; observing distinctions and the nature of the matter." Good diction, leisurely and clear enunciation, and unaffected delivery were essential to the effective interpretation of both literary forms.

Reading of prose versus poetry

James Cleland

John Brinsley

The leaders of Renaissance education emphasized the influence of the classics upon English thought and the educational philosophy of the period, but the pendulum swung too far. A growing sense of nationalism brought resistance to the classics. This reaction was inevitable when England became a strong nation and produced some literature of her own of which she could justifiably be proud. Many parents began to complain that their children were required to learn Greek and Latin despite the fact that they could not speak or write their own language properly. More and more, objections began to be voiced that the "heathen poets were affecting manners rather than advancing virtue." In 1582, the Privy Council ordered that *Anglorum Praelia,* an English history in verse by Christopher Ocland, be used in schools. With this decree the growing spirit of nationalism received official expression.

Growing interest in English speech and literature

Educators, too, were aware of the need to emphasize English literature. Sir Humphrey Gilbert, in *Queen Elizabeth's Academy,* presented a plan for the education of her majesty's wards, and recommended that the exercises and orations be given in English saying, that regardless of the language in which learning was attained, it was to be used principally in the vulgar speech, as in preaching, in parliament, in council, in commission and other offices of the nation.

Gilbert

Richard Mulcaster was another who saw the need to train pupils first in English before putting a language barrier between them and the knowledge they were to acquire. By 1580 William Bullokar had published a book "for the Amendment of Orthographie for English Speech," a project which he undertook because he found so many pupils mispronouncing words when they read aloud in English. This work was very important in the transitional period of English when the language was in a fluid state, and as we read in verse by M. Timperley in Simon Daines' *Orthoepia Anglicana,*

Mulcaster

Bullokar

> England has had so many Tongues as men,
> And every one his way of speaking.

Coote's *English Scholemaister* (1596) was also intended to promote "the framing and sweet tuning of thy voyce" and "the natural reading of any English." According to the author, this was such a good book that teachers need only follow its precepts to achieve their goals. He particularly recommended it to a new group of teachers who were emerging. These were men and women engaged in trades or crafts who, apparently, would listen to pupils recite while they, the teachers, plied their trades. In the preface Coote said:

Coote

> . . . men and women of trades, as Taylors, Weavers, Shop-keepers, Seamsters and such other as have undertaken the charge of teaching others . . . . thou maiest sit on thy shop-bord, at thy Loomes, or at thy needle, and never hinder thy worke to heare thy scholers, after thou hast made this little booke familiar unto thee.[30]

Meagre as this education must have been, it was another step towards the democratization of education and an added reason for using English rather than Latin as the medium for instruction.

Bacon

One must not conclude, however, that the anglicizing of education in language and literature was primarily for the benefit of those who had not mastered the classics. Far from it. Even Francis Bacon, scholar though he was, felt that the exclusive use of ancient literature for forming style was not entirely advisable. In *The Advancement of Learning* (1605) he put forth the idea that this practice overstressed eloquence and encouraged excessive interest in phraseology, word choice, and rhythm at the expense of subject matter and meaning.

Gill

In 1619 the *Logonomia Anglica* of Alexander Gill appeared, using quotations from such poets as Sidney, Daniel, and Spenser to illustrate rhetoric and grammar. This further strengthened the interest in English literature. Some men, for instance George Fox (1624-91), sought to keep Christian literature to the forefront. In his *Warning to All Teachers* Fox demanded that the telling of tales, jests, rimes, and fables cease, and that religious books be read to children.

The Bible

The classical revival did not diminish religious zeal. By liberating men from a blind acceptance of tradition, it encouraged the questioning spirit and was a part of the movement towards a more enlightened study of man's ideals. The awakening mind of the Renaissance, studying and revering the Bible, lay behind the great political upheavals, the religious experiments and the readjustments so typical of that era. Most people were convinced that salvation depended on obeying the rules of conduct laid down in Holy Writ. Among the general public the desire to read the Scriptures was the chief motivation for learning to read at all. Those who could read had a duty to read to those who did not have this skill, so that as many people as possible could know, and do, the will of God.

The English Bible has many connections with oral reading; and a brief study of this relationship will emphasize the unbroken partnership between oral literature and religion which began long before the advent of Christianity and has continued to this day. For long years the Roman Church had carefully withheld the Bible from the man in the street, on the grounds that he was incapable of understanding it without the proper guidance. This idea was perhaps not without merit, but such a practice was not in tune with the Renaissance spirit, and there were strenuous efforts to make the Bible available to as many people as possible.

Wycliffe

The idea that English should replace Latin was not new. As early as the fourteenth century John Wycliffe had translated both the Old and the New Testaments into English. But Wycliffe was ahead of his time, and this remarkable achievement was regarded with alarm.

Tyndale

Over a century later William Tyndale fell foul of the church by translating the New Testament. He was exiled and continued his work in Antwerp. There, on Sundays, it was Tyndale's custom to go to a merchant's house and read aloud to the assembled company the parts he had completed. In 1535, Miles Coverdale published in England the first complete English Bible. This enabled the average man to read the Bible for himself or to listen while others read it aloud.

Coverdale

Henry VIII, who appointed himself head of the English Church in 1534, decreed that every parish buy a large Bible and put it in the church for all to read. The "Great Bible" printed in 1539 was enthusiastically received. Crowds thronged to read it or to hear it read, and six copies of it were chained to the walls of St. Paul's Cathedral. A favorite reader in St. Paul's was John Porter, whose fine voice and skill in reading never lacked an audience. Throughout the land people gathered to hear the Bible read aloud by the ablest readers in the parish.

The "Great Bible"

Even this seemingly commendable thirst for knowledge of the Bible, however, was not without its drawbacks. Such was the exuberant zeal of the readers, on occasion, that the reading of the Bible constituted a veritable breach of the peace. Over-zealous recitation in some part of the sanctuary sometimes disturbed priest and congregation during divine service, and the offenders were wont to resent any interference with their activities. In 1534 it is recorded that, in Langham, some girls who were reciting their matins were ordered by an attendant to leave the church. The girls complained that they were not allowed to stay in the church and read "pryvlidged bookes."

Nor was Bible reading only a church and Sunday pastime. A London clergyman, Robert Wisdome, was said to have told his parishioners to use the Scriptures when they gathered in taverns on Sunday and holidays. This might have passed without censorious comment had not the readings gone beyond peaceful discussion to pugnacious argument and uncomplimentary names.

Although Henry VIII himself is not reputed to have been a paragon of pious decorum, he was swift to act when word of such disorderly brawls came to his ears. He issued a proclamation commenting upon the unseemly arguments which so frequently arose in churches, taverns, and alehouses. While he had wanted to make the Bible available to his subjects, he could not approve its being read in "undue time and places," and he sought to remedy the situation by decreeing that no one except curates, graduates of Oxford and Cambridge, or such as had a license to preach or teach the Bible might read it aloud in public. No one was to read the Bible in English in churches, chapels, or elsewhere "with any loud or high voice, (and especially) during the time of divine service or celebrating and saying of masses."[31] However, he also made it clear that he approved of people reading the Bible provided they did not disturb others.

Bible reading in public

The King's decree

In 1542 Bible reading was further encouraged when it was decreed that, each morning and evening, a chapter of the New Testament be read in every parish. On Sundays and Holy days the curate was to read, in English, in the course of the year, first from the New Testament, and when it was completed, to begin with the Old Testament. Such practices did not spread without resistance on the part of some clergymen, however, who maintained that the people could not understand the Scriptures. Still striving to maintain high standards of oral reading, others objected on the grounds that too many readers were not adequate to their task. The Bishop of Salisbury, despite the King's injunction, would not permit a certain monk to read until "he be of better judgment; yea, and of more insight in Scripture than he is yet like to be."

Religion continued to be a stormy subject throughout the Tudor period, and by the time Elizabeth, the third of Henry's children to ascend the throne, became queen, many churches were without priests–some were dead, some were fled, and some were banished, for no man of strong will or high principles could have pleased all of the Tudors. Since the universities needed time to educate more men for the church, Elizabeth, in 1559, decreed that persons who were capable readers, even if laymen, should be appointed to read the church services. She took the precaution, however, of forbidding the readers to preach or interpret the Bible, or to express themselves on matters of doctrine. The reader's duty, in toto, was to read "plainly, distinctly and audibly, that all the place may hear and understand." To prevent the mushrooming of opportunists in this emergency measure, it was further decreed that the reader should receive no emoluments for his services and that lay readers should be employed only in the poorer parishes when no clergyman was available.

Readers in the church

Despite the well-meaning efforts of both the state and the individual, these readers were not too satisfactory. Many were completely untrained and were subjected to sharp criticism not only for lack of reading skill but also, in some cases, for facing the altar, "after the old way," when they read. So great was the need for readers, however, that they continued to be used, at least in Scotland, as late as 1621. When *The Buke of Discipline,* by John Knox, was published in that year, Knox recommended that, if no minister were available, the Common Prayers and Scriptures be read "distinctlie" by "the most apt men" in the community. The lay readers, of course, were not alone in finding their activities closely supervised. Strict rules also governed the curates and other clergymen; in large towns the clergy was to give either a sermon, say the Common Prayers, or read the Scriptures daily. The Bible was to be read in order; that is, "some one buke of the Auld and the New Testament be begun and ordourlie red to the end."[32]

John Knox

Memorization of large parts of the Bible was considered so desirable that, in 1542, all of the priests in London under Bishop

Bonner were required to know, from memory, the entire New Testament. This memorization continued to be favored; even a decade later all vicars, up to the age of forty, were ordered by the Archbishop of York to learn by heart one chapter of the Epistles of St. Paul in Latin each week, and even those over forty were to be able to recite some of it.[33]

Bishops' Bible

New versions of the Bible appeared – the Bishops' Bible in the reign of Elizabeth and the still popular King James version in the reign of her successor. The ancient practice of reading aloud to obtain criticism was put to good use in compiling the King James version of the Bible. The best scholars in the land were chosen, and each scholar was given a certain portion to translate; as each section was completed the whole group assembled to hear the new translation read aloud. Suggestions and corrections were made which helped the new version to attain a unity which would have been difficult to achieve without the opportunity for group discussion provided by the oral reading.

King James Version

Educators as well as churchmen were interested in fostering reading, and the interest in reading aloud spread from church and school to the home. From nobleman's castle to the worker's cottage it became a daily ritual to gather round the literate members of the family to listen to them read from the Scriptures.

The pride of parents whose children could read was equalled only by the pride of the children themselves, and it was an occasion for rejoicing when hesitant stumbling changed into relatively fluent reading. Such progress was noted in memoirs and diaries, and many were the reminiscences about the pleasures of children in reading to their admiring families.

The duty of the literate to spread the knowledge of the Bible was taken seriously and conscientiously carried out through reading aloud. In some aristocratic families a chaplain read the Bible and gave religious instruction, but in others this task was performed by the noblewomen themselves or by their children. The diaries of Lady Hoby, Lady Falkland, Lady Anne Clifford, and the Duchess of Suffolk all tell of this practice. Nor did the audience listen in bored indifference. The words they heard could, they believed, mean the difference between salvation and eternal damnation so that it was important to pay attention. A happy incident is related by Thomas Traherne, who testified that as he listened to the Bible, he was transported in ecstacy to other worlds and other days, experiencing the "joys and triumphs of God's people; all of which entered into me and God among them."

While the Bible seemed, in some quarters, to be the absorbing concern of sixteenth century England, and while the church strove to keep religious ideals to the forefront of men's minds, there was nevertheless a vast fund of literature and a vigorous theatre to show that other interests prevailed as well. No longer crowded together into castle and keep for protection against aggressors, the more widely dispersed population could not be so easily reached by the minstrel type of entertainer and relied more heavily on local readers and story tellers for the vicarious excitement of a well-told tale.

Story telling in the home

For many people, literary interests had not changed from what they had been in medieval days. There was, of course, more literature and more to challenge the intellect of an increasingly educated public, but people still had a keen desire to hear about the wonders of the world. The familiar legends of Celtic and Norman origin, of Greece and of Rome, still held many an audience spellbound. The ever-popular stories of ghosts and goblins, and the adventures of Sir Topas, Bevis of Southampton, and Guy of Warwicke were beloved tales not lightly to be cast aside, and although the minstrels had become decadent and had gone down in the world, the fireside narrator took over where the old minstrels left off and kept those tales alive. Campion, describing the simple folk of the day said,

> Well can they judge of nappy Ale,
> And tell at large a Winter's Tale . . . . ,[34]

and it is easy to see from the writings of the time that these "winter tales" were a standard part of every festive gathering. Although Shakespeare might say, in his *Winter's Tale,* that "a sad tale is best for winter," not all of them were sad by any means. Tales went with games and dancing, wassail, cakes and ale to make Christmas one of the merriest seasons of the year. Tales also served to lighten more serious events; according to Ben Jonson, the ability to tell "many a merry tale" was one of the qualifications required of that "queene of Gossips"–the midwife, and it was a talent appreciated in many other walks of life.

There was also much fine literature being written in the sixteenth and seventeenth centuries, so that narrative, in fact, literary fare in general, was more plentiful and varied than it had ever been before. As in former times, much of this was enjoyed as oral literature. No less a scholar than Erasmus, moving in the highest intellectual circles, took for granted that guests at a feast would take turns entertaining the company by relating stories of their youth, of danger, adventure, or other interesting subjects.

Education of a gentleman

So important was story telling in the education of a gentleman that a number of so-called "courtesy books," popular at that time, treated it in some detail. Castiglione's *Book of the Courtier,* and *Galateo* by de la Casa (1576) gave advice to young storytellers, cautioning them against rough language and unseemly gestures. A gentleman, they advised, should stay within the limits of propriety at all times and not, "like a commune Jester passe his boundes."

Authors continued to be conscious that they were writing for a listening as well as a reading public, but may have been unaware of how rapidly the reading public was growing. However, some, such as Alexander Barclay, (1475-1552) and Sir John Harington were conscious of this at an early date. Barclay, in his "Egloges" addressed those who "shall here and rede," this book, and Harington, god-son of Good Queen Bess, wrote that although some writers did not enjoy his efforts, "the readers and the hearers like my books." *Wonders Worth Hearing* was the title Nicholas Breton (1545-1625) gave to his book. He recommended it for reading aloud round a winter fire, or in the fields of summer, "to purge melancholy from the minde and grosse humours from the body." Thomas Campion (1567-1620), telling of the popular pastimes of the day wrote:

> All do not all things well;
> Some measures comely tread;
> Some knotted Ridles tell;
> Some Poems smoothly read.[35]

Later, Lady Anne Clifford, in her diary of the early seventeenth century, made countless references to reading aloud. Her reading covered the Bible, "a great part of the History of the Netherlands," Montaigne's Essays, Spenser's *Faeirie Queen,* Ovid's *Metamorphosis,* and Josephus' history. Sir John Evelyn (1620-1706), mourning for his deceased daughter, wrote in his diary that no one could read prose or verse better or with more judgment. She had the talent of rehearsing a comical passage or a poem which was more delightful than one would hear in the theatre.

Samuel Pepys

A more renowned diarist Samuel Pepys (1633-1703) had much to report on storytelling and reading aloud. When he and his cronies gathered for an evening of good cheer they would, in addition to drinking great quantities of sack and ale, entertain each other with many a merry tale. When Pepys spent a quiet evening at home, he and his wife frequently read aloud to each other. Pepys, a man with a mind of his own, did not hesitate to comment with candour on what he heard or read; he said of one biography of the queen that "it was so sillily writ that we did nothing but laugh at it." He also took some delight in *Cabala,* "A merry book against the Presbyters."

While the homefolk were content to hear or recite what others had written, the more urbane or ambitious fancied themselves quite able to write their own poetry. There were many amateurs with considerable talent, and almost everyone seemed to be writing verses. Schoolboys, no doubt under duress, had to write verses in English, Latin, or Greek which they read to their masters; gentlemen, with a new poem in their pockets extolling their dearest friends or newest loves, would read to their friends for criticism or acclaim.

Even Henry VIII prided himself on his skill as a poet, and with his court jester, Will Somers, composed and recited verses in turn.

A favorite entertainment was "capping" verses. This was a pastime in which one person would start out by composing a line or couplet orally and the next in line would add to it. At one such session Ben Jonson was capping verses with his friend Sylvester. Sylvester began with the line, "I, Sylvester, kissed your sister," to which Jonson responded, "I, Ben Jonson, kissed your wife." At this point Sylvester objected because the line did not rhyme. "I know it," admitted Jonson, "but it's the truth."[36]

"Capping verses"

Not only amateur poets but also many serious writers read their efforts aloud. Erasmus read his verses to his friend William of Gouda, and Edmund Spenser (1552-1599) matter-of-factly suggested that Bryskett, who translated Giraldi's *A Discourse of Civill Life,* either read his translation aloud or recite it to him from memory. Inns and taverns, the precursors of the later clubs, were favorite meeting grounds for those discussing philosophy, literature, politics, or gossip; and in them the oral traditions were adapted to meet the needs of the day. Of such gatherings Ben Jonson, in merry mood, says in "Rules for the Tavern Academy":

Inns and taverns

> Let raillery be without malice or heat
> Dull poems to read let none privilege take.
> Let no poetaster command or intreat
> Another extempore verses to make.

Later, when Robert Herrick paid tribute to Ben Jonson, he recalled these happy meetings and longed for the days when, at the Sun, the Dog, or Triple Tun "each verse of thine Outdid the meat; out-did the frolick wine."

While such gatherings in taverns were relatively common-place and relieved the monotony of daily existence, recitation had a much more colorful role to play in the great pageants which were so prominent a feature of Tudor England. These pageants, always very elaborate, took place at coronations and other royal celebrations. In 1533, when Anne Boleyn, Henry VIII's second wife, was crowned, there were pageants along the way from the Tower to Westminster Abbey. At one of these, "well-apparelled" scholars from St. Paul's recited English translations of Latin poets, and from a tower near Ludgate Hill, four persons representing the cardinal virtues recited orations in honor of the ill-fated Anne.[37] Just twenty-five years later, as Queen Elizabeth's coronation procession wended its way through Cheapside, the new queen was presented with an English Bible. Elizabeth kissed it and held it to her breast declaring that she would often read it.

Pageants and progresses

Throughout Elizabeth's reign pageants were frequently given. When Elizabeth visited her nobles, a pageant was usually staged in her honor. These "progresses," as they were called, no doubt delighted the queen not only for the entertainment they provided, but perhaps also because they were, along with all of the other hospitality provided for her majesty, so costly that even the most powerful noble was considerably less powerful financially by the time the celebrations were over. The entertainment at such events had often a classical or patriotic theme, and sometimes an uneasy union of both. On one occasion, Neptune recited a long poem in the queen's honor, and on another, Venus greeted the monarch in a burst of poetry and proffered her Venus' own sceptre in deference to her majesty's beauty. When Elizabeth went to Kenilworth Castle in 1575, George Gascoigne himself recited some verses in the masque which he had written for the occasion. At Elvetham, she was greeted with an oration in Latin.

Queen Elizabeth

At castles

Elizabeth also made frequent descents upon the universities of Cambridge and Oxford. At Cambridge in 1564 the public orator met her at King's College Chapel and praised her in Latin for a full half hour. Greeted with verses in Greek at Christ's College, Elizabeth promptly replied in Greek. Orations and disputations followed, and then her majesty topped things off with a speech in Latin at St. Mary's Church.

Cambridge and Oxford

The polite impassivity expected of modern royalty was not a characteristic of Good Queen Bess. At Oxford, in 1592, when the famous Thomas Smith spoke, she remarked that he was taking too long for her liking, and on another occasion, the active lady twice sent word to an orator that he was to stop, for she wanted to make a speech herself.[38] However, the persistent gentleman, with his carefully prepared oration, was determined to deliver it and continued to the end in spite of the queen's impatience. Many a greater man would have dared far less.

In her old age, when she was frail and ill, Sir John Harington tried to amuse Elizabeth with his verses, but she replied with a smile, "When thou dost feel creeping tyme at thye gate, these fooleries will please thee lesse; I am past my relish for such matters." Nevertheless, in 1603, when she knew death was near and no longer had joy even in the affairs of state, she turned again to poetry, to Chaucer's *Canterbury Tales,* and listened attentively to the reading of the stories she loved. She was a fitting monarch for England's great age of literature, and although pageantry and poetry survived her, something of their splendor died with her.

The usual celebrations were held when her successor James I was crowned and again recitation was an important part of the program. When the new king arrived at Fleet Street, a "poetical oration" written by Thomas Middleton was delivered by a figure representing Zeal. When James' queen came south to join him, Ben Jonson provided entertainment for her at Althorp where, as the entourage

James I

approached her host's house, a satyr leaped out and spoke verses to her majesty.

A royal entertainment

In 1606 the state visit of the King of Denmark to James' court was also the occasion for much celebration. The Earl of Salisbury entertained the royal visitor, and as the exalted guests entered the inner courtyard, verses of congratulation by Ben Jonson were recited. There was also a great feast given at the court for the royal Dane which seems to have deteriorated into a magnificent orgy. Both performers and spectators unfortunately imbibed too freely, and the result was disastrous. The "Queen of Sheba," forgetting the steps, upset wine, cream, jelly, and viands into his Danish majesty's lap, and then fell at his feet. King James, deciding to dance with Sheba, collapsed when he tried to stand up and had to be carried out. "Peace," finding her entrance obstructed, took her olive branch firmly in hand and hit on the head those in her path. Faith, Hope Charity, and Victory were all supposed to recite, but by the time their turn came they were beyond speech, and so they are mentioned more for their good intentions than for their actual performance.

Entertainment, literary criticism, religion, and education were but a few of the uses to which oral literature was put; its role in publication, propaganda, and matters of health continued to be very important.

Reading and reciting as physical therapy

With the rediscovery of the classical world interest revived in the use the ancients had made of reading and reciting to promote good health. In Italy, Guarino, and Vittorino da Feltre were convinced that reading was a means of increasing bodily heat, stimulating circulation, and helping digestion. In England, Sir Thomas Elyot, in *The Castel of Helth* (1534) recommended reading, singing, and crying for "Exercise of the brest"; men with feeble bodies, he said, "must read oftentimes loude, and in a base voyce, extending out the wind pipe and other passages of the brethe." Moreover "by high crieing and loude redinge are expelled superfluous humors." This advice was to be repeated in Thomas Cogan's *Haven of Health,* published in 1596. Their contemporary in the educational world, Richard Mulcaster, was a confirmed believer in the therapeutic power of speaking and reading aloud. He reported that physicians were prescribing these exercises just as had been done in the days of Seneca and Celsus. Mulcaster described two kinds of reading which the medical profession recognized in his day, the one being "quiet, caulme and staing" and the other "quicke, cleare and straining."[39] This latter type was believed to be an aid to the bodily functions and to improve the health in general. Specifically, said Mulcaster, it "stirreth the lungs," refreshed "the inward parts of the breast," it was good for a dry cough, and could even check some kinds of consumption. Moreover, it so benefited circulation that it "purgeth all the veines, openeth all the arteries," and did not allow "the superfluous humors to thicken." Seneca himself used this kind of reading to combat "the rewme and distillation from the head which troubled him sore."

Should the patient's malaise stem from a mental condition, the doctor was equally likely to suggest reading aloud. It was frequently used as therapy for "frenzies and troubled mindes." In such cases the patient was to be given material to read which would not, because of difficulty or because of its subject matter, tax a weak or sensitive mind. Rather, it was to be "pleasaunt and plaine" whether it was designed to treat a simple headache or relieve the "frantike from madnesse."

As mental therapy

In the more ordinary disturbances suffered by many people, Hoole found that reading aloud was a great help, especially in overcoming bashfulness and helping pupils to adjust to their environment. He reported that when his shy pupils competed in reciting Latin and Greek verses, they were so filled with enthusiasm that they contended like nightingales.

To summarize, it may be said that the period of the Renaissance in England was one of the crystallization of a great nation at a time when that nation became fully aware of its inner strength, its present power, and its future possibilities. This awareness gave vent to creative and imaginative expression in the realm of architecture, government, religion, the theatre, education, and literature. It was in the last five that oral expression in its several forms was to be a vital force. The sixteenth and seventeenth centuries laid the groundwork for developing theories, methods and practices of oral expression. These were to be clarified and made more explicit in the eighteenth century.

References

1. *The Epistles of Erasmus,* tr. Francis Morgan Nichols (New York, London: Longmans, Green and Company, 1918), Vol. III. Ep. 810. p. 434.

2. Battista Guarino, "De Ordine Docendi et Studendi," *Vittorino da Feltre and Other Humanist Educators,* ed. W. H. Woodward, Classics in Education, No. 18 (New York: Bureau of Publications, Teachers' College, Columbia University, 1963), p. 174.

3. Aeneas Sylvius Piccolomini, "De Liberorum Educatione, 1450," *Vittorino da Feltre and Other Humanist Educators, op. cit.,* p. 143.

4. Juan Vives, *Instruction of a Christian Woman,* tr. Richard Hyrde (London: John Danter, 1592), Ch. 11.

5. John Strype, *Ecclesiastical Memorials* (Oxford: Clarendon Press, 1822), Vol. I. Part I. p. 577.

6. *The Epistles of Erasmus, op. cit.,* p. 434.

7. Stephen Hawes, *The Pastime of Pleasure* (London: Early English Text Society, Oxford University Press, 1928), lines 1189-1211.

8. Erasmus, *Apophthegmes, 1564,* tr. N. Udall (Boston: Lincolnshire, Robert Roberts, 1877), Bk. I. p. 89. Suggested by Robert R. Kidder.

9. Erasmus, "De Pueris Instituendis," *Desiderius Erasmus Concerning the Aims and Method of Education,* ed. W. H. Woodward, Classics in Education, No. 19 (New York: Bureau of Publications, Teachers' College, Columbia University, 1964), p. 212.

10. Erasmus, "The School Master's Admonitions," *The Colloquies,* tr. N. Bailey (London: Gibbings & Co., 1900), Vol. I. p. 78.

11. Erasmus, *The Praise of Folly, 1509,* tr. John Wilson, 1688, ed. Mrs. P. S. Allen (Oxford: Clarendon Press, 1925), p. 131, pp. 135-136.

12. Thomas Wilson, *The Arte of Rhetorique* (London: John Day, 1553), Folio 104.

13. Richard Rainolde, *The Foundacion of Rhetorike* (London: Kingston, 1563), Folio 5.

14. Karl Wallace, "Rhetorical Exercises in Tudor Education," *Quarterly Journal of Speech,* Vol. XXII. Feb. 1936. p. 31.

15. *Ibid.,* p. 34.

16. Roger Ascham, *The Scholemaister* (London: John Day, 1570), Preface.

17. Thomas Wilson, *op. cit.,* Folio 118.

18. Edmund Coote, *The Englishe Scholemaister* (London: Widow Orwin, 1596), Preface.

19. John Brinsley, *Ludus Literarius* (London: Thomas Mann, 1612), p. 50.

20. Balthazar Gerbier, *The Art of Well Speaking* (London: Ibbitson, 1650), p. 4.

21. Thomas Wilson, *op. cit.,* Folio 119.

22. *Ibid.,* Folio 118.

23. Abraham Fraunce, *The Arcadian Rhetorike* (London: Thomas Orwin, N.D.), Bk. II. Ch. V.

24. *Ibid.*

25. John Bulwer, *Chirologia* (London: Tho. Harper, 1644), title page.

26. John Bulwer, *Chironomia,* pp. 6-7.

27. Obadiah Walker, *The Art of Oratory* (London: 1659), p. 126.

28. Baldassare Castiglione, *The Book of the Courtier,* ed. W. E. Henley, tr. Sir Thomas Hoby, 1561 (London: David Nutt, 1900), Vol. 23, p. 162. Suggested by Louis Mushro. See William E. Buys, *Speech Education of the English Gentleman in the Tudor Age,* Ph.D. Dissertation, University of Wisconsin, 1952.

29. James Cleland, *The Institution of A Young Nobleman* (Oxford: Joseph Barnes, 1612), p. 76.

30. Edmund Coote, *op. cit.*

31. John Strype, *op. cit.,* Part II, pp. 434-37.

32. John Knox, "The Buke of Discipline, 1621," *The Works of John Knox,* ed. David Laing (Edinburgh: James Thin, 1895), Vol. II, p. 240.

33. Frederick Harrison, *Life In a Medieval College* (London: John Murray, 1952), p. 207.

34. Thomas Campion, "The First Booke of Ayres," *Campion's Works,* ed. P. Vivian (Oxford: Clarendon Press, 1909), p. 127.

35. Thomas Campion, "The Third Book of Ayres," p. 166. Suggested by John Gore. Dr. Gore also suggested several diaries.

36. Mary I. Curtis, *England of Song and Story* (New York, Boston: Allyn and Bacon, 1931), p. 446.

37. John Nichols, "Coronation of Anne Boleyn 1533," *The Progresses.... of Queen Elizabeth* (London: John Nichols and Son, 1788), Vol I, p. 10.

38. *Ibid.,* "The Queen at Oxford," Vol. II, p. 21.

39. Mary I. Curtis, *op. cit.*

Mrs. Siddons Reading. Copyright. Courtesy The Tate Gallery, London.

Chapter V
EIGHTEENTH CENTURY

Near the beginning of the eighteenth century (1702), Queen Anne ascended the throne of England. During her reign, living conditions improved, farms prospered, and better roads made communication easier between towns and villages. Beautiful new homes, planned for comfort rather than for protection, dotted the landscape. But more important than the external and physical changes were the changes in the country's intellectual and social flavor. Within the aristocracy a group of highly educated scholars arose whose interests were almost equally divided between classical learning and practical affairs of state. Anne's reign, and those of the Georges who followed her, saw the rise of many important names in the fields of speech, theatre, and literature.

Importance of speech arts

The speech arts of elocution, reading, oratory, and acting were of interest in the eighteenth century for a number of reasons, not the least of which was that England had become more strongly unified as a nation, and a deepening national consciousness reflected itself in those arts. Language was becoming standardized, and the public, not satisfied with the endless variations of provincial dialect, was interested in learning to pronounce and articulate its language correctly. This interest gave rise to a large number of teachers. Another important factor was the rise of democracy, which brought public speaking to the fore and sent many a hopeful young man in search of a speech teacher as his first step on the road to political fame. Oratory, he realized, was of prime importance to an aspiring statesman. The home, too, fostered the development of speech; still the center of entertainment for many people, the fireside was often the site of reading and storytelling for friends and family. And, of course, a growing theatre was much preoccupied with the problems of effective speech. The church, too, had good reasons for turning to speech for help. All in all, it was a challenging age for teachers of oral art. These teachers came from many different cultural backgrounds; from education; from the church and from the theatre, as well as from public life; and although at times it seemed as if there were as many theories as there were books and teachers, a very definite philosophy of speech expression developed in the eighteenth century.

Oral reading and religion

The close relationship between oral reading and religion which has been evident throughout other epochs, was maintained in this century. The Age of Reason, however, had to mold and adapt oral art to suit its own concepts of what was effective and acceptable. One aspect of oral practice, which again came in for much scrutiny, was its use in the church services. Characteristic of this period was the laity's increasing dissatisfaction with the way in which the Bible and liturgy were being read in church. This was perhaps to be expected, for, as noted in the preceding chapter, Bible reading was increasingly practiced in homes and schools and beyond the walls of the church. Excellent readers, who were not necessarily churchmen, had educated popular taste to the point where poor delivery was a distraction to the listener, and church practice being no longer as inviolable as it had been heretofore, an articulate public made its displeasure known. The Church of England found itself open to attack from many quarters. Dissenters had gained recognition by the Toleration Act of 1689, which permitted them to worship as they chose provided they believed in the Trinity, and loyal churchmen were increasingly dismayed to see how rapidly the Dissenters gained in numbers. The Church began to think seriously about the situation which Milton had deplored fifty years earlier when he wrote, "The hungry sheep look up and are not fed." Since there was general dissatisfaction with the fare which was being offered, the age of reason set about discovering why the flock remained unsatisfied. The conclusions reached were, in general, that the oral presentation of the church service was at least partly to blame. The poor reading of the Bible and liturgy and the ineffective delivery of the sermons were widely and frequently criticized, often by prominent citizens whose words carried weight in the land.

Toleration Act, 1689

Reading of Bible and liturgy

Both clergy and congregation were well aware of the problem, and it was the subject of much discussion. *The Spectator* and *The Tatler,* under the guidance of Addison and Steele, bluntly asserted that the rise of the Dissenters was directly traceable to the incompetence of Church of England clergy in oral delivery. Addison and Steele quoted a certain gentleman to the effect that, if the clergy improved so that the speakers learned to speak and the readers learned to read, within less than a year there would not be a dissenter. But, even while Church of England clergy were being raked over the coals for "dispassionate indolence," the dissenting ministers were being criticized for wasting "a lively vehemence" on unimportant words and phrases. In short, criticism of church services was widespread and varied.

Spectator and Tatler

Some clergymen, often classical scholars, affected a "certain gentleman-like familiarity of tone," and read a prayer with no more feeling than if it were a newspaper. They would not have dared read their beloved Vergil or Martial with as little taste as they read the church service. If, said Addison and Steele, clergymen would but hear an excellent reader, they would learn to read clearly with sufficient strength, as well as with religious intensity. One minister was suggested as a suitable model because he responded to the emotional spirit of the liturgy in joy or sorrow. He had good diction, appropriate tempo, variety, correct cadence, proper emphasis, and other vocal skills which contributed to his success as a minister.

Good models needed

John Henley, who had been educated as a clergyman, had not received instruction in the art of preaching, or praying, or reading. His own problems and experiences led him to conclude that the liturgy could best be improved by applying to it the principles of elocution. A minister, he said, should first strive to know and understand the liturgy, and then, when every part of it had been impressed on the mind and heart of the speaker, he could read it with clarity and propriety and impart its message to his hearers.[1]

John Henley

Under-standing

A major cause of dissatisfaction was the style in which sermons were delivered. Thomas Betterton, the actor, said that sermons were at once uninspired and uninspiring, an opinion which found an echo in many quarters. Some critics thought the sermons too abstract; some thought they were ill-prepared; some thought they were too learned; others simply thought they were too long. Many people, including Betterton,[2] objected to the clergyman reading his sermon, feeling that to be acceptable, it should be memorized and should give the impression of being a spontaneous address.

Reading versus memoriza-tion of sermons

Jonathan Swift, himself a churchman, deplored the fact that sermons were often badly read. Swift, although he felt that reading is to speaking as a copy is to an original, did not condemn reading as such provided it was skilfully done. Swift found no excuse for those who were hesitant in reading or whose posture was so slovenly that they kept their heads "within an inch of the cushion," thus muffling their tones and making themselves inaudible. Equally annoying were those who looked up and down as they read like indolent school-boys. To correct poor delivery, Swift recommended that greater care be given to the preparation of a sermon. He told of one clergyman who wrote his sermon in large script, and then, on Sunday morning, went over it five or six times before delivering it to the congregation. As a result, this reader looked at his manuscript with such ease that the congregation was not aware that he was reading rather than speaking. Swift had no objection to this style of reading.

Jonathan Swift

A new approach

Nearly everybody, it seemed, had advice for the clergy; the general theme being that spontaneity, logical treatment, and emo-tional expression were lacking. The result of such deficiency was a stilted and artificial style of delivery. Having recognized that oral practices were bad, the next step was to determine why they were bad. *The Spectator* attacked the way in which The Common Prayer was often read and blamed early school training for the lamentable state of oral delivery; too much emphasis was still being placed on reading Latin, and not enough emphasis on the elements of reading itself. Out of this imbalance arose the speech faults most commonly found among clergymen–a lack of distinctness, too little volume, rapid speech, and sudden, irrational changes in tempo and volume.

Schools blamed

Thomas Betterton agreed with Steele and Addison in laying much of the blame on the schools. He said that the lack of vocal expression arose from the practice of permitting children to recite their lessons in an unvarying tone, a practice which eventually became a habit. A natural communication of sincere feeling was the ideal towards which actors, preachers, and elocutionists alike were striving, but it was easier to define this goal than to achieve it. Speakers and readers struggled with this problem throughout this century and the next. The honest desire of clergy, actors, and others to improve their standards gave rise to an increasing number of teachers of elocution. These teachers won fame in their immediate circles through their teaching, and earned a place in history by publishing books explaining their theories and methods. Many teachers and critics, like John Mason, were convinced that both reading and speaking should have their roots in conversation. James Burgh, for example, said that reading was neither more nor less than simply speaking what one sees in a book. Most teachers agreed that to sound natural a reader should seem to be expressing his own ideas in his own words.

John Mason: reading and conversation

John Rice

John Rice, in 1765, published *An Introduction to the Art of Reading,* which was outstanding in its day partly because it was devoted exclusively to the art of reading. Rice sought spontaneity of expression–the same animation in reading that would be natural if the reader were uttering his own words, or as he says "to give the energy of the living voice to the precision of the dead letter."[3] In *The Art of Delivering Written Language (1775)* William Cockin, a contemporary, agreed to some extent that reading should sound like conversation, and advised that sermons be read "like any other book" in the capacity of "one who is content to entertain and instruct his hearers with reading to them his own or some other person's written discourse."[4] However, Cockin had some reservations about how far reading should simulate speaking and sought to formulate the idea of aesthetic distance. While agreeing that the tones used by the reader should come from common speech, he felt that they should be "more faintly characterized." Emotions should be more restrained than in real life. He saw oral reading as an art of suggestion rather than as a realistic art. He likened it to a reflection of reality or to a copy of an original, and therefore, somewhat less animated.

William Cockin

Thomas Sheridan

One of the most outstanding teachers of the eighteenth century was Thomas Sheridan, father of the playwright, Richard Brinsley Sheridan. Thomas Sheridan shared the common concern over the way in which divine services were conducted, feeling that they lacked solemnity and propriety. To remedy this lack, he wrote lectures specifically for the purpose of improving the art of reading in the church, and he appealed to the bishops to make "propriety of reading" a requirement for all clergymen.[5] Sheridan, however, did not regard good reading as an end in itself but merely as a necessary stepping-stone to the ultimate goal which was, in his opinion, the recitation of the church service from memory. He admonished, "it is impossible whilst the eye is on the book that the heart can be upward."[6]

Memorization

We see then that speaking, conversation, or "common speech" were used as a guide in determining the standard for reading. Interestingly enough, while common speech was an accepted yard-stick, learning to read was recognized as a preliminary step to speaking. Dodsley presented this viewpoint in *The Preceptor* (1748). Later Walker and then Rippingham subscribed to the same theory; Walker saying that "good reading . . . . is not so much a picture of what speaking is, as of what it ought to be," and that the rules used in the art of reading could be applied in learning to speak effectively, and Rippingham stressing that effective reading was one of the necessary skills an orator must master. Nothing could more clearly demonstrate the inter-relation between these two aspects of oral communication than the fact that there was considerable concern as to which should first be mastered, reading or speaking.

Standard guide for teaching

Although John Locke, philosopher and educator, died in 1704, his influence was to be felt for centuries thereafter. He was typical the transitional period in many ways inasmuch as his philosophy presented both aristocratic and democratic viewpoints. It was his belief that the best place to start educating the "abhorred rascality" was in the ranks of the aristocracy. He said: "That most to be taken care of is the gentleman's calling. For if those of that rank are by their education once set right, they will quickly bring all the rest into order."[7]

John Locke

Locke was a fit spokesman for the Age of Reason because he based his whole theory of education upon the importance of reason. He said that children understand reasoning as early as they do language and love to be treated as rational creatures sooner than one realizes. With such a philosophy, he naturally gave understanding a place of prime importance in the learning process. This attitude is readily discernible in two of his studies, *Essay Concerning Human Understanding* and *Conduct of the Understanding,* both written to explain his theories on the best way of achieving understanding.

Reason

Locke particularly objected to the emotionalism and superstition which persisted in his day. With a philosophy based on reason, he was naturally opposed to the legends and tales of fantastic adventures, the stories of ghosts and goblins, witches and warlocks which

Popular stories

were still the nightly fare around many cottage firesides and in some noblemen's halls. A servant or older brother could still find an eager audience for the supernatural tales which sent many a child, tingling with excitement, up a long dark stairway to a cold, clammy bed. Even Lady Mary Wortley Montagu, famous for her letters, related that it was common for the governess to tell some spine-chilling ghost story to her charges, who were just as eager to be scared as were their ancestors in bygone ages. In revolt against such a literary diet, Locke urged that stories for children deal with reality, with "anything they know". Actually, he disapproved of nearly everything but Aesop's fables, which was then circulating under the guise of children's literature. But Locke's reason was no match for popular desire, and despite his disapproval, tales of the supernatural did not die out. In the nineteenth century, Wordsworth was to credit the fairy tales and ballads he heard as a child with contributing to the development of his imagination, and even twentieth century tales are not lacking in creatures unknown to man or boy. However, despite Locke's difficulty in exorcising the supernatural, his philosophy of reason and understanding found ready support not only in England, but also on the continent where Voltaire became an ardent exponent of rationalism.

Rousseau

In 1712, shortly after Locke's death, his disciple, Jean Jacques Rousseau, was born in Geneva. He was to exert an influence on educational thought in both the eighteenth and nineteenth centuries. Rousseau championed a natural approach to life, contending that man is born a pure animal but is corrupted by civilization. Rousseau was in favor of directing man's natural impulses but was in no way an advocate of suppressing them; rather, he preached a greater emotional freedom. Rousseau argued that in order to protect a child from the unnatural life of the times, he should be sent to a rural environment, there to live a simple life unfettered by the stultifying influences of the city. He believed also that understanding was the foundation upon which to develop a vigorous and alert mind, a theory which was quite in accord with trends in the Age of Reason.

The elocutionists were among those who came under the spell of Locke, Voltaire and Rousseau. John Henley, John Mason, James Burgh, John Rice, Thomas Sheridan, William Cockin and even John Walker stressed understanding as the basis of learning. With understanding achieved, it was the task of the interpreter to communicate that understanding or sense to the hearer, and as Cockin reminded his readers, neither "stops", nor punctuation, nor any other mechanical device could be substituted for this essential element.

Reason being so firmly established at this time, one might well wonder about the importance of emotion. Was it to be disregarded, stifled, and driven from the creative world of art? Such might have been its fate if cold intellect alone had triumphed, but thanks to Rousseau as well as to the basic makeup of man, the eighteenth century was, as noted, also dedicated to the philosophy of following nature. With Rousseau at the helm emotional reaction was not only acceptable, it was natural and therefore highly desirable.

This balance between the rationalism of Voltaire and the emotional freedom of Rousseau was good for oral reading and recitation and for all of the arts. Until a writer has evoked an emotional response, he does not have a living story. The oral reader must pass along to his listeners the emotional reaction supplied by the author. Since some of man's deepest emotions are those which touch upon his religion, it is not surprising to find that the liturgy was again under scrutiny in this respect, and that it was precisely the lack of this emotional element which called forth much of the criticism noted above. The relatively few clergymen who were able to convey to their congregations the emotional richness of the oral part of the church service had no difficulty in winnning the approval of their hearers.

Emotion

Emotion has always been the life-blood of literature and of the oral rendition of literature. This has been true from the days of the *Iliad,* the *Aeneid,* and *Patient Griselda,* to *Pamela, David Copperfield,* and the works of modern authors. Such a vital attribute of oral communication naturally attracted the attention of those dedicated to the furtherance of the oral arts in he 18th century, and most authorities had much to say about the nature and degree of emotion required in the art of reading. There was general agreement that there should be emotional response on the part of the hearer who, as Mason said, should be so affected by what he heard that he actually experienced the emotions presented by the author.[8] The difference in teaching methods which evolved came about as a result of differing theories as to how this effect on the hearer should be achieved.

Lord Kames

In an age of rationalists it was to be expected that some people would be wary of too much emotional feeling and advise the performer to stand aloof, directing and playing upon the feelings of his audience through the skilfull use of technique; others felt that to move an audience the reader must first be moved himself. Lord Kames recommended relating the various emotions to their vocal counterparts by, for instance, raising the voice for elevated words and thoughts and lowering it for dejection. Undoubtedly for the same purpose of affecting the hearer, James Burgh went to some lengths with his marginal notes to depict the effect of emotion upon the body. But, while it was generally accepted that the hearer should be emotionally moved, the old controversy arose as to whether or not the performer should be affected and, if so, to what extent. There were those, such as John Mason, with strong so-called natural

Emotional involvement

leanings, who maintained that only if the reader himself experienced the author's emotions or "affections" he then in turn could arouse them in his hearers. Sheridan, true to his basic philosophy, advised the reader to feel and to understand the author's sentiments; this done, he said, good vocal expression must perforce follow as correct emphasis, and tone, grow out of the meaning and spirit of the author. Even Walker, the rationalist who tended to think that a fair part of life could be built on rules, encouraged the reader to experience the emotions he was attempting to arouse in his audience. Walker realized, of course, that this was not always easy and offered some suggestions as to how the reader might stimulate his own emotions. He advised him to recall events and emotions in his own life similar to those described in his material. If this should prove beyond the reader's powers, then he should at least try to imitate the emotion involved, in the hope of arousing it, and to prove his point, Walker cited Edmund Burke's belief that one could not assume the attitude of an emotion without having that emotion, to some extent, conveyed to the mind.[9] This was an earlier concept of the principle later propounded in the James-Lange theory.

Imitation of emotion

A word of caution against too much emotion was voiced by John Rice in *An Introduction to the Art of Reading* (1765). Rice agreed that some emotion was essential, but he pointed out the dangers of excessive emotion in reading such literary forms as the soliloquy. True to much of the eighteenth century philosophy, he pointed out that it is just as natural for men "to reason as to rave".[10] In reciting or reading, he said that the reader may actually be, or **seem** to be, affected by the emotion, but he must be careful not to be so deeply moved that he loses control of himself. In fact, he held that the reciter did not actually need to be affected. Repetitious and overlapping as the theories of some of these writers were, yet, by their careful analysis and appraisal of the factors involved in making a successful appeal to the emotions of both reciter and audience, these men molded the art of oral interpretation and created of it a medium through which mood and philosophy might find expression.

Emotional control

In the spirit of Rousseau, "follow nature" became the clarion cry of the eighteenth century. At first glance this would seem a simple, straightforward piece of advice, but "follow nature" was just vague enough to defy clear definition, and confusion arose as one authority after another tried to explain what it really meant. Present-day definitions are by no means unanimous, and it is perhaps hazardous to try to pin down just what the phrase meant two centuries ago. Yet it is clear that the eighteenth century was far from interpreting "follow nature" as sanctioning a free and easy abandonment to impulsive and unbridled expression. In an age when mannerisms and affectations were the fashion in polite society, the

Follow nature

emphasis on nature was primarily a reaction to the artificiality of the day. To the Age of Reason "nature" was synonymous with order, form, and plan. Nature itself showed reason and order at every turn, thus "following nature" meant obeying law and reason. The restraining influence which enabled man to follow nature with intelligence recalled the classical philosophy described by Pope:

> Those rules of old discovered, not devised,
> Are Nature still, but Nature methodized;
> By the same laws which first herself ordained.
> Hear how learned Greece her useful rules indites
> When to repress and when indulge our flights.

Essentially this same idea was expressed by Sheridan when he said that the Greeks based their principles of art upon reason which, in turn, dictated that nature's law must be followed.

How far eighteenth century elocutionists succeeded in following nature is hard to say; with the exception of some limited attempts by men like Joshua Steele to apply musical notation to spoken words, we have no exact means of appraising their actual oral reading and speaking. Occasionally, however, we can suspect that "follow nature" was no more than meaningless cant, some of the elocutionists pretending to follow a "natural" approach while pursuing the methods of the mechanical enthusiasts. Any teacher, for example, who told his pupils to count "one for a comma, two for a simi-colon [sic]" and so on, could scarcely be described as a pillar of the natural school.

Mechanical vs. Natural schools

The whole division of eighteenth century elocution into two schools, Mechanical and Natural, has occasioned much controversy. Some authorities claim that the distinction between the mechanical and natural concepts actually constituted two schools of thought so sharply defined that they met at few points; others believed that these differences had been greatly magnified and really existed to a limited degree. As early as 1810 John Quincy Adams remarked that the differences between the two schools were neither easy to discern nor as great as some supposed. It is probably true that the division into schools meant no more than that some favored a preponderance of mechanical elements in delivery while others sought to keep these to a minimum. Assuredly a study of eighteenth century authors reveals none who were purely mechanical and very few who might be considered purely natural. Mattingly says that the mechanical school supported the dictum "follow nature" but believed that Nature alone could not accomplish everything and needed assistance.[11] Probably most readers and teachers used elements from each school in order to achieve their ends.

Early in the century Robert Lloyd, in *The Actor,* declared that"Nature's true knowledge is the only art," and this was certainly the basic premise from which the natural school took its direction.

The mechanical school put more emphasis on such elements of speech as vocal modulation, punctuation, inflection, and standardized gesture, seeking to establish specific rules for expressing thought and emotion. Vandraegen says that "rules, external patterns and uniformity" characterized this school.[12]

Symbols and notations

One aid to expression which some eighteenth century writers sought to develop was a system of symbols, notations, and gestures to guide the reader in expressing the author's thought. Thomas Sheridan, often regarded as the high priest of the natural school, nevertheless favored some signs, or marks, by which the voice might be guided in delivery. He worked out a scheme for marking to indicate emphatic words, pauses, and degrees of tone suspension. Cockin and Rice, on the other hand, true to the natural approach, favored greater freedom of expression and wanted the principles of reading set forth "on a more rational and extensive foundation."

Opposition of Cockin and Rice

Cockin, an opponent of mechanical methods, did not believe it possible to establish a system for charting either vocal or bodily expression because of what he called the "indefinite variety which Nature delights to display in these provinces."[13] Rice, too, opposed any "mechanical system, or arbitrary mode of pause and cadence,"[14] be it in prose or poetry. This viewpoint was later carried on by John Lettice, who also believed that no rules for modulation could be prescribed because all the subtle changes of voice could be achieved only through deep feeling and understanding. With these elements present he had no doubt that Nature, and Nature alone, could determine the range of expression.

In the first half of the century, however, such writers as John Henley and John Mason partook of both philosophies; though they are both regarded as belonging to the natural school, some of their views are mechanical in flavor. Henley relied on numerous rules, and Mason was not unwilling to relate punctuation and pausing. It was he who observed that at a comma the voice is withheld "while we may privately tell one, a simi-colon [sic] two; a colon, three, and a Period four,"[15] but he then said that pauses must be determined primarily by the sense. Mason's main theme was natural expression. He recommended the study of Nature and stressed the importance of thought and feeling in conveying "the full sense" and "Spirit of your Author."[16] He particularly wanted the reader to be free of mechanical limitations in order that he might arouse in the hearer the same ideas and passions that the author had aroused in the reader.

Joshua Steele

Joshua Steele is another who may, at first glance, appear mechanical, for he used musical notation along with some other symbols as the basis for his approach. Yet, while his system has mechanical elements, there is no evidence that he intended it to replace the thinking process or to put excessive emphasis on methodology. Rather, he was interested in recording, by means of symbols, how certain selections were delivered by famous people such as David

Garrick. Steele's influence can be seen later in John Thelwall's interest in cadence, meter, and quantity, and in his respect for Steele as an authority; it is also evident in James Chapman's specific attempt to apply Steele's principles of music to reading and speaking.

Chapman, however, credited John Walker with contributing more than anyone else to the improvement of elocution. Walker provided explicit guidance in the mechanical approach, defining reading as "that system of rules which teaches us to pronounce written composition with justness, energy, variety, and ease."[17] Walker demanded a study of sentence structure, punctuation, and the forms of inflection -- the upward and downward, which he regarded as the "axis . . . , on which the force, variety, and harmony of speaking turns" for reader or speaker.[18] He developed a system of marking inflections and defended it on the grounds that such marks should impede the reader no more than ordinary punctuation everyone accepts. He pointed out that his system was not intended to restrain the skillful reader, but rather to help the beginner.

John Walker

Having seen some of the mechanical tendencies in the treatment of voice, action or gesture should be studied to see to what extent they were treated mechanically. In James Burgh we find a fusion of natural and mechanical elements. Burgh's influence was extensive during his lifetime and was to outlive him through his book, *The Art of Speaking.* His basic tenet certainly has no quarrel with the Natural School, for he held that reading was "nothing but speaking what one sees in a book, as if he were expressing his own sentiments, as they rise to his mind."[19] Understanding was Burgh's touchstone for good reading. Since one cannot speak well upon that which one does not understand, neither can one read well until the subject matter has been thoroughly digested. Burgh voiced his objection to the dogmatic rule of so many counts for certain punctuation marks suggested by earlier writers. When he discussed emotion and gesture, however, he showed definite leaning toward the mechanical school. He described the various emotions and indicated the position or action of the head, eyebrows, eyes, mouth, arms, and entire body for each emotion.

James Burgh

Walker so admired Burgh's treatment of gesture that he referred to *The Art of Speaking* as "a very ingenious performance" and admitted his own indebtedness to it. Yet Walker confessed that he had made a few changes – and improvements – on this admirable work. Like Burgh, however, Walker believed that the emotions should be classified, with each emotion having "a particular attitude of the body, cast of the eye, and tone of the voice, that particularly belongs"[20] to it. All such gestures should be practised before a mirror. He believed that the expression of every emotion ought to come from within. Walker's commendation of Burgh suggests that he had cautious enthusiasm for somewhat set, mechanical gestures, for

Walker on gesture

he believed that assuming the external appearance of an emotion helped arouse that emotion. And, strangely enough, the principle, if not the complete practice in all of its details may have had some merit; many decades later the James-Lange theory was to give psychology's blessing to the idea that the bodily position, which appeared to suggest a certain emotion, could in fact be an aid to inducing that emotion. Both the nineteenth and twentieth centuries will show some teachers continuing to defend mechanical practices.

Degree of gesture

Cockin, convinced as he was of the futility of trying to chart human emotions precisely, asked only that gesture and tone be moderate in expression and without grimace and affectation. Others, either disregarding or merely mentioning any graphic system, concerned themselves not with specific gestures, but rather with a degree of action. In general, gestures modified to a much greater degree than those used in acting were favored in reading. John Walker, whom we might well expect to favor more rather than less gesture, shared the view that there should be less action in reading than in speaking and at the same time advised both readers and speakers to make use of no more action than they can help. Perhaps nothing more clearly shows the overlapping of the "mechanical" and the "natural" than to find John Walker, leader of the so-called mechanical school teaching that if readers and speakers are "in earnest as they ought to be, some gesticulation will naturally break out; and if it be kept within bounds it will always be tolerable."[21] Action is fine, said the arch-mechanist, if it be fitting and natural.

Whether or not the mechanical or natural aspects of speech or reading can be regarded as separate schools is relatively unimportant. Certainly some mechanical tendencies and concepts arose in the eighteenth century. These may well be attributed to the attempts of the age to solve the issues of life through cool, calculated rational means which considered everything as objectively as possible. It is, of course, ironic that these ideas were often pushed beyond the bounds of reason and sometimes resulted in the very thing they sougnt to avoid, namely the acceptance of arbitrary rules in place of sober judgment in dealing with the problem at hand.

Imitative school

One method of teaching which has been practised in varying degrees in many periods of history was the imitative method. It had its advocates in the eighteenth century. Cutting across the so-called natural and mechanical schools, it was regarded by many eminent people as the best means of teaching elocution; John Mason and John Walker were among those who favored it. Walker advocated that pupils imitate their teachers so carefully that their very inflections would be identical. Walker's acceptance of the imitative mthod does not, of course, negate his interest in the mechanical devices already discussed. William Cockin in *The Art of Delivering Written Language* also advocated imitation. Even *The Spectator,* at the beginning of the century, had urged the imitation of good models as a means of improving the reading of the clergy.

Imitation, however, despite its illustrious supporters, has never been able to achieve universal acclaim, and in the eighteenth century those opposed to it were as significant as its supporters. Robert Dodsley warned students never to copy a voice, and John Rice considered mimicry a danger. John Herries and Thomas Sheridan also opposed imitation. In the early nineteenth century two clergymen, the Reverend James Chapman and Archbishop Whately, offered further opposition to this method. If the reader grasped the meaning and concentrated, said Whately, he would not imitate.[22] Although twentieth century philosophy is generally opposed to imitation, it is still used in varying degrees.

Methods of performance

Just as there were different theories of teaching, there were also methods of performance. Two of these methods, reading and recitation, flourised side by side in the eighteenth century; some were prone to argue the merits of one over the other, many considered both practices acceptable.

Memorized recitation

Memorized recitation, the older form, was used for many different purposes and occasions. As noted earlier, the clergyman who could memorize his sermons was held in greater esteem than one who, too obviously, read them. The views of Swift and Sheridan on this matter found support throughout the century from such men as Enfield, Campbell, and Blair. All of these men agreed that reading a sermon was second best to delivering it from memory, and that the ideal effect to be sought, in either case, was that of spontaneous speech. Enfield not only favored memorizing sermons, but actually blamed reading for the affected manner seemingly peculiar to oral readers. Blair approached the matter from a different angle; he saw memorization as a different skill and believed that persuasive discourse profited by memorization and lost power when read. Cockin and Sheridan accepted memorization, but felt that this should be undertaken only after the pupil had mastered the art of reading. The rhetorician, Campbell, on the other hand, said that he could find six good readers to one "who repeated tolerably," and he was quite willing to accept good reading rather than endure poor memory work. Those who actually preferred reading to the older art, often blamed memorization for many of the glaring faults so frequently encountered in its delivery. They accused memorization of fostering in children a sing-song tune as well as causing the monotone so often found in children's reading. In adults, memorization encouraged a stilted and unnatural delivery.

Reading

While these attacks upon both forms of delivery were in progress, a more positive attitude was being taken by such men as John Rice and William Cockin, each of whom wrote a book dealing with reading as an art. Of the two, John Rice was the more uncompromising in his insistence upon the value of reading. In *An Introduction To The Art of Reading* (1765), he says, "there are few or none who have treated professedly" this art.[23] William Cockin, in *The Art of Delivering Written Language* in 1775, was not quite so rigid in his preference for reading. He was willing to concede that plays and orations might well be given as an actor would give them, implying memorization, although they, too, could effectively be read in a simple style.

Categories of delivery

Many believed that the type of material could, in some measure, determine whether memorization or reading was to be preferred. This led inevitably to the familiar practice of dividing delivery into its various forms. Going back to ancient Greece and Rome, to Aristotle, Cicero, and St. Augustine, the eighteenth century paid homage to the classical age by reviving and elaborating upon ancient tradition. Several methods of classification were possible. Material might be grouped according to its literary genre: poetry, prose, comedy, tragedy, orations or sermons. Rice suggested a division into the five categories: poetry, narrative, description, public speaking (including sermons), and theatrical declamation. For all of these categories, Rice favored reading over memorization, and he gave advice on how the different types should be delivered.

Recognizing that the delivery must be suited to the material, Rice wanted narration and inanimate description to be given in a simple manner without any trace of declamation. However, he warned the performer to distinguish between a desirable simplicity and an unwarranted familiarity; the pompous must not be discarded merely to make way for the vulgar. He had no use for an affected pomposity, as can be seen again in his remarks on poetry. He ridiculed without mercy those who took a simple message, or couplet, and mouthed it with all the dignity and oratorical display suitable to the epic grandeur of great tragedy. As to his other classifications, one cannot do better than to quote his own words. Comparing theatrical declamation to the simpler forms, he said:

> . . . . in the recital of mere narratives, of descriptions, and of argumentative or persuasive Discourses, the Reader stands in the Place, and speaks in the Person of the Writer; but in the Rehearsal Conversation-Pieces, he must diversify not only his Mode of reciting, in Conformity to the Subject but also in Conformity to the Character.[24]

In all dramatic composition he cautioned the performer never to address himself to the audience.

These various attempts to establish little compartments into which the different forms of reading or reciting could be placed, appealed to the eighteenth century mind with its love of order, organization, and logical thinking. While some of the distinctions might seem picayune, the classification of reading styles continued to interest scholars such as Austin and Whately in the nineteenth century; nor is it far removed from some of the distinctions which have been made in the twentieth century such as interpretative reading, personation, impersonation and mono-acting.

Differences in reading prose and poetry

In addition to the various forms of delivery, the differences in rendering poetry and prose were of major importance in the eighteenth century. Poetry, of course, had held sway for many centuries as the acme of literary achievement, but the age of reason say English prose coming into its own and producing significant novels, essays, diaries, and letters of high literary value. These literary forms rivalled poetry in popularity as material for readers and reciters alike, and much time and thought was spent to determine what distinctions, if any, should be observed in the delivery of prose and poetry. There were those who favored differentiating between the two by using entirely separate reading methods for each, but opinions varied widely. Sir Joshua Reynolds, the painter, viewed poetry as an artificial form of expression divorced from the usages of common speech in measure, rhyme, accent, and pause; he wished to see this artificiality preserved because it was precisely this artificiality which raised poetry above the level of common speech. He desired a "sense of congruity, coherence, and consistency" which not only increased the artificiality of the poem but also added to its artistic value.

Since many thinkers were struggling hard to throw off the shackles of artificiality which plagued the fashionable world, many tried to minimize these same elements in poetry by reading it as much like prose as possible. They argued that if the meaning of a literary work was brought out clearly, the form of expression, whether poetic or prosaic, was of small moment.

Final pause

One of the main points at issue was the treatment of the pause at the end of the poetic line. Should there be a slight pause at the end of the line to accentuate the rhyme and the rhythm, making it quite clear that poetry and not prose was being read, or should the reading flow so easily from one line into the other that it minimized the rhyme and sometimes even the rhythm of the poetry and so almost obliterated the difference in the two forms of literature? Some thought that this pause, even if the sense did not require it, was absolutely essential, and they would approve of no reading of poetry which did not observe it. Isaac Watts, early indicating some directions already mentioned in connection with the mechanical school, stipulated that at the end of a line there should be a slight pause, about half the length of a comma. Many important names in reading such as Cockin, Sheridan, Priestley, and Enfield were champions of the final pause. Not to observe this pause, said Sheridan, was to reduce verst to a "hobbling" metre.

Caesural pause

The caesural pause, the pause in the middle of the line which is an ancient device in the history of poetry, was traditional and, to many, so fitting and proper that without it poetry ceased to be poetry. Sheridan, Walker, and Enfield all required the reader to observe it when reading aloud. Austin supported this opinion, along with all of Sheridan's rules for reading verse.

The pause and meaning

However, unanimity was not achieved on the treatment of pauses. The controversy arose, as a rule, whenever a pause, either final or caesural, interfered with meaning. Why pause at any specific point in a line, many asked, when the idea is carried through from one line to another? John Mason would tolerate neither pauses nor a too obvious rhyme if they impaired meaning. Rice was so concerned on this point that he proposed a method for clarifying the meaning of verse and for reducing the danger of too sharp a beat. He suggested that verses which do not rhyme be written in lengths consonant with their meaning, rather than arbitrarily following the length of the line chosen by the poet. Lord Kames and Joseph Priestley felt that the solution lay in having the meaning and the pause coincide.

John Walker on prose and poetry

This ideal, however, was not always attainable and, as John Walker pointed out, it was not the pause which distinguished poetry from prose, but rather "the adjustment of the accented syllables, which forms a regular return of stress, whether the line be long or short."[25] The pause, he observed, was often natural at the end of a verse line, and its duration should be determined by the connection in thought between the two lines, but, he added significantly, it must never be allowed to interfere with the sense. If one's ear is not sensitive to poetic sounds, it is better to read poetry as if it were prose, even though this is an error. In general the eighteenth century tendency was to prefer that the pause elucidate the meaning, when possible.

Prose or poetry first

Another question which teachers debated at this time was whether prose or poetry should be tackled first by the budding reader. Opinions differed as to which form was the more difficult to read. Some teachers took the view that prose, because of the irregularity of its cadences, was more difficult to read than poetry and should therefore be studied first. John Mason and William Cockin were in favor of studying prose first. Cockin argued that poetry is to ordinary speech as dancing is to walking; it requires special consideration and, therefore, should be tackled last. Mason suggested that pupils begin with those works which most nearly resemble ordinary conversation; he recommended *Pilgrim's Progress,* the *Family Instructor,* or an "innocent" novel, as possibilities.

The discussion continued well into the nineteenth century with Thelwall and Lettice. They wanted the student first to master the art of reading poetry. Thelwall believed that the effective reading of prose could not be achieved through reading prose alone, but if one learned to read poetry he would certainly be able to read prose. Lettice, who set high standards for reading, said that if one could read Milton's *Paradise Lost,* the most difficult reading material in English, he would certainly have no difficulty in reading prose.

Sheridan and Walker, both of whom firmly believed that poetry was more challenging to read than prose, presented rules for reading poetry. Sheridan, condensing the number of rules to four, proposed the following:

Sheridan's rules

1. All the words should be pronounced exactly in the same way as in prose.
2. The movement of the voice should be free from accent to accent, laying no stress on the intermediate syllables.
3. There should be the same observation of emphasis, and the same change of notes on the emphatic syllables, as in prose.
4. The pauses relative to the sense only, which I call sentential, are to be observed in the same manner as in prose; but particular attention must be given to those two peculiar to verse, the caesural and final, as before described, which I call musical pauses.[26]

Walker's rules

Walker, unable to limit himself to four rules, made several proposals for the reading of verse. He recognized that finding the precise tone of a poem was not easy and accordingly advised the reader to begin a poem very simply and prosaically. He went on to say that in reading verse the same syllables and words would have the accent as they would in prose; the weak vowel *e* in words like "dang'rous" or "gen'rous" should be sounded; most verses permit a caesura or pause in the middle of the line which must be respected to maintain harmony and distinctness; at the end of each line there should be a pause, the length depending on its relation to the next line; the falling inflection should be used in the caesura of the next to the last line to maintain cadence; a simile should be read in lower tone than the preceding passage; when there is no sense pause at the end of a verse the last word should have just the same inflection as in prose; and, finally, "sublime, grand, and magnificent description in poetry, frequently requires a lower tone of voice, and a sameness nearly approaching to a monotone, to give it variety." [27]

Readers and reciters

So much discussion and controversy over different aspects of oral delivery meant that professional readers and reciters, whether in church, hall, or drawing room, had to be prepared to face a critical and discriminating public. Many of these professionals were well-known actors or teachers of elocution who were quite able to meet the challenge of the age. Among the theatrical celebrities who won renown as readers were James Quinn, John Henderson, John Philip Kemble, and Mrs. Siddons. In the field of elocution, Thomas Sheridan and John Walker were as famous for their reading as for their teaching. Sheridan, at least as early as 1769, gave a recital at Foote's theatre. John Walker's reputation was solidly built upon his readings of Milton and other poets, and upon his rendition of the

Lord's Prayer. This last was so impressive that he was regarded as a fit model for the clergy.

There was already a distinction made in the minds of some spectators, whether clergymen, elocutionists, or discerning laymen, as to the differences between acting and reading. Dr. Johnson, for example, regarded Quinn and Henderson as using more of the actor's art than that of the reader. David Garrick, the actor, was described as reciting with superior skill and feeling. He gave an ode at the Shakespearian Jubilee in 1769 with such sensitivity that Boswell likened the event to "an exhibition in Athens or Rome," with Garrick seeming to be transformed into a demi-god. Garrick's reading of the liturgy earned such acclaim that Richard Cull published a book, *Garrick's Mode of Reading the Liturgy,* in which he attempted to analyze Garrick's performance for future generations.

David Garrick

Such presentations by professional people attracted much attention from the public, aspiring actors, readers, the clergy, and amateurs who wanted to improve their skill in telling tales and reading to family and friends. Many maintained that they could learn as much from observing these living models as they could from a teacher or book.

Authors

Another group which contributed to the reading or recital of literature was made up of the authors of the day who were eager to read their works, either to obtain criticism or as an act of publication. Many who could not interest a publisher in their work insisted upon inflicting it on friends and acquaintances, in much the same manner that had galled discerning Romans in earlier days. Early in the century *The Tatler* cast derisive glances upon the ubiquitous "Mr. Softly" type of author who frequented coffee houses, taverns, and other gathering places in search of any audience he could find. Amid stifled laughter, the hapless poet bravely, or perhaps naively, poured out his verses to his critical, yet indulgently amused listeners. Goldsmith also described a group of "authors" in *The Citizen of the World* some of whom offered riddles or stories at their weekly meeting at "The Broom" in Islington. In addition to the "Mr. Softly" types, rife in every village and shire, there were many competent writers whose works still find favor today, who read aloud to willing and sympathetic ears. MacPherson and Goldsmith read their poetry to Boswell, and Mrs. Sheridan, together with her husband, also read aloud her play, *The Discovery,* to Boswell.

Unfortunately, being an author did not make a man automatically a good reader, and although some could enhance the beauty of their works by skillful reading, there were others whose works had to survive through sheer worth in spite of having been read aloud by their writers. John Dryden's poor reading abilities caused Colley Cibber to find *Amphytrion* dull when he heard it read aloud by its author. Equally uninspiring were the readings of Congreve, Addison, Thomson, and Oliver Goldsmith who read in a "slovenly" fashion and with a strong Irish brogue.

Fortunately some authors charmed their listeners more successfully than did these gentlemen; perhaps one reason Dryden's reading annoyed Colley Cibber was that the latter was himself a reader of great ability. Although he preferred the old and more formal style of delivery to the new familiar mode favored by Garrick, he was an accomplished and respected reader. Alexander Pope was said to have the "voice of a nightingale," a statement which drew from Lady Mary Wortley Montagu the caustic remark, "very true, indeed, all sound and no sense." [28] Despite the lady's opinion, we may assume that Pope's pleasing voice enhanced his poems. Rowe did such a good job of reading his own plays that the actress, Mrs. Oldfield, readily acknowledged him as her model. The old complaint noted in ancient Rome was heard again in eighteenth century England, that when the reading was given with great artistry, it was hard to isolate tone from words and to criticize the selection strictly as a piece of literature. When Hooke, the historian, read his lectures aloud, the critics could scarcely decide whether they were being charmed by the history or by the voice of the historian. In any case, eager audiences could be found for good readers in oaken tavern, Chippendale drawing room, or the bustling coffeehouse which was so much a part of eighteenth century life.

Coffee-houses

The Tatler under Addison and Steele, set out to bring philosophy out of libraries and educational institutions "to dwell in clubs and assemblies, at teatables and in coffeehouses". Among the topics discussed in *The Tatler* were several concerned with oral delivery; for example, the inadequate delivery of sermons by the clergy and the reciting and reading habits of certain individuals. Addison and Steele also encouraged another speech activity, the reading aloud of periodicals within the various coffeehouses. It was the custom for a young man to stand and read the news aloud to the assembled guests while they enjoyed their potations. Quite naturally, *The Tatler* was interested in the continuance of this practice. It recommended that a pulpit be erected in every coffeehouse, and urged the public to repair to the coffeehouse of its choice. The very first issue of *The Tatler* gave a description of the various coffeehouses, summarizing the particular part played by each one:

> All accounts of gallantry, pleasure, and entertainment shall be under the article of White's chocolate-house; poetry, under that of Will's Coffeehouse; learning under the title of Grecian; foreign and domestic news, you shall have from St. James' Coffee-house . . . . "[29]

Such offerings for the replenishment of mind and spirit did not exhaust the benefits of oral reading, since in this century again it provided services to the body as well. From the days before Celsus down to the present day, reading and reciting have been considered to have therapeutic value in the treatment of certain ailments. John Henley, in 1727, was advising the orator to practice reading in "as high a voice as nature will bear" to improve his health at the same time that he advanced his education. This practice may have strengthened the orator but, for obvious reasons, it was not always popular with the neighbors. One Londoner, in what must have seemed an excess of zeal, opened wide his windows in the morning and, after a relatively harmless half hour of deep breathing exercises, shouted "fifty verses as loud as he could bawl them for the benefit of his lungs." He resorted to none less than Homer for this morning activity, contending that the Homeric tones were deeper, more resonant, and "more conducive to expectoration" than those the other poets could offer.

John Herries, who wrote *The Elements of Speech* (1773), was just as convinced that Homer was good medicine for both mind and body. Herries quoted the verse:

> Read aloud resounding Homer's strain,
> And wield the thunder of Demosthenes,
> The chest, so exercised, improves its strength;
> And quickly vibrations through the bowels drive the
> restless blood.[30]

Therapy

Mental therapy was, and is, another recognized function of oral reading and recitation. Kings and warriors, churchmen and children have all wooed relaxation and restful sleep through the good offices of a bed-time storyteller. James Boswell prevailed upon his barber to read to him until he fell asleep. Further, and perhaps more significant, uses for the recital of literature were suggested by James Burgh who regarded the recitation of classical literature as a means of developing confidence in the reciter, an aspect of oral literature which was to grow in importance in the next century in an awakening America.

Early America

English influences

The English elocutionists naturally set the standards for reading and speaking in colonial America. Despite the growing tension, the intellectual and emotional bonds with England were strong. The same names were known in elocutionary circles. Sheridan and Walker were often used as authorities by those seeking to establish elocution in the new world, and Sheridan's *Lectures on Elocution*, was prescribed for use by the Brown University Laws of 1783.

Speech teachers were also familiar with the theories of Burgh, Steele, Blair, Kames, Enfield, Rice, and Cockin. In step with the times, Daniel Staniford and other American writers gave wide acceptance to the idea that Nature was the best guide for the art of speech. The term "propriety" crossed the seas unscathed, and Increase Cook struck a familiar note when he defined reading, as Cockin had done, as the "art of delivering written language with propriety, force, and elegance." Exhortations to the reader to "enter into the feelings of the author, whose sentiment he professes to repeat," were imports from the Mother Country. They thrived in the new soil.

Nature

Propriety

Oral delivery had an honored place in the school curriculum; and even Benjamin Franklin took time to formulate his theories on the teaching of speaking and reading. His *Sketch of an English School For the Consideration of the Trustees of the Philadelphia Academy* (1779) outlined the objectives to be attained in each class, from the beginners who were to be guided not to read too fast and to observe the stops and pauses, to the relatively accomplished speaker who could address an audience. Like some of the English authorities, Franklin believed that reading should precede speaking and he supported the school of opinion that stressed understanding as the *sine qua non* of good oral delivery.[31] With this emphasis it is perhaps the more surprising to find that he favored learning by imitation. He reported on pupils who had listened attentively to their esteemed master Mr. Dove who read aloud to them, after which they imitated his reading so carefully that they soon "caught his manner" and thereby gained Franklin's approval. Good habits, Franklin was sure, could be learned by imitation.

Benjamin Franklin

The seats of higher learning in America did not ignore the speech arts. The Harvard College laws of 1642 required the prospective student to be able to "make and speake true Latin in verse and prose."[32] In the mid-seventeenth century Harvard students "were practiced twice a day in reading the Scriptures," repeated sermons "publicly in the hall," heard lectures on rhetoric and had "practice of poesy" in their second year.[33] Declamations were to be given periodically in Latin and Greek, and by 1766 a tutor was giving instruction in elocution, English composition and rhetoric.[34]

Harvard

Extra-curricular activities such as the Harvard Speaking Club, founded in 1770, also contributed to the American interest in speaking and reciting. This group's programs included readings from such authors as Shakespeare, Milton, Pope, Steele, Addison, Thomson, and Young. By 1773, the Harvard Overseers noted improvement in the elocutionary standards at Harvard's annual exhibition,[35] due no doubt both to the instruction and to such extra-curricular activities as the Speaking Club.

Other colleges, too, paid more than token respect to speech. At Brown University, for example, the Laws of 1783 provided for instruction in Greek and Latin literature including Homer, Vergil,

Reciting and reading

and Cicero, much of which would have involved oral reading and reciting.[36] Yale required Scriptural reading, disputations and the recitation of the Catechism in Latin.[37] The College of New Jersey (Princeton) encouraged declamations and introduced contests in reading aloud.[38]

Commencement exercises have remained a favorite exhibition ground for speech activities from Harvard's first commencement at which Latin and Greek orations and declamations were given. Poems were recited at later commencements. At the Yale commencement in 1717 an oration and disputation were held "as usual." Other colleges followed this tradition, and to this day many students expect to hear a speech as part of the farewell to their alma mater.

American publications

While many of the books used in eighteenth century America were those of the English elocutionists, books by American writers began to appear. Many of those published after the American Revolution appealed to the national pride of the young democracy. Caleb Bingham, for example, achieved national fame when he published *The American Preceptor* in 1794[39] and the *Columbian Orator* in 1797,[40] in which he encouraged the use of American literature. Some other books which appealed to this patriotic fervor were Joseph Dana's *A New American Selection of Lessons,*[41] and Alexander Thomas' *The Orator's Assistant.*[42] There were many others, some of which dealt more directly with reading.

Lindley Murray

There was, in fact, enough interest in reading to warrant the publication of books specifically on that subject. In 1799 Lindley Murray's *English Reader* appeared.[43] The American-born Murray, known as the father of English grammar, regarded the purpose of his book as threefold: "to improve youth in the art of reading; to meliorate their language and sentiments; and to inculcate some of the most important principles of piety and virtue." Murray, confused in his own mind concerning the mechanical and natural approach, believed, on the one hand, that it was not possible to give fixed rules for pauses, emphasis and tone; on the other hand, he believed "some rules" on loudness, distinctness, slowness, pronunciation, and emphasis as well as on the manner of reading verse would be helpful.

Increase Cooke

At the turn of the century James Abercrombie and Increase Cooke, whose influence was felt well into the nineteenth century, also contributed to the study of reading. Cooke, although his interest was mainly in the realm of oratory, observed in *The American Orator*[44] that reading, recitation, and declamation were often used as preparatory exercises, as well as on "real occasions." Abercrombie was a clergyman noted for his reading of the Bible. In 1803 Abercrombie wrote *Two Compends For the Use of the Philadelphia Academy,*[45] which included sections on elocution and natural history. *Lectures on the Arts of Reading and Speaking,* was

James Abercrombie

published in *The Port Folio* between 1809 and 1811. His works show that there was concern for the way in which the Bible, as well as other literature, should be read. Whereas in early New England no one was permitted to read the Bible publicly without an exposition, this limitation was later removed, and therefore the need to maintain standards of reading became a challenge to teachers.

Daniel Staniford

In 1807 Daniel Staniford published *The Art of Reading,*[46] which was in the English tradition of propriety, elegance, the conversational manner, and some elements of both the natural and mechanical approach. This book was largely an anthology for orai reading.

Although early America did not contribute much that was original in the field of speech, it became increasingly aware of the importance of this study; and it did transplant and nurture the English traditions, keeping them alive until they could be modified to suit the philosophy and needs of a young and different land.

Theories and ideas do not begin or end with dates or the change of centuries; many of the trends noted in this chapter continued well into the nineteenth century and the more durable philosophies are still in favor today.

References

1. John Henley, *The Appeal of Oratory To the First Stages of Christianity* (London: 1727), p. 73.

2. Charles Gildon, *The Life of the Eminent Tragedian, Mr. Thomas Betterton* (London: Ptd. for R. Gosling, 1710), p. 79.

3. John Rice, *An Introduction to the Art of Reading With Energy & Propriety* (London: J. & R. Tonson, 1765), p. 195.

4. William Cockin, *The Art of Delivering Written Language* (London: H. Hughes, 1775), p. 134.

5. Thomas Sheridan, *Lectures on the Art of Reading* (Dublin: Samuel Whyte, 1775), p. IV.

6. *Ibid.,* (London: Dodsley, 1775), p. 283.

7. John Locke, *Some Thoughts on Education* (Cambridge: University Press, 1895), p. LXIII.

8. John Mason, *An Essay on Elocution* (London: M. Cooper, 1748), pp. 19-20.

9. John Walker, *Elements of Elocution* (London: J. Johnson, 1806), 3rd ed., pp. 286-287.

10. John Rice, *op. cit.,* p. 305.

11. Alethea S. Mattingly, *The Mechanical School of Oral Reading in England, 1761-1821* (Unpublished Ph.D. Dissertation. Northwestern University, 1954), p. 311.

12. Daniel E. Vandraegen, *The Natural School of Oral Reading in England, 1748-1828* (Unpublished Ph.D. Dissertation. Northwestern University, 1949), p. 4.

13. William Cockin, *op. cit.,* p. 125.

14. John Rice, *op. cit.,* pp. 152-153.

15. John Mason, *op. cit.,* p. 22.

16. *Ibid.,* p. 28.

17. John Walker, *op. cit.,* p. 1.

18. *Ibid.,* p. 56.

19. James Burgh, *The Art of Speaking* (London: T. Longmans, 1761), p. 9.

20. John Walker, *op. cit.,* p. 279.

21. *Ibid.,* p. 282.

22. Richard Whately, *Elements of Rhetoric* (Cambridge: James Munroe, 1834), p. 272.

23. John Rice, *op. cit.,* p. 1.

24. *Ibid.*, p. 291.

25. John Walker, *op. cit.*, p. 254.

26. Thomas Sheridan, *Dictionary of the English Language, to which is Prefixed A Prosodial Grammar* (London: Charles Dilly, 1797), 4th ed., Vol. I. p. LXXXVII.

27. John Walker, *op. cit.*, p. 260.

28. William Cooke, *Memoirs of Samuel Foote* (London: Richard Phillips, 1805), Vol. II. p. 203.

29. *The Tatler*, No. 1, Tuesday, April 12, 1709.

30. John Herries, *The Elements of Speech* (London: Edward and Charles Dilly, 1773), p. 103.

31. Benjamin Franklin, "Sketch of English School," *The Works of Benjamin Franklin*, ed. Jared Sparks (Boston: Hilliard, Gray and Co., 1836), Vol. II. p. 127.

32. *New England's First Fruits* (London: Overton, 1643), p. 13.

33. Josiah Quincy, *The History of Harvard University* (Cambridge: John Owen, 1840), Vol. I. pp. 190-191.

34. *Ibid.*, Vol. II. p. 133, Appendix XIV.

35. S. E. Morison, *Three Centuries of Harvard* (Cambridge: Harvard University Press, 1936), p. 140.

36. Walter C. Bronson, *The History of Brown University* (Providence: The University, 1914), p. 103.

37. F. B. Dexter, *Documentary History of Yale* (New Haven: Yale University Press, 1916), pp. 32, 158, 267.

38. George V. Bohman, "Rhetorical Practice in Colonial America," *History of Speech Education in America*, ed. Karl Wallace (New York: Appleton-Century-Crofts, Educational Division, Meredith Corporation, 1954), p. 63.

39. Caleb Bingham, *The American Preceptor* (Boston: Manning and Loring, 1797), 4th ed.

40. Caleb Bingham, *Columbian Orator* (Boston: Manning and Loring, 1797).

41. Joseph Dana, *A New American Selection of Lessons* (Exeter, 1799), 3rd ed.

42. Alexander Thomas, *The Orator's Assistant* (Worcester, Mass.: I. Thomas, Jr., 1797).

43. Lindley Murray, *English Reader*, ed. Jeremiah Goodrich (Saratoga Springs, N.Y.: Samuel Newton, 1825), Preface.

44. Increase Cooke, *The American Orator* (Hartford: O. D. Cooke, 1814), 2nd ed., p. 13.

45. James Abercrombie, *Two Compends for the Use of the Philadelphia Academy* (Philadelphia: H. Maxwell and Wm. Fry, 1803). Suggested by Porter Perrin.

46. Daniel Staniford, *The Art of Reading* (Boston: John West and Co., 1810), 7th ed.

Charlotte Cushman Seated, Reading. Copyright. Courtesy Theatre Collection, The New York Public Library at Lincoln Center, Astor, Lenox and Tilden Foundations, New York, N. Y.

Chapter VI

NINETEENTH CENTURY AMERICA

The nineteenth century in America was an age of growth and expansion. Not only had the population of the young country increased with incredible speed from a mere four million in 1789 to twenty-three million by 1850, but the nature of the population was changing as well. To the Anglo-Saxon pioneers had been added other ethnic groups with other customs, other languages, other culture patterns, and other literary backgrounds. Along with this physical growth there developed a national consciousness which, in turn, brought an awareness of the need to unify both the language and the thinking of this heterogeneous population if political democracy and national unity were to be maintained. The ability to express oneself clearly with voice or pen was again of prime importance; thus a sound educational system, a free press, and able speakers were necessary.

Young America grew larger and stronger, and education began to burst the bonds of class as it had never done before. As the frontier moved steadily westward, attempts, though meagre, were made to carry education and a respect for learning to the deep forests and distant prairies, so that the rising generations might be prepared for the tasks which lay ahead. In time, railroads, steamboats, and machines began to push back the frontier and change a rural nation into a complex and increasingly urban civilization.

English influences

All of this expansion had its effect on art and expression inasmuch as systems and philosophies of expression arise as a reflection of current trends of thought. In keeping with the times, therefore, nineteenth century concepts of oral expression in America arose to embody some of the religious, philosophical, scientific, psychological, and aesthetic thinking of the day. These various approaches, important as they were, were never quite strong enough to eradicate the deeply-rooted ideas of the famous English leaders of the eighteenth century, and much of nineteenth century thought continued to reflect eighteenth century ideas. "Follow Nature" still sent writers in search of Nature's ways, and even at the end of the nineteenth century Alfred Ayres, a leader in elocution, advised the would-be reader to observe, study, and copy nature. However, the need to define one's terms was still a major problem among educators; more than ever before, "nature" and "natural" meant different things to different people. Some sought nature by way of the emotions, others through dogmatic rules which often obscured the issue instead of clarifying it, while still others turned to science, to the occult, to philosophy, to religion, or to the new psychology to explain what nature and natural meant. Some distinguished between "natural" and "unnatural" by saying that a good reader is "natural" when he has freed himself of his eccentricities and faults in delivery, and "unnatural" when he has failed to do this. Even the faults themselves were elusive because what pleased some critics displeased others.

Joshua Steele

Among the eighteenth century writers whose influence was still strong in nineteenth century America was Joshua Steele. Men like Jonathan Barber, Epes Sargent, Merritt Caldwell, and George Vandenhoff were in his debt. James E. Murdoch, one of the leaders in the field, said that Steele's theory was one of the most outstanding contributions to the field of spoken language ever to appear in that it completely established the theory that the tones of the voice in speech can be definitely measured and given visible notation, as in song.

Thomas Sheridan

John Walker

Thomas Sheridan, also, made a noticeable impact on nineteenth century thought, but even greater was the influence of John Walker, who was quoted, lauded, and censured throughout the century. One of Walker's early admirers in America was Ebenezer Porter, who combined emotional expression with the principles set forth in Walker's *Elements of Elocution.* Porter was credited by William Russell with having done more than anyone else to simplify some of Walker's complex procedures. Many others accepted Walker's approach either fully or in part, so that James Rush, as late as 1859, was able to say that, for much of the century, Walker's ideas were the basis for most of the books on elocution both in Britain and America.[1] Murdoch, in 1883, called Walker "the father of the English system of elocution," a description which caused S. S. Curry to observe that Walker was "only the father of mechanical elocution." In actual fact, Murdoch's devotion was to James Rush rather than to John Walker, and when Murdoch was offered the presidency of the Philadelphia School of Oratory, he accepted the position on the understanding that only the philosophy of James Rush would be taught. When he discovered that Walker's methods and not those of Rush were being used at that institution, he promptly resigned.

Gilbert Austin

Gilbert Austin, an Englishman whose book *Chironomia* has been mentioned, made a significant contribution to American nineteenth century thought. William Russell recommended *Chironomia* to his students, saying, ". . . here you will find the best treatment extant of the subject of gesture."[2] In 1845 Merritt Caldwell wrote that Austin's book "for nearly forty years has been the common source from which have been derived the principles of gesture." And, it can be added, after yet another forty years had gone by, Moses True Brown still considered it pre-eminent.[3] Austin had set himself the task of devising a system for recording bodily action just as Steele had earlier attempted to do for voice. The result was a mechanical complexity so involved, yet so impressive, that it sustained Austin's influence not only throughout the nineteenth century but also well into the twentieth century. Not everyone, of course, was enthusiastic about such an approach, but Austin's influence was sufficient to prompt S. S. Curry, not an admirer of Austin, to observe that "hundreds of authors, in fact, nearly all, especially in the realm of gesture, have followed Austin as an absolute authority."[4]

Classification of styles

Austin made a meticulous and detailed study of the various styles of reading. He altered the terms used by eighteenth century writers and classified reading as intelligible, correct, impressive, rhetorical, dramatic, and epic in form. Intelligible reading, such as that used in business by a clerk, or in the reading of a parliamentary bill, he regarded as the lowest form of reading. Slightly above this he placed correct reading, which has the elements of intelligible reading plus appropriate emphasis, good delivery, and suitable manner. Although this style was often used in the church, Austin felt that it was "dry and cold." Impressive reading, in addition to the elements found in correct reading, required, he said, an expressive voice and countenance, "direction of the eye," variety in tempo and the proper use of pauses. It required but little gesture. Austin recommended impressive reading for use in the church. Rhetorical reading he considered somewhat similar to impressive reading, but it required some gesture and a more expressive countenance. The material used in rhetorical reading should be very nearly committed to memory. This was an interesting compromise between reading and memorization and a technique which has proved popular with speakers in almost every age. Dramatic reading, he said, required consistency in voice and countenance, appropriate tempo and accent, and a moderate degree of gesture to suggest a specific character.

The reading of epic poetry should, Austin felt, be quite different. The epic demanded great dignity, a more exalted quality, a great range of emotion from the pathetic to the awful, and a measure of enthusiasm like unto that of the poet himself. He believed that epic gesture should have grandeur and grace along with simplicity and precision. Inasmuch as Austin regarded novels as the tools of Satan and also opposed them because they encouraged rapid reading, it is not surprising that he offered no advice as to how they should be handled.

Other scholars made less elaborate classifications. Dodsley in the eighteenth century and Archbishop Whately in the nineteenth century followed the example of Cicero and St. Augustine and divided delivery into only a few styles. Dodsley spoke simply of the familiar, solemn, and pathetic style. The familiar style was that used in reading a paper or letter and required the least skill. His solemn style, used in serious narrative, demanded uniformity, steadiness, clarity, and calmness, while the pathetic style, which might be used in some orations, permitted the expression of the emotions through voice. Whately used the terms correct, impressive, and fine reading to denote the three categories into which he divided the delivery of literature. "Correct" reading, to Whately, meant reading which would convey by the voice everything that a silent reader would get were he to peruse the selection himself. Impressive reading he defined as simply adding to correct reading "some adaptation of the tones of voice to the character of the subject, and of the style." "Fine" reading followed a slightly different course and imposed upon the reader the additional role of critic. Here Whately said that the reader might seem to direct his hearers as if saying to them, "This deserves your admiration;–this is sublime;–this is pathetic, etc."[5] American writers would also give much thought to classification of reading styles. They would devise new terminology according to their various philosophies of oral reading, as will be seen later in this study.

Definitions of elocution

Definitions of "elocution" varied at this time. Some restated the ideas of the eighteenth century and some sought to encompass the widening interest of the day. Early in the century Samuel Kirkham defined elocution as the setting down of principles or rules to teach one to "pronounce either extemporaneous thoughts, or written composition, with justness, energy, variety, and ease"–a typical eighteenth century definition. He regarded the object of elocution as first, to make a good reader, and then second, to make a good speaker. His contemporary Ebenezer Porter said that elocution involved the utterance of one's own thoughts or those of others. In the 1860's Anna T. Randall and Allen A. Griffith defined it similarly. Alfred Ayres regarded it as an intellectual art, so fraught with difficulty that up to his day he considered America to have produced only a few readers of the first rank.

Elocution involved many things. It usually covered the expression of thought by means of both body and voice. In references to bodily action the authority was usually Austin. Russell, Andrew Comstock, and Caldwell all based their theories on his. Later Delsarte continued to stress action as a part of expression.[6] Emotion, as well as thought, persisted as one of the basic elements in the philosophy of Rush, Donald Macleod, and S. S. Hamill; Alexander Melville Bell stated this philosophy of emotion aptly and simply when he said that the student must "learn to feel." The realm of the soul was encompassed, too, for the Transcendentalists were increasing in number. Shoemaker said, "Elocution concerns the commerce of mind and soul,"[7] while E. B. Warman, in turn, pontificated that the greatest orators, ministers, readers, and public speakers were those whose words shine through "a clean, pure, white soul—ay, breathing, as it were, the very breath of the Divine." S. S. Curry, founder of the Curry School of Expression, reflected this attitude.

"Elecution" as a term

Despite these various interpretations of the term there was a growing dissatisfaction with the word 'elocution.' Some, like E. B. Warman, were content to modify it. Warman distinguished between "true" and "false" elocution and was careful to indicate that in his *Lecture–True and False Elocution.* Obviously he was opposed to the undesirable aspects of the elocution of his day, and, in some respects, he does go beyond the elocution of that time. S. H. Clark, at the end of the century, sought to avoid the unpopular implications of the word by referring to the "old" and the "new" elocution. The old, he said, dealt with voice as voice, and often succeeded in separating the voice from the man. The new, however, had educational principles and emphasized self-expression. He and his co-author, W. B. Chamberlain, defined elocution as "a study of thought processes in their relation to utterance." This definition echoes the principle offered by Ebenezer Porter, and it was often repeated thereafter, with slight variations on the amount of emphasis to be given to thought and utterance.

Imitation

While the imitation of definitions seems to have been a popular pastime in the nineteenth century, there was widespread dismay that imitation in delivery should find such ready acceptance as a means of training elocutionists. Dodsley, in 1748, had advised teachers to warn their pupils against the dangers of copying, but the practice still flourished in the next century and shows signs of life today. Some teachers, such as Andrew Comstock, frankly favored imitation. Comstock advised teachers to read a selection aloud and then have the pupils repeat it in unison with such gestures as the material should require. In England John Lettice in 1822 gave support to this method when he recommended that at Oxford and Cambridge Milton's *Paradise Lost* be read aloud annually. An able reader should be chosen for this task, and the students should repeat aloud what they had heard. In America William Russell was willing to compromise, taking the view that though he did not approve of imitation, it was acceptable for a teacher to show the pupil how to present a piece of literature. This little concession might seem ingenuous enough to disarm everybody, but it did not. There was a considerable and significant group either completely opposed to imitation, or holding such a different concept of it that, in the ordinary sense, it was not imitation at all. The opposition to copying slavishly what one heard and saw came from many of the leading nineteenth century authorities. Bell maintained that imitation encouraged the pupil to copy his teacher's bad qualities as well as the good, a danger while George Vandenhoff also sought to avert when

Bell's viewpoint

he advised pupils not to try to "catch and imitate the tones and peculiarities of any other man."[8] As Bell pointed out, the pupil would substitute his teacher's eccentricities for principles of correct delivery and end up with no basic standards except the manners of his teacher. This approach, he believed, was what had given elocution its doubtful reputation.

A different concept of imitation was held by some of the more able teachers whose interests extended to philosophy and aesthetics. They seem to have interpreted the word in its Aristotelian sense, which does not imply a literal imitation of nature as we ordinarily think of it, but rather an idealization of it. However, S. S. Curry's skepticism seems well founded: that many who practiced imitation in its common interpretation merely quoted Aristotle to appease their own consciences.

James Rush

James Rush objected to imitation primarily because critics could not agree on any single individual as a suitable model for imitation. Imitation was accepted, Rush argued, before there was any realization of "a **common source** of knowledge in the few and classified constituents of speech." Since Rush had devised a system which both gave this knowledge and classified it, he thought he had, *ipso facto,* rendered imitation obsolete. His book, *The Philosophy of the Human Voice,* published in 1827 was one of the really significant books in the field of speech.

One of the outstanding characteristics of the nineteenth century was the tremendous growth of the scientific spirit. Rush was a man attuned to his century. He was a physician, a graduate of Princeton and Pennsylvania, a student at the University of Edinburgh and an original thinker with a deep interest in science. This interest in science led him to forsake his medical practice and turn his considerable talents to research and writing. In *The Philosophy of the Human Voice* he set forth the various aspects of voice, providing nomenclature to describe vocal processes in an attempt to show that "elocution can be scientifically taught" by establishing principles based upon scientific knowledge.[9]

To embark upon his scheme, he tried "to establish a system of directive precepts, and of elementary instruction," based upon a foundation of physiological history. Like his predecessors, Rush accepted the premise that Nature was the standard of judgment in elocution as it was in the other arts, and he contended that his system was founded upon, and originated in Nature. To find Nature, however, Rush went a step farther than anyone else had gone, up to this time. He sought it in the realm of science and physiology. Though he approached his study from a scientific viewpoint, it was upon elocution as an art that he was to build his philosophy. His physiological studies were but a means to an end, and that end was to give the **art** of elocution a sound scientific foundation based upon Nature.

His study of the voice applies to the arts of speaking and acting as well as of reading, but he had much to say which is of interest to the oral reader. Rush included the following aspects of practice to develop the art of reading–training in the vocal sounds, time elements, vanishing movement, force, stress, pitch, melody, cadence, tremor, quality, and rapidity of utterance. The perfect reader required a great number of skills, many of which, Rush believed, could be developed. Perhaps it is as well to present Rush's own summary of these abilities, for it also shows some of his ingenious terminology:

> It will be little more than recapitulation therefore to say; the faultless reader should have the various qualities of voice from the full laryngeal bass of the orotund, to the lighter and lip-issuing sound of daily conversation. He should give distinctly that pronunciation of single elements and their aggregates, both as to quantity and accent, which accords with the habitual perceptions of his audience. His plain melody should be diatonic and varied in radical pitch, beyond discoverable monotony. His simple concrete should be equable in the rise and diminution of its vanish. His tremor should be under full command for occasions of grief and exultation. Discrimination and taste must have fixed the places of emphasis, and a knowledge of its forms and degrees, have afforded the means for a varied and expressive application of them. He should be able to prolong his voice through every extent of quantity in the wave, and in every concrete interval of the rising and falling scale. He must have learned to put off from the dignified occasions of reading, everything like that canting or affected intonation, which the artful courtesies and sacrificing servilities of life too often confirm into habit; and to avoid in his interrogations the keenness and excesses of the vulgar tongue. He should have for this, as for every other Fine Art, a delicate sense of the Sublime, the Graceful, and the Ridiculous. A quick perception of the last is absolutely necessary, to guard the exalted works of taste, from an accidental occurrence of its causes.[10]

Rush was aware of the importance of both mind and emotions in speech. The range of thought and emotions should find expression through the five aspects of voice which he listed as quality, time, force, abruptness, and pitch. For example, he described the whisper, falsetto, orotund, guttural, and natural qualities of voice; relating the whisper to secrecy, the falsetto to fear, or surprise, the orotund to dignity, deliberation, "solemnity and grandeur," and the natural to "familiar" reading. The orotund he described as "an improved quality of the speaking voice." He regarded it as the only voice

Qualities of voice

suitable for epic and dramatic reading, for the church service, and for Shakespeare and Milton because of its greater musical elements, its increased volume, its expressiveness, and its aid to diction and vocal control. Little did Rush realize that his words would be taken so seriously in the nineteenth and even in the twentieth century that the orotund, in many cases, was almost accepted as the normal quality. Such was not Rush's intention.

His terminology for force and pitch did not make such impact, but when he devised his method of stress, it equalled in strength his dictum on quality. For at least a century we find the radical, median, vanishing, compound, and thorough stress mentioned so often that many teachers throughout America never questioned that these were the traditional and accepted forms of stress.

No other book on the speech arts exerted such an influence in the nineteenth century as *The Philosophy of the Human Voice.* Its merit derived from the scientific attitude of its author, and his determination to approach his subject with scientific objectivity; its weaknesses were no fault of its own but arose rather from its mis-use as a practical textbook by admirers who did not fully understand Rush's intent.

Rush's influence

As frequently happens when a creative mind tries a new approach which catches the public fancy, there were soon disciples who believed that Rush had found the only way to teach speech. Such a disciple was Dr. Jonathan Barber, who was, according to Rush himself, the first to follow Rush's principles. Barber, like Rush, was a physician. A member of the Royal College of Surgeons in London, he came to America and taught at various colleges including Yale and Harvard. Barber believed in a careful analysis of the material and rigorous vocal training for those who would learn to speak effectively. In his book, *An Introduction to the Grammar of Elocution,* he highly recommended Rush's work to all prospective teachers, praising particularly Rush's lucid and precise terminology. Disciples do not always receive the blessing of their masters, but Barber was recognized by Rush as a faithful follower, and he soon was joined by many others. Olney, and then Samuel Kirkham, joined the Rush coterie, and in 1835 Donald MacLeod journeyed all the way to Cincinnati to praise Rush and his philosophy in an address before the Western Literary Institute and College of Professional Teachers. Six years later, Sullivan H. Weston was extolling both Rush and Barber for their "elegant and masterly essays," and calling Rush's treatise "the most perfect work of the kind in any language." Two more physicians, Andrew Comstock and H. A. Apthorp, joined the ranks of Rush admirers, but perhaps the greatest triumph for Rush was the approval of William Russell, called "the father of American elocution." Russell was a particular asset to Rush because he appreciated the real purpose of Rush's work, which was to present a philosophy of voice rather than to produce a book of practical rules.

Many other names – Day, Raymond, Frobisher, and Monroe, for example – could be added to the list of Rush's disciples. One of the most ardent of all was James E. Murdoch. He was so devoted that he avowed he would gladly end his days in support of Rush's system. This system, which held that each mental state had corresponding vocal signs in some of the various forms of pitch, force, time and quality gave vision, said Murdoch, to the older concepts of elocution.[11]

Inevitably there was another side to the picture; and it would not be completely accurate to suggest that Rush was universally hailed even in the nineteenth century. He was criticized for being too detailed, too meticulous, too mechanical, too artificial, that he presented too many rules, and was, in fact, impractical. Edward P. Thwing attacked him as being "full of conceits, odd phrases, and irrelevent matter." Perhaps the most balanced evaluation was made by S. S. Curry, who regarded the mechanical aspects of Rush as the antithesis of sound educational principles, yet believed that the field of speech was greatly indebted to him for his scientific approach to its problems.[12]

Attempts were also made to fuse Rush's theories with those of others such as Walker and Sheridan. Later in the century, Robert I. Fulton and Thomas C. Trueblood attempted to combine the scientific approach of Rush with the philosophical and religious approach of Delsarte – an attempt which Maud May Babcock described as trying to "mix the unmixable." The enthusiasm for Rush waned with the century, partly because Delsarte's star was rising by that time and partly because of the growing interest in psychology. Men like S. S. Curry challenged the mechanical aspects of his work, yet his decline was gradual and is still incomplete; the philosophy upon which his fame was built is still recognized and accepted by many.

Francois Delsarte

American educators and readers were developing their own theories and philosophies, but influences from abroad were sufficiently important in America to demand consideration. The Frenchman Francois Delsarte, although he never saw America, found more support for his philosophy in the new world than he ever enjoyed in his native France. Delsarte was apparently led to work out his own system, or philosophy, of voice training because he himself had suffered the loss of his voice while studying at the Paris Conservatoire, and he blamed the methods used there for his misfortune.

Steele MacKaye

Delsarte owed his fame in America to an enthusiastic young actor, Steele MacKaye, who went to France to study acting. There MacKaye "discovered" Delsarte and became his devout and dedicated follower. Convinced that he was offering to his fellow-Americans nothing less than the key to self-expression, MacKaye became Delsarte's first disciple in America; this energetic enthusiast spread the master's fame from coast to coast. Yet, despite this fame, Delsarte has always had an aura of mystery about him. He published nothing during his lifetime, and although he did leave a number of so-called "literary remains," we are largely dependent on his followers for an explanation of his philosophy. The "literary remains" were published in a book entitled *Delsarte System of Oratory* which also included two lengthy discussions of his philosophy by two of his students, M. L'Abbe Delaumosne and Mme. Angelique Arnaud. From this, and other books on Delsarte, it can be seen that he built a system of expression based upon a philosophical and religious concept derived in part, it would seem, from Catholic doctrine and from the theories of Emanuel Swedenborg. Swedenborg taught that everything in the natural world derives its existence from a corresponding element in the spiritual world. In natural man the spiritual world is reflected in his speech, face (which he calls the index of the soul), and gesture.

Delsarte System of Oratory

Delsarte was also influenced by Swedenborg's belief that everything that is complete is a trinity, be it the soul, body, and the "operation" in man, or the trinity of "infinite love, infinite wisdom, and infinite power," or the Father, the Son and the Holy Ghost.[13] On the question of whether or not Delsarte himself was a philosopher, Angelique Arnaud replied that if the meaning of the word was limited to aesthetics, then he was a philosopher. Delsarte saw art as an idealization of nature. He believed that art was divine in all its aspects and that there was an underlying unity, relationship, and interdependence among all arts. Mme. Arnaud explained that "the principle of the system lies in the statement that there is in the world a universal formula which may be applied to all sciences, to all things possible:- this formula is **the trinity**,"[14] each part of which requires the other parts for its existence. Delsarte carried this idea into all phases of his philosophy, holding that the three principles of man's being are life, mind, and soul; that beauty is based upon three elements – clearness, integrity, and proportion. All tones, he said, consist of three parts, the tonic, the dominant, and the mediant; the tonic being the "father," the dominant the "son," and the mediant the Holy Ghost. Delsarte used this principle of the trinity in his first and greatest law, namely that "the sensitive mental and moral states of man are rendered by the eccentric, concentric, or normal form of the organism."[15] His second law stated that each form of the organism becomes triple by borrowing the form of the two other forms.

Emanuel Swedenborg

He saw the body as being divisible into nine parts, among which there is an interrelationship or "intertwining."[16] In Delsarte's chart, which S. S. Curry included in *The Province of Expression,* Curry states that the lower part of the chart is concerned with the "agents of the body," while the upper part explains man's psychic makeup.

Much more has been said upon Delsarte's system than upon his actual teaching practices, but a little is known of his methods – methods which seem to have been much less highly systematized than later descriptions of his philosophy would indicate. Mrs. Steele MacKaye says that Delsarte started his class with a philosophical discussion, the presentation of theory, or the study of a chart. This was followed by practical work, such as the recitation of a fable, a scene from a play, or even a song by master or pupil. Among Delsarte's favorite selections were passages from Greek drama, from Meyerbeer or La Fontaine, in all of which he used a remarkable range of expression from the sublime and tender to the ferocious.[17] In his private teaching he used selections with open vowels for voice training. In narrative passages he advised that the speaker's eyes meet the eyes of the audience to gain attention and sympathy, but, according to Shaver, Delsarte was interested in recitation only as a medium for teaching acting.[18]

Though largely due to Steele MacKay's support, and to the fact that France still spelled culture to many Americans, the popularity of Delsarte sprang from a more basic fact. He came to the forefront at a time when the old standards of an agricultural community were being pushed aside by urban and industrialized power, and neither the Age of Reason nor the scientific spirit could comfort a society regimented to the rhythm of a soulless machine. Escape from this growing monster was sought in a re-birth of romanticism and a revival of the Gothic spirit. Delsarte caught the mood of the times with his philosophical and religious ideas, his devotion to art, and his desire to help men express themselves freely and fully. His philosophy seemed to offer a sense of order to philosophical thought, a consolation to a world faced with the more unfathomable elements of science.

Delsarte influence

A list of all the Americans who were influenced by Delsarte would read like pages from the nineteenth century *Who's Who* in the field of expression. Among them were the Reverend William R. Alger, who gave up his ministry to preach the philosophy of Delsarte, Louis Baxter Monroe, who helped found the Boston University School of Oratory, and Steele MacKaye. These men were called "the founders of the 'new elocution'."[19] Monroe especially exerted a tremendous influence on the rising generation of teachers: E. B. Warman, Charles Wesley Emerson, S. S. Curry, Anna B. Curry, Leland Powers, and Franklin Sargent all came under his spell. Warman travelled from ocean to ocean to spread the new gospel, and Moses True Brown rejoiced that a new star shone over the land. Brown lamented that, until Rush broke the spell, most Americans were content to teach "the thread-bare" techniques of the English elocutionists and offered students little more than a watered-down version of Steele, Walker, and Sheridan. Delsarte changed all that and earned from S. S. Curry the title of "the most original investigator in the department of delivery of any teacher or writer during the present century." Curry applauded him for the stimulus he gave to the study of the entire body, and his help in the study of the mind and nature. Curry, along with his approval of these values, voiced his disapproval of other aspects of Delsarte. He regarded Delsarte's study of pantomine as mechanical. Curry placed Delsarte in the "speculative" school and regarded his method as artificial, based as it was on the inflexible concept of a trinity rather than upon nature.[20]

Different teachers accepted Delsarte for different reasons. Moses True Brown regarded Delsarte as a great seer rather than a significant philosopher. Delsarte's insight, said Brown, surpassed his reason. Many, with less imagination and less understanding, paid little attention to Delsarte's philosophy, but stressed his study of gymnastics. This resulted in a revival of the old mechanical system, despite the insistence of Delsarte's daughter that gymnastics was not a part of the Delsarte system, and the observation of Genevieve Stebbins, a pupil of Steele MacKaye, that Delsarte, as far as she knew, did not "elaborate any gymnastic system to develop perfect body and soul". MacKaye gave her a few gymnastic exercises of Delsarte, but they "were not worthy of the name of system." Esthetic gymnastics, she said, were first suggested by MacKaye and perfected by other Americans.[21]

Since the time of the Renaissance man has been struggling to free his mind from superstition and from enslavement to blind authority. Success in this endeavor freed him for further investigation of nature's phenomena; thus we find nineteenth century man branching out into avenues of thought which his forbears would not have dared to contemplate. Charles Darwin, Johann Friedrich Herbart, and William James opened doors through which the timid feared to pass.

Science

However, the interest in science took such a hold on the public mind that the word 'art' was often replaced by the word 'science,' and we find many references to the science of elocution or the scientific aspects of elocution. Rush had broken the ground for the scientific approach to speech. Anatomical and physiological studies of the vocal organs and the muscles of respiration were now carried on; at least one person, Erasmus North, claimed that elocution was a branch of physiology.

Darwin

Darwin's theories of evolution, according to Brown, made possible a 'science' of expression.[22] His application of the principle of evolution to expression, said Brown, was the first step of the new advance.

Charles Wesley Emerson

The idea of evolution, it seems, led Charles Wesley Emerson, a pupil of Monroe, to relate this principle to the art or science of expression. While ancient peoples maintained that their heroes were children of the gods, modern man believed that the individual underwent a process of evolution. Emerson applied this philosophy to his subject and build upon it his theory of expression later expounded in his *Evolution of Expression.* In this study he started with the premise that the history of the race is repeated in the life of man, and he saw in both a similar sequence which he described as, "first, animation, next, manifesting his objects of attraction, third, displaying his purposes, and finally, putting forth his wisdom in obedience to the true, the beautiful, and the good."[23] Emerson applied these steps to the study of oratory, in the belief that the young orator must progress through the same stages in his growth as those through which the race had progressed. He insisted that "the steps of natural evolution" be followed, and in his books the selections for study were chosen on this basis. He was known as an outstanding teacher, and his school has supplied many teachers in American educational institutions ever since he founded it.

At about the same time S. S. Curry was also interested in studying certain aspects of Darwin's work. Darwin believed that the emotions were so intimately connected with expression that if the body was inactive, the emotion was almost non-existent. Curry used this in showing the relationship and interdependence of bodily response in the art of expression.

Psychology

Another aspect of science, the study of mental processes, was making a sharp impact on the thinking of educators, philosophers, and scientists in the nineteenth century. In 1816 Johann Friedrich Herbart published the first textbook in psychology, *Lehrbuch zur Psychologie,* in which he presented his theory of the subconscious; and in the latter part of the century William James, through his *Principles of Psychology,* exerted a strong influence upon concepts of learning and upon the nature of the mind. James was concerned with such issues as the fringe of consciousness, mental activity, attention, the adjustment of the organism, the relation of the bodily state to emotion, and the neurological aspects of habit. Habit, he said, was the most precious conservative agent of society. His ideas, as well as his terminology, were to reach out in many directions, and not the least to be affected was the field of oral expression.

William James

Oral expression was ready for a new stimulus at this time; Rush's ideas began to appear outdated in the light of the scientific advances which were being made. In like manner, enthusiasm for Delsarte began to wane. Transcendentalism, which appealed to the philosophical and religious mind, still had a considerable hold. In this situation, the oral interpretation of literature needed to be re-evaluated in terms of the new emphasis in order to make it vital, comprehensible, and acceptable to the rising generation. Psychology was best able to do this. Teachers of oral expression began to look at their field through the eyes of science, and particularly of the science of psychology. They began to speak in terms which must have fallen strangely on Delsartian ears. Preoccupation with the law of correspondence and the trinity gradually gave place to discussions on mental speculation, mental activity, mental processes, the organism, stimuli, response, and habit. In 1870, at Princeton

J. H. McIlvaine

University, J. H. McIlvaine was already interested in the mental processes involved in reading and discussed them with remarkable lucidity in his *Elocution: The Sources and Elements of Its Powers.* Just eleven years later J. W. Shoemaker spoke of the role of habit in speech, and in 1892, shortly after James' *Principles of Psychology* appeared, Julia and Annie Thomas published *The Thomas Psycho-Physical Culture.*

Charles Wesley Emerson

Emerson, always alert to the new developments in science or philosophy, spoke with ease of the nervous system, impulses, reflex actions, and the motor sensory system. He believed that too much emphasis on mechanical action interfered with the normal response of the sympathetic nervous system, and also that emotional response, without control, could jeopardize clear thinking.[24] Thus he made a frontal attack on two major tendencies of the age: 1) set, prescribed, and formal gestures; and 2) the use of emotion without control.

Mary Blood and Ida Riley

Emerson's interest in psychology seems to have inspired two of his students, Ida Riley and Mary Blood, to build their philosophy on this new approach. They defined it in *The Psychological Development of Expression* and applied it at their school in Chicago.

Individual growth

The emphasis in oral recitation began to shift as interest grew in studying the mind of man. Formerly, concern had been centered on the audience; the air of the reader was to affect his hearers; and voice, diction, and action were often taught in terms of entertaining, or impressing, an audience. This was a valid approach. Now it became clear that oral literature might have a value for the student himself, aside from the usual applause and parental pride which it called forth. Thus the objective changed from pleasing an audience to developing an individual. The question now being asked was the following: What is his training doing for him as a person? This was, in part at least, the concept which S. H. Clark had in mind when he decried the type of elocution which separated the voice from the man, and was the concept which gave the art of expression a firmer footing in the educational world. When it was shown that the art of oral expression could help a student's development as an individual, as well as train him to express himself orally, the prestige of the discipline as an educational medium rose, and colleges and universities began to look on it with increasing favor.

S. S. Curry

S. S. Curry, whose school later sent many teachers to colleges and universities throughout the country, published *The Province of Expression* in 1891, and it, too, showed the impact of psychology. The author described expression as "the presentation of a vast complexity of physical actions which are directly caused by psychic activities."[25] He believed that the action of the mind should bring about the response of voice and body, and that training in expression should be as much concerned with mental as with physical activity. Curry regarded man's actions as of two kinds: the voluntary, controlled by the will; and the involuntary or reflex over which the will had little, if any, control. The latter he considered to be important in the spontaneity essential in developing freedom of expression.

Emphasis on the role of the mind continued. The noted drama critic and teacher, Alfred Ayres, saw elocution as primarily an intellectual art. In fact, he concluded rather sadly that "the poor devils that have no brains to use will always have to read badly–i.e. artificially – or not read at all."[26] William B. Chamberlain agreed with him that the subject "needs to be more fully intellectualized." Along with S. H. Clark with whom he collaborated in writing *Principles of Vocal Expression* (1897), Chamberlain saw psychology as the meeting ground of the mental and physical, which were so closely linked that it was hard to consider either one of these elements as a separate unit. And thus, through the works of one writer after another, ran the thread of psychology inextricably interwoven into the warp and woof of oral reading. To this day it has remained one of the dominant factors in the approach to this art.

Alfred Ayres

W. B. Chamberlain

S. H. Clark

Underlying these various influences–Rush, Delsarte, the Transcendentalists and the psychologists – certain basic concepts, taught since the days of Quintilian, still remained valid. Nothing had been invented or discovered to replace thought and understanding. Some indifferent and inconsequential readers tried, apparently, to get along without these fundamentals even though their importance continued to be stressed by many writers. In ninety-six out of one hundred and fifty-two textbooks written between 1785 and 1855, Erickson found the authors trying to impress upon their readers the value of reading "thought by thought," as Alexander Melville Bell put it.[27] Readers were warned that, unless oral reading went hand in hand with thinking, it became mere mechanical utterance. Emerson College built its philosophy of expression upon the need to "trust in the power of thought," and S. S. Curry described expression as "simply thinking aloud."

Thought and understanding

A. M. Bell

Emerson College

S. S. Curry

Among English scholars whose influence was substantial in nineteenth century America were several who emphasized the need for understanding. Among them were John Thelwall, leader of a fashionable London school, and John Lettice, interested in helping the clergy to achieve better speech. Both men reiterated Cockin's belief that, for the development of subtle expression, no amount of technique could take the place of complete understanding and feeling for the material. In the early nineteenth century Richard Whately's advice to readers to concentrate upon meaning and not upon the voice was widely accepted and helped discourage an excess of mechanical rules in the teaching of reading. Archbishop Whately, like Austin, was dedicated to the theory that inner emotional feeling was the well-spring from which would come satisfactory expression.

Whately

In reading the Bible, or any words which the reader himself had not written, Whately says he "should deliver them as if he were **reporting** another's sentiments, which were both fully understood and felt in all their force by the reporter."[28]

Emotion

Feeling continued to be a necessary companion to thought. Austin had stressed the need for the emotional involvement of the reader. He taught that in reading epic poetry the interpreter should, like the poet, be "alive and feeling," inspired and filled with enthusiasm. In reciting memorized selections the performer should go even further; he "must appear altogether to adopt and feel, and recommend" the sentiments as if they were his own. Rush had defined elocution as the use of the voice to express thought and passion; and Murdoch had taken Walker to task for failing to explain the relation of voice to the passions, saying that the emotions and the imagination compose a great part of man's makeup. Certainly the elocutionists did not underate emotion. They believed that, in oral expression, the language of the passions was to be found in vocal quality, pitch change, inflection, articulation, emphasis, and bodily action. Alexander Melville Bell said that the pupil must "learn to feel; and to keep the fine-strung organs of expressiveness in a state of delicate susceptibility."[29] No system, it was felt, could take the place of feeling, and it was the complaint of some teachers, including William Russell, that their students shrank from a full expression of feeling.

A. M. Bell

Too much of anything, of course, is too much, and the gross excesses frequently offered in the name of art led some critics to conclude that emotional expression had become so exaggerated, such a "painful exhibition of precocious hot-house passion," as F. Townsend Southwick said, that it should be completely rejected.[30] When one sees sketches of some of the reciters, or reads some of the sentimental novels of the period, one is inclined to agree. Valid objections were raised against attempts to falsify emotions, to pretend to deep emotional involvement where none was felt. Antics of emotional display, devoid of real feeling, were prevalent in this era and were rightly condemned by those who wished to keep emotional response controlled and genuine.

False emotion

Comparisons between the arts of reading and speaking continued, and opinions differed as to which should be studied first. Ebenezer Porter, among others, considered that the "art of reading well is indispensable to one who expects to be a public speaker; because the principles on which it depends are the same as those which belong to rhetorical delivery in general, and because nearly all bad speakers were prepared to be so by early mismanagement of the voice in reading."[31] The ideal in reading was still thought to be so perfect a facsimile of correct speaking that, as Bronson said, "if one should hear you without **seeing** you, he could not tell whether you were **reading** or **speaking**."[32]

Reading and speaking

Among the differences noted between the two arts was the amount of emotion and the amount of emotional control involved in each. Merritt Caldwell and J. E. Frobisher agreed with the opinion that reading required less emotion, but greater restraint, than speaking; and this was essentially what North meant when he said that reading requires "less force of emphasis" than speaking. In a more penetrating analysis, J. D. McIlvaine differentiated the two arts according to the origin of the idea which they expressed. The spontaneity of speech comes from the fact that the speaker is expressing ideas which he himself has created, whose style is his own, and whose meaning is clear to him from the beginning. In oral reading, on the other hand, an idea is taken in by the eye, understood by the mind, and communicated by the voice. The mental activity required to get the meaning from an outside source makes reading more subdued, the tones less full, the inflections more tempered, the articulation less sharp, the emphasis is less pronounced, and the gesture, if any be allowed, is more subtle than in speaking. All this, as McIlvaine said, makes reading less demonstrative than speaking. Since reading involves simultaneously taking in and expressing meaning, he regarded it as a more difficult art than speaking, even though familiarity with the material reduces the complexity of the operation.

Degree of emotion

McIlvaine's approach

Comparing reading to conversation, John Pierpont, in *The American First Class Book* (1829), said that both were probably learned more from example than from rules. Many teachers advised their pupils to read as they would converse–assuming, naturally, that they conversed well.

In this century there was more controversy than there had been for some centuries as to the relative merits of reading from a printed page and memorization. Recitation had the tradition of thirty centuries behind it. The very act of memorizing demanded some degree of sacrifice in time, effort, and concentration, a fact which earned respect for it; while reading, it seemed to many, was but child's play by comparison. Memorization was also favored by those who were eagerly striving to "free the body"; and by many who wished to relate physical culture to the speech arts. Memorization freed the performer to express with his entire body the ideas and emotions in his material, and this very freedom demanded a well-trained body which could respond to emotion with ease.

Memorization

This emphasis on action and gesture was largely due to the influence of Austin, as both William Russell and Moses True Brown were ready to testify. Austin, and to a lesser degree Delsarte, had so many disciples all stressing action that there came a time when instead of action for meaning's sake, there was, among the less discriminating teachers and performers, action for action's sake. Stock directions used year after year still survived from Georgian England. Pupils were being told to raise the hand for a sublime thought and lower it for a grovelling attitude. This made the judicious wince, since the tendency to exhibitionism waxed strong To those in favor of precise and exact movements, a book was, of course, an encumbrance, and they demanded memorization rather than reading.

The material had to be precisely memorized so that there would be no hesitancy in its presentation, and the ideal state was reached when the memory of the lines had been submerged into the subconscious; then, and only then, could the reciter devote himself completely to expressing the sentiment. This much was necessary if recitation was to deserve the name of art; such was the attitude of those who demanded memorized recitation. This group, moreover, was neither small nor insignificant in the quality of its adherents. Bronson, for example, in 1845, advised ministers to memorize Biblical passages for oral presentation. Julia and Annie Thomas believed that "To memorize and recite the best thoughts of the best authors or poets is also most refining and cultivating to the entire body."[33]

Reading aloud

Although this creed was honored by many, there were equally fine teachers both in America and in England who believed that reading from a book had great values, maybe even greater values than memorization. Others believed that the choice depended upon the material and the situation. The reading enthusiasts blamed recitation for most of the faults prevalent in the oral presentation of literature, and they had ample reason for this view, since memorization often put such a strain on the reciter's memory that he failed to cope adequately with the meaning. Austin, in England, recommended reading for certain types of material, and in America there were many who supported it as a school exercise, as preparatory training for public speaking, as a necessary aid in the church service, and as an art medium for the presentation of literature. Reading was accepted by leaders such as Alexander Melville Bell, L. B. Monroe, E. B. Warman, Hiram Corson, Alfred Ayres, and S. H. Clark; and in the latter half of the century interest in reading grew to such an extent that it was preferred by some of the greatest solo performers such as Charlotte Cushman, George Riddle, J. W. Churchill, and Bertha Kunz-Baker.

The nineteenth century is frequently associated with an exaggerated artificiality in standards and manners generally referred to as "Victorian." Some of the unhappy characteristics of this age in relation to the speech arts were tone for tone's sake, exaggerated diction, and gestures as artificial as the age they represented. Murdoch, in 1883, said that the tendency of reading, at that time, was towards poor acting than good reading.

Yet the Victorian Age was not all sham by any means. The true values of the age were expressed in England by such men as Tennyson, Carlyle, and Ruskin, and in America by Emerson,

Thoreau, and Whitman, to name a few. The new idea of man presented by the psychologists helped to defeat the bombastic display artists. A greater desire for simplicity and a new rationalism gradually brought the speech arts close to man's mode of expression in daily life and resulted in the substitution of the "talk element," as Brown called it, for "exaggerated strut and bombast." F. Townsend Southwick strove to remove from elocution the expression of artificial emotion.

Advantages of reading

This new approach lent itself to reading rather than to a too-obviously memorized rendition. Alexander Melville Bell called reading "the chief of all the arts of life"[34] and likened it to a painting "in which only select forms are introduced and in which the hard outlines of reality are softened by blending touches while all necessary accessories are subordinated to the central dominant object of the picture." Bell liked reading, not only because the book gave the performer confidence, but also because it enabled one to interpolate, to make comments on his material, a risk which he who memorized would never take. The memorizer, he said, was "on a rail" and dared not saunter or pause, and was, indeed, more dependent on the unseen book than if he actually held it in his hand. E. B. Warman said that all readings which were didactic and did not require gestures "should not be given without the book either held in the hand or lying on the desk." The reader, he said, stands alone without special costuming or scenic effect. He has only his array of imaginary characters to call forth his power; by his voice and action he must so vividly convey both characters and scenery that the spectator forgets the reader and lives in the world of his characters.

Hiram Corson's view

Readers who could do this successfully, said Hiram Corson, were the bulwarks of oral interpretation, for they helped to keep it within its own form of expression, rather than going into the realm of acting as did the reciters who performed with "limbs all going like a telegraph in motion and straining after effect."[35] This view was shared by S. S. Curry, for he, too, regarded reading as a subjective, more manifestive art, than acting. Curry held that, "In proportion as anything is representative it can be seen at once; in proportion as it is manifestive it can only be realized imaginatively, mystically."[36] Given freedom of movement over any part of the stage, reciters often ended up either acting or trying an unsatisfactory combination of reading and acting.

Clark and Babcock

S. H. Clark and Maud May Babcock, devoted followers of Alfred Ayres, were earnest supporters of reading. Clark, who taught at the University of Chicago, strove to free delivery from its artificial elocutionary trappings, and consistently presented a strong case for interpretative reading. Whether or not the reader memorized his material was of secondary importance. The main thing was that his presentation should have the **appearance** of reading.

This interest in the "new art" made reading very popular with two groups: those experts who were interested in an honest, simple, yet subtle presentation of the author's meaning without decorative baroque trimmings, and those who naively believed that reading was so easy that anyone could do it. This second group brought before the public many "readers" who had neither the talent nor the training for the interpretation of literature. This practice, naturally, brought temporary disrepute upon the art, but eventually, trained readers were to show that good reading did have the power, as Bell said, to annihilate for the mind all obstacles of time and space. Reading was to triumph in the twentieth century, and the words of Joseph Emerson are as applicable today as they were in the early decades of the last century:

> Consider well, who and where and what, was the speaker or writer, and who and where and what, were the persons addressed, as well as what was said and the particular occasion. Let the eye of imagination point to the fancy, as far as may be, every important object, and most striking circumstance; and then let your mental eye affect your heart. Would you read the Sermon on the Mount, go in imagination to Immanuel's land.[37]

Hiram Corson said that spiritual education is the indispensable condition of good oral reading. Communication, observed Charles Wesley Emerson, depends upon the reader's awareness, deep within himself, of the "truth which he interprets."[38] and his realization of the listener's need for that truth.

Erasmus North

J. E. Frobisher

With such principles as a guide, what was considered the essence of good reading? According to Erasmus North it must have a meditative quality which should put the audience in a reflective "complacent, gratified state of mind," while J. E. Frobisher described it as similar to the "conversation of an **earnest** person **thinking to himself** aloud."[39] Moreover, it required less forceful gestures than are usually required in public speaking. Curry, Emerson, and others, whose observations have been noted on this topic, added to and amplified these ideas.

Classifications of reading

Beyond these basic ideas a further stratification of reading was developed, often based upon traditional classifications. For example, where Austin had listed six categories–intellectual, correct, impressive, rhetorical, dramatic, and epic, Porter listed but two–correct and rhetorical. Correct meant plain and unimpassioned, and was suitable, he said for reading public documents and for those Psalms and Proverbs having short sentences and with no particular emphasis. But rhetorical reading was another matter and demanded not only intelligibility and feeling, but beauty, force, and variety to combine the aesthetic with the intellectual element. William Russell also made three classifications of Biblical narrative–familiar, middle, and elevated styles. As examples of the familiar style he suggested such selections as Abraham's sacrifice of Isaac, the Prodigal Son, and passages that required "a **deeper, softer,** and **slower** voice . . . . . the whole style **vivid, earnest,** but **subdued.**" The middle style, suitable for the story of David and Goliath, or the Raising of Lazarus, was characterized by a "**deeper, firmer and more uniformly sustained**" tone. The sublime elements in the elevated style made it suitable for reading the stories of the Creation, the Flood, the Passage of the Red Sea, and Paul's defence before Agrippa. The elevated style required "a **deeper, fuller, slower, more forcible** and **impressive** manner" than the other styles.

Personation and impersonation provided another subject of interest at this time. About the middle of the century John Hanbury Dwyer defined personation as the representation by a reader or speaker of the words and actions of one or more persons, as if he or they were themselves reading or speaking; in other words, "giving form to fancy, and embodying thought." In his mind, personation seemed to be akin to what the classical rhetoricians had called prosopopoeia. E. B. Warman tried to point out the differences in reading, recitation, and impersonation. He described reading as applying to the presentation of didactic material not requiring gestures. Recitation required "gestures of description and often strong heroic attitudes." Impersonation, more dramatic in style, called for more careful training in voice, gestures, and attitudes. Shakespeare, he ruled, should be impersonated.

Some of these forms of presentation were not too well received. J. H. McIlvaine, one of the best thinkers in the field, wrote from his Princeton study that declamatory reading displayed a lack of culture. Perhaps Bell had the same thing in mind when he said that "bad reading compels one to notice manner in the first place. Good reading should fix the thought upon the matter only."[40]

Bell

In the continuous discussion of the different forms of oral delivery one opinion which remained reasonably constant was the following: if reading was to be classified as an art, it would have to be built upon technique. An unbalanced insistence upon this fact caused many people to focus so much attention on technique that the result of their efforts was sometimes a nice display of vocal and bodily gymnastics without the necessary creative spark, the imaginative stimulus, to give their reading life and meaning. Nevertheless, technique, though not the only requirement, was usually regarded as a valuable and helpful part of the reader's training during various stages of his education. For the beginner such matters as whether he should stand or sit, whether his book should be in his hand or on a desk, could pose a problem. Nor was there always unanimous agreement on these matters. For example, while many teachers approved only of standing, Charlotte Cushman, one of the greatest readers of the day, sat when she read from Shakespeare.

Technique

The relation of the reader to his audience also raised questions. What should this relationship be and how should it be established? Erasmus North said that reading should have some element of address to an audience, albeit neither so direct nor so earnest as in speaking. The eyes played an important part in establishing this relationship, and there was discussion as to whether or not the reader should look directly at his audience. Elsie Wilbor, echoeing Delsarte, said that the eyes of the speaker should meet the eyes of the audience, for this enables him to hold attention as well as win sympathy.

Bell felt that simple etiquette demanded that one should look at his hearers. Most authorities advised the reader to have his eyes on the audience rather than on the book or, at the very least, to look up as frequently as possible to establish what North called the element of address in reading, which, though less direct than in speaking, must be present.

Dialoque narration

Technique also helped a reader faced with the problems of representing two or more characters in a play or dialogue, or in differentiating between narration and impersonation where both were employed in the same selection. One suggestion was that the reader should turn the head at an angle when reading the character and face front for descriptive passages. Whatever the technique used, the reader's job was to take the author's place, as Warman said, and to create characters so that the reader himself was forgotten. Murdoch ruled that the author must not be made obscure by an "obtrusion of the reader's personality." The interpretation of the author was the real key to reading and was the creative process which made reading an art and not an empty exhibition.

Reading poetry

Attempts were again made in the nineteenth century to decide how poetry should be read. Since keeping both the metrical flow and the sense was not easy, opinions differed widely as to which should take precedence and as to how metre, rhyme, and pauses should be handled. James E. Murdoch compared poetry and conversation. Poetry, he said, should not be read as one ordinarily converses because such a mundane approach would fail to acknowledge the elevated nature of poetry. Ebenezer Porter, for one, favored the traditional observation of the caesural and final pauses "where it is fitting," holding that these preserved the harmony of poetry. This opinion was also held by North, who asserted it was an inexcusable error of style to make poetry sound like prose. Some tended to do this when they ignored the pauses. A middle way was proposed by Frobisher, who said that the pauses should be of a "suspensive kind" to suggest the continuation of the idea. Warman went a little farther, asking for a "delicate poise" rather than an actual pause.

Another teacher who was anxious to preserve poetry as a distinct form was Vandenhoff, who sought to bring out its musical qualities by insisting that the metrical movement, of pulsation, was a necessary characteristic of the poetic form, and must therefore be observed. There were some who carried this insistence on metre so far as to alter the pronunciation of a word if the metre required it. A compromise was offered by Russell who thought it enough merely to suggest the metre rather than to feature it.

Some writers observed that, in reading poetry, work-groupings needed more careful attention because, if the metre is strong, there is a tendency for a reader to connect words in accordance with the metre rather than on the basis of sense. Russell and Dwyer both objected to any mechanical observance of the "jingle" which jeopardized clarity of thought. Compromises and modifications were proposed to bridge the gap between those who sought to emphasize the framework of poetry and those who put understanding so far ahead of every other consideration that they would rather destroy the rhyme and rhythm of a poem than risk losing one iota of the "meaning."

Bell, who found that the principle was the same in reading both poetry and prose, advised his public to unite no words that have no mutual influence in expressing sense. He believed that reading can never be good, that is regulated "either by lines in poetry or periods in prose."

Sidney Lanier: relation of prose to poetry

In *The Science of English Verse,* Sidney Lanier's illuminating discussion on poetry, the author struck a modern note when he said that both prose and verse have rhythm, melody, and tone color; often, in fact, the two are very close to each other. He defined prose as "a wild variety of verse."[41] This idea was similar to that discussed later by Chamberlain and Clark, who regarded prose rhythm as less regular than that of poetry and determined more by the reader's interpretation. The two literary forms also differed in tempo and inflection. A slower tempo for poetry, with more prolonged sounds and more time between each word and each sentence, was recommended by a considerable number of people, including Dwyer and Russell. As to inflection, Porter, for example, preferred a rising inflection for delicate, plaintive poetry. Others looked for a rising inflection at the end of the first of two rhyming lines. Lanier, interested in the relation of the voice to poetry, saw a relation of phrasing in poetry to pitch changes. In general, this was a period in which the traditional rules for the reading of verse were gradually being broken in favor of a less artificial style.

Differences

Oral reading and recitation, though recognized as arts in themselves, continued to serve as training methods for orators and public speakers, as they had done through the ages. Books on oratory and elocution containing many selections for recitation were used to train famous speakers like Jeremiah Sullivan Black, Abraham Lincoln, Henry Clay, Wendell Phillips, and Albert J. Beveridge.

The history of a subject cannot be gleaned from its textbooks alone. Behind the books on speech arts were the writers and

Private schools

institutions which they represented. Speech education, either in specific courses or in extra-curricular activities, was offered in a number of colleges, universities, and private schools. Some of the best work at this time was being done in the private schools. This is not surprising since many of the names mentioned in this chapter were associated with such schools: the School of Practical Rhetoric and Oratory (Murdoch and Russell), the Vocal and Polyglot Gymnasium (Comstock), the College of Oratory and Acting (Frobisher), the Monroe College of Oratory (later the Emerson College of Oratory – C. W. Emerson), the Cumnock Conservatory (Robert McLean Cumnock), the Columbia School of Expression (Mary Blood and Ida Riley), the Byron King School of Oratory, and the Curry School of Expression. These schools helped to put speech training on a professional basis; and they turned out trained men and women to teach in colleges and universities, where they not only gave speech stronger academic status but also broadened its scope. But, in addition to the schools, two other organizations must be credited with bringing the oral arts before the American people; namely the Lyceum, founded in 1826, and the Chautauqua, established in 1874. These organizations presented lecturers, humorists, readers, and reciters as well as musicians.

Lyceum

Chautauqua

Chautauqua, from its very simple beginning with four Bible readings given by clergymen, grew to include many types of reading and many famous readers. In 1878 Lowell Mason gave elocutionary readings, to be followed by A. P. Burbank, Professor J. W. Churchill, and Robert McLean Cumnock, all of whom were giving Chautauqua programs by 1885. Among the menbers of the instructional staff were S. S. Curry and S. H. Clark. The interest in reading expanded, and when the Chautauqua circuit was established, inspiring and aspiring readers were brought before a culture-thirsty, and appreciative audience. Presentations of *Macbeth, King Lear,* or *Hamlet* on the Chautauqua circuit inspired many youthful spectators to test their own histrionic powers and brought new talent to the reading field. Professional reading and reciting were so popular in nineteenth century America that these arts spilled over from large cities – Boston, New York and Philadelphia – to remote towns and hamlets all across the nation in answer to the growing demand for education, culture, and entertainment. School attendance was often erratic or of short duration in isolated areas, and the visiting reader was as popular as his minstrel ancestors in their heyday. Many townhalls, church auditoriums, and school rooms resounded with recitations – good, bad, or indifferent. These were sometimes given by local talent trained either in the city, or by itinerant teachers.

In addition to the conscious search for culture, there was, and always would be, a large public seeking relaxation and entertainment. Probably more came for amusement than for education, as is true in every age. The problem then was not so much how to hold the interest of a mass of people, for that was almost a certainty, but rather how to maintain, for the discriminating, a standard of excellence in both the performers and the material. This goal was often achieved, since many of the readers and reciters, and many persons in the audience, were people of some taste and refinement; but when it was not achieved, the results could be appalling. Some performers lost all sense of form and style, sometimes overstepping the limits of reading by going into acting or vaudeville routines, or doing something to make the spectators roll with laughter, cry copiously, or scream in fear. This type of entertainment satisfied the vanity of the performer and swelled his receipts, but it did real damage to art, education, and oral literature by making them seem ridiculous. Material was often written to display extremes of emotion without any semblance of logical development, and absurdities of character and situation were presented without a true sense of comedy.

In Victorian days the theatre was frequently frowned upon as the habitat of evil, and Harriet Beecher Stowe, for example, was reluctant to permit adaptation of *Uncle Tom's Cabin* for stage presentation. In fact, when it was produced, she wore a veil over her face and sat unobtrusively in a box when she went to see it. Such widespread aversion to the theatre was another reason why reading and reciting flourished at this time, offering, as they did, substitute entertainment in the chaste milieu of school room and church hall where the most sanctimonious could enter with a free conscience.

Public readers

It would be wrong to leave the impression that inferior oral art and hypocritical audiences completely dominated the scene; many performers were good and now a few were great. They included actors, professors and teachers of elocution, professional readers, reciters, and authors who recited their own works. Among professors and teachers of elocution who won fame as readers are many of those mentioned in this chapter. The public flocked to hear such well-known figures as Solymon Brown, Dr. Barber, the Vandenhoffs, J. W. S. Hows, the Frobishers, Allen A. Griffith, L. B. Monroe, William Russell, and James Murdoch. One of Murdoch's activities was giving readings for soldiers in camp during the Civil War. Later in the century E. B. Warman, Locke Richardson, George Riddle, S. H. Clark, Robert Raymond, Anna Baright Curry, Leland Powers and many others were added to the roster. Professor Raymond, for one, was able to draw three thousand people to hear him read in Cooper Institute in the season of 1878-79, which indicates the popularity of his programs. Maud May Babcock described Clark's presentation of *King Lear* as the finest public reading she had ever heard.

Teachers

Authors

Authors, some of whom were excellent readers, could also attract large audiences. Names of international renown came to the fore when Charles Dickens, Harriet Beecher Stowe, Ralph Waldo Emerson, and Mark Twain travelled over the country reading and reciting their own works. They added the applause of a listening audience to the adulation of the reading public. Close behind them came Anna Cora Mowatt, F. Hopkinson Smith, Frank Dempster Sherman, George Cable, James Whitcomb Riley, Eugene Field, Will Carleton, and Ella Wheeler Wilcox.

Actors

Actors and actresses, many of them famous personalities such as Mrs. Barrymore, William Charles Macready, Edwin Forrest, Sarah Bernhardt, Josef Kainz, Fanny Kemble, and Charlotte Cushman appeared on the reading platform to the delight of great crowds. One of the most talented was Charlotte Cushman, whose skill in reading brought her unlimited praise from the crowds that thronged to hear her. Her first appearance, at Providence in 1871, started her on the road to fame. She was considered Fanny Kemble's equal in creating characters and her superior in comprehension of the material. Like Edwin Forrest she carefully worked out every inflection, every pause beforehand, to ensure a perfect performance. Alfred Ayres, drama critic and teacher, considered that Forrest surpassed Miss Cushman in scholarly approach, but Sidney Lanier was so enthralled by her reading that he described it as a new art composed of speech tunes, and vowed that "when Charlotte Cushman reads *Macbeth* . . . it is really a great cast."[42] Seated at a reading table, she was able to carry her hearers far beyond the confines of any hall and lead them through the tragic corridors of Elsinore, or leave them on a windswept heath in England. Such was the fare she offered her audience with the consummate skill of a perceptive and sensitive artist.

Literature presented

Other readers besides Miss Cushman offered their patrons literature of high quality. In the early part of the century, many of the English and French classics were presented – the works of Shakespeare, Dryden, Milton, Burns, Southey, Collins, Campbell, Scott, Corneille, Racine, Voltaire, and Rousseau were all offered. Later, works of Keats, Byron, Tennyson, Browning, Thackeray, and Rosetti shared the limelight with the plays of Sheridan, Lessing, Goethe, Hugo, Schiller, and Ibsen. The merits of the American authors were recognized with selections from Washington Irving, Edgar Allan Poe, William Cullen Bryant, Henry Wadsworth Longfellow, Oliver Wendell Holmes, and Francis Scott Key.

An age of tremendous activity, the nineteenth century had reason for pride and reason for chagrin in its reading and reciting; pride in its expanding horizons, its scientific and aesthetic developments, and its many fine teachers; chagrin in its exaggerations, its relentless exhibitions, and its tedious books and artificiality. Despite these weaknesses and because of these strengths, it made many worthy contributions.

In the nineteenth century oral reading and recitation served some, but not all, of the purposes it had served in earlier centuries. It continued to entertain, it continued to serve religion, but probably less than before did it serve purposes of criticism. It did achieve a new dimension when, with the advent of science, and particularly psychology, it focussed attention not only on the pleasures of the listeners but on the development of the individual personality. It laid the foundation for much that has been done in the twentieth century.

References

1. James Rush, *The Philosophy of the Human Voice* (Philadelphia, J. B. Lippincott & Co., 1859), 5th ed., p. 480.

2. Moses True Brown, *The Synthetic Philosophy of Expression,* as applied to the Arts of Reading, Oratory and Personation (New York, Houghton Mifflin, 1886), p. 144.

3. *Ibid.,* p. 159.

4. S. S. Curry, *The Province of Expression* (Boston: Expression Co., 1927), 19th ed., p. 155.

5. Richard Whately, *Elements of Rhetoric* (Louisville, Morton & Griswold, 1854), Reprinted from 7th ed., p. 236.

6. M. L'Abbe Delaumosne and Mme. Angelique Arnaud, *Delsarte System of Oratory* ... with the Literary Remains of Francois Delsarte (New York: Edgar S.Werner, 1887), 3rd ed., p. 466.

7. J. W. Shoemaker, *Practical Elocution* (Philadelphia: Penn Publishing Co., 1881), p. 17.

8. George Vandenhoff, *The Art of Reading Aloud* (London: Davison, Low et al, 1878), p. 164.

9. James Rush, *op. cit.,* p. xxxv.

10. *Ibid.,* p. 555.

11. James E. Murdoch, *A Plea for Spoken Language* (Cincinnati, New York: Van Antwerp & Bragg, 1883), pp. 73-74.

12. S. S. Curry, *op. cit.,* p. 325.

13. Emanuel Swedenborg, *True Christian Religion* (New York: Houghton Mifflin, 1907), Vol. 30. No. 166, p. 272.

14. Genevieve Stebbins, *Delsarte System of Expression* (New York: Edgar S. Werner, 1902), 6th ed., p. 111.

15. M. L'Abbé Delaumosne and Mme. Angélique Arnaud, *op. cit.,* p. 4.

16. Claude L. Shaver, "Steele MacKaye and the Delsartian Tradition." *History of Speech Education in America,* ed. Karl Wallace (New York: Appleton-Century-Crofts, 1954), p. 205.

17. Percy MacKaye, *Epoch: The Life of Steele MacKaye* (New York: Boni and Liveright, 1927), Vol. I, pp. 136-137.

18. Claude L. Shaver, *op. cit.,* p. 204.

19. *Werner's Magazine,* Vol. 14. March 1892, p. 59.

20. S. S. Curry ,*op. cit.,* p. 358,360.

21. Genevieve Stebbins, *op. cit.,* p. 400.

22. Moses True Brown, *op. cit.,* p. vi.

23. Charles Wesley Emerson, *Evolution of Expression* (Boston: Emerson College of Oratory, 1901), 18th ed., Vol. I. p. 8.

24. J. E. Southwick, *The Emerson Philosophy of Expression* (Boston: Expression Co., 1930), p. xi.

25. S. S. Curry, *op. cit.,* p. 25.

26. Alfred Ayres, *Acting & Actors, Elocution and Elocutionists* (New York: D. Appleton & Co., 1894), p. 61.

27. Marceline Erickson, *Speech Training in the Common Schools, Academies and High Schools from 1785-1885 As Revealed by a Study of the Books Used in the School* (Doctoral Dissertation, University of Wisconsin, 1948), p. 705.

28. Richard Whately, *op. cit.,* p. 243.

29. Alexander Melville Bell, *The Principles of Elocution* (Salem, Massachusetts: 1878), p. 113.

30. F. Townsend Southwick, *Elocution and Action* (New York: Edgar S. Werner & Co., 1890,1894 & 1903), p. 2.

31. Ebenezer Porter, *The Rhetorical Reader* (New York: Mark H. Newman, 1834), 220th ed., p. 13.

32. C. P. Bronson, *Elocution: Or Mental and Vocal Philosophy* (Louisville: Morton & Griswold, 1845), 30th ed., p. 57.

33. Julia and Annie Thomas, *Thomas Psycho-Physical Culture* (New York: Edgar S. Werner, 1892), p. 127.

34. Alexander Melville Bell, *Essays and Postscripts on Elocution* (New York: Edgar S. Werner, 1886), p. 135.

35. Hiram Corson, *The Voice and Spiritual Education* (New York: Macmillan & Co., 1896), p. 24.

36. S. S. Curry, *op. cit.,* p. 107.

37. Joseph Emerson, *The Poetic Reader* (Wethersfield: 1832), p. 13.

38. Charles Wesley Emerson, *Six Lectures on Pulpit Elocution* (Boston: Everett Press, 1909), p. 65.

39. J. E. Frobisher, *A New and Practical System of the Culture of Voice and Action* (New York: Ivison, Phinney, Blakeman Co., 1867), p. 29.

40. Alexander Melville Bell, *op. cit.,* p. 147.

41. Sidney Lanier, *The Science of English Verse* (New York: Charles Scribner's Sons, 1907), p. 57.

42. *Ibid.,* p. 262.

Chapter VII

EPILOGUE: THE TWENTIETH CENTURY

In the twentieth century the term "elocution" continued to lose favor and "expression," "expressive reading," "oral reading," or "interpretative reading" took its place. Thomas C. Trueblood at the University of Michigan did not object to "elocution." However, he said, "Let us get rid of that abominable name 'elocutionists' that is down in the mud. We have tried for fourteen years to pull it out of the mud and it will not pull, it is there – not 'elocution,' but 'elocutionists.' Let us get it out."[1] The use of the book by the reader, instead of memorization, contributed to breaking down the old elocutionary style; it was this that prevented "limbs all going like a telegraph in motion," as Corson described it.

Reading had begun to lose some of its artificial and mechanical qualities even in the nineteenth century, and this trend continued. There were a number of reasons for this. First of all, the elegance and the predilection for form in the nineteenth century began to give way to the direct approach of a new age. Clothing became simpler, architecture became less ornate and more functional. More positions were open to women in the business world than ever before. The population was increasing at a tremendous rate, and a higher percentage of people were attending school than in the past. Moreover, there was the problem of assimilating in the school system a large population of non-English speaking background; this, too, made reading of more practical value than memorized recitation. The relative merits of reading versus memorization continued to be debated for at least three decades of the new century. As late as 1922 Rollo Anson Tallcott believed that the presentation of memorized material should be pursued for "years" before reading from the printed page could be successfully achieved.

Psychology

The field of psychology has had such a profound effect upon most of twentieth century thought that it was inevitable that interpretative reading would also feel its influence. Psychology was closely connected with the increasing interest in man and his personal problems. Behaviorism, the James-Lange theory, and the Gestalt theory were studied to make clear philosophies of expression for teachers and students. Fortunately, the influence of psychology was not usually carried to the extreme of making interpretative reading merely a scientific experiment; in general, its contributions were very helpful. Certainly it was so strong a current that it would have been impossible, as well as unwise, to have resisted it. Other psychological research included *Experimental Studies in Vocal Expression* by Andrew Thomas Weaver (1924),[2] *Motor Control and Ability in Interpretation* by William John Miller (1926),[3] *Incipient Motor Responses in Oral Interpretation of Literature* by Elsie Viola Haney (1927),[4] and *A Description and Application of the Significant Contributions of Psychology to the Problems of Interpretative Reading* by E. M. Cogswell (1931).[5] Psychological principles are still recognized as important to oral interpretation.

Therapeutic values

Related to the interest in psychology was the concept of oral reading as a therapeutic activity. This continued from the time of Celsus on and into the Renaissance, and it came to the foreground again in the twentieth century. Numerous teachers regarded oral interpretation as the best way of helping the individual student realize his potentialities. The same concept was often used in "educational" dramatics. The therapeutic values of oral reading were stressed in terms of giving confidence and poise to the pupil and helping him to suggest personality traits unlike his own, thereby broadening his own perception and insight. This interest continued into the fourth decade of the century.

Graduate studies

Graduate studies in the field of oral interpretation have increased considerably since 1930, although some significant studies were made before that date. Studies in silent and oral reading, testing, educational values, literary analysis and criticism, aspects of literature, psychology, physics, social sciences, philosophy, semantics, linguistics, and aesthetics have been made in relation to oral interpretation.

Historical studies

The history of oral reading and recitation aroused little interest in earlier centuries, and even in the nineteenth century extensive knowledge of its background was slight. In the twentieth century this interest began to expand, and a number of studies were made. Curry, in *The Province of Expression,* made a useful analysis of the various schools of speech in the eighteenth and nineteenth centuries.[6] In 1909 Charlotte Stewart wrote a *Brief History of Elocution in the United States.*[7] Other studies followed this, which were, however, more concerned with rhetoric and public address than with oral reading.

Several studies have been made of oral interpretation in certain eras. In 1932 an article, "Interpretative Reading in Ancient Greece," was published in *The Quarterly Journal of Speech.*[8] This seems to be the first study in the field of oral interpretation to survey classical backgrounds of reading. In 1937 an article, "Interpretative Reading in Classical Rome," was also published in *The Quarterly Journal of Speech.*[9] In 1941 Mary Margaret Robb published *Oral Interpretation of Literature in American Colleges and Universities in Nineteenth Century America.*[10] This book was a milestone in the historical study of the oral interpretation of literature. In 1946 a comprehensive historical study entitled *A Study of Comparative Speech Forms of Delivery With Special Reference to Interpretative Reading* was written by William J. Farma.[11] Other significant studies of oral reading and recitation were made near the middle of the century including *The Natural School of Oral Reading in England, 1748-1828,* by Daniel Vandraegen (1949);[12] *The Mechanical School of Oral Reading in England, 1761-1821,* by Alethea Smith Mattingly (1954);[13] *Oral Interpretation in Anglo-Saxon England,* by Patricia Morford Evans (1957);[14] *A Study of Interpretative Speech in England, 1860-1940,* by Evelyn M. Sivier (1961);[15] *A Historical Study of Oral Interpretation as a Form of Professional Theatre in London, 1952-62,* by James R. L. Linn (1964);[16] and *The Development of Imagery as an Integral Element in Interpretative Reading, 1900-1960,* by Henry J. Jisha (1965).[17]

Interpretative reading and impersonation

In the twentieth century the relative merits of interpretative reading and impersonation as art forms and educational media were a major issue. Many who favored impersonation felt that it alone was worthy of the name of art, and that interpretative reading was only a poor attempt to cover up lack of skill which would eventually lead to the death of the art of expression. One of the advocates of impersonation in the reading of plays was Phidelah Rice, an able reader, who thought of impersonation as a mental and imaginative process, to which were added some vocal and bodily activity as well as costume and make-up. Leland Powers was generally recognized as one of the ablest readers in the use of impersonation. Maud May Babcock defined impersonation as literal in voice and action, employing make-up, costumes, stage setting, and furniture. This mode attempted to bring the character literally before the spectator's eyes. She opposed impersonation because it emphasized method and broke the unity and harmony of a selection by its sudden changes from one character to another. She maintained that "the good reader dominates the character, the good actor is always dominated by the character." She was one of the most active champions of interpretative reading. She defined interpretation as the rendition of any of the types of literature without benefit of special dress, stage properties, settings, make-up, or realistic use of voice and action; she regarded it as the art of suggestion directed to the imagination.

Phidelah Rice

Leland Powers

Maud May Babcock

Rollo Anson Tallcott

Another able reader and teacher, Rollo Anson Tallcott, classified the types of performance as interpretative reading or pure reading, impersonative reading, straight personation and acting. He included under interpretative reading that material which is concerned with thought and emotion, rather than character. Impersonation, he believed, may be used in plays and novels in which character types were particularly important. Personation, however, was not the medium for material in which there must be sudden changes of character, for personation was literal in the use of voice and body. Tallcott did not follow the dictum that personation was less artistic; he believed that the nature of some material is such that personation was preferable; moreover, it could serve to lead a hearer toward interpretative or pure reading.

Many other prominent educators in the first third of the century were interested in the relative values of impersonation and interpretation. Gertrude Johnson believed that the nature of the material itself was the primary determinant in the type of presentation to be used. A play **may**, but not necessarily **must**, be given impersonatively. She regarded complete impersonation to be acting and suitable only for monologues or material with one character. She agreed with Tallcott in proceeding from the literal elements of impersonation to the suggestive nature of interpretation. In all of her own public programs she used the interpretative approach.

Gertrude E. Johnson

Impersonation as an art was not generally popular in the academic world in the second quarter of the century, despite the fact that there were several excellent performers in the early part of that period.

The recording of readings from literature has fluctuated in popularity from the early days of the phonograph. Interest in such recordings increased in the second quarter of the twentieth century, although many a family had gathered around the phonograph in the earlier part of the century to hear the poems of James Whitcomb Riley, Biblical readings, and selections from drama and poetry. In 1937 Kimball Flaccus established the Phonographic Library of Contemporary Poets, consisting of various types of recordings, including readings by forty-five poets.[16] Dr. Cabell Greet and Professor Frederick Packard were pioneers in the effort to make recordings of poets reading aloud, and as early as 1932-33 Professor Packard recorded T. S. Eliot. Altogether there have been many recordings of poetry, drama, and literature, including those of the poets reading from their own works.[17]

Recordings

There was a growing interest in the application of the principles of aesthetics to reading in this century. One of the major exponents of the aesthetics approach to reading was C. C. Cunningham, whose *Literature as a Fine Art* was the first book to treat interpretation primarily from the aesthetics viewpoint.[18]

Aesthetics

Public reading and recitation were popular in the twentieth century and often attracted relatively large numbers of people. In the early part of the century reciters and readers appeared in Chautauqua programs at Chautauqua, New York, and throughout the country as they had done in the nineteenth century. These programs were a far cry from the wandering minstrels of ancient Greece, but in a sense, they served a similar purpose. By moving from place to place they brought theatre and culture to areas which otherwise must have been denied these opportunities. Some of the outstanding readers in the first half of the century included S. H. Clark, Anna Baright Curry, H. L. Southwick, Leland Powers, Rollo Anson Tallcott, Phidelah Rice, Maude Scherer, Mary Agnes Doyle, Ralph Dennis, Gertrude Johnson and Davis Edwards.

Literature and literary criticism

In the latter half of the century there has been a close alliance with the study of literature and literary criticism. The schools of criticism, based on a knowledge of the author, on what the literature is saying, on the rhetoric of literature, and on psychological implications have assumed increasing importance. There have also been studies in imagery, prosody, figures of speech, and reading as a communicative art. At the same time there seems to be increasing latitude in the methods of oral presentation.

Verse Choir

One form of presentation that was well received was Verse Choir or Choral Speaking – the group reading of poetry, prose, and certain parts of drama. This came into favor in the 1920's, due to the pioneering of this form in England by Marjorie Gullan. Particularly successful with certain types of narrative, lyric, and antiphonal poetry, it was used extensively for several decades and is still used considerably.

Radio

When the scientific world exploded into prominence with the advent of radio in the twentieth century, it gave rise to another use of reading aloud. The majority of the radio programs involving speaking were read aloud and can be classified as oral reading. The range of such oral reading was extensive, going from matter-of-fact presentations of stock, grain, and news reports to the oral reading of speeches and literature. Special techniques for reading over the radio have been taught in courses and discussed in textbooks on speech, interpretation, and radio. Of the utmost importance was good diction, for especially in the early days of radio, the microphone magnified every error in diction. Certainly the popularity of radio in the twentieth century brought a new challenge to the art of interpretation. Could the voice alone, without bodily response, and with no visual element, convey the meaning? Secondly, could literature stand on its own as a program presented over radio? The answers seemed to be in the affirmative. In numerous cases literature was presented to a musical background to strengthen both mood and attention values. It is interesting to note how literature, especially poetry, has throughout the centuries frequently associated itself with music. While some specific programs of poetry lasted for years on radio, they gradually began to disappear. However, incidental programs of literature, or readings from literature as a part of a program, have been popular throughout radio history, and poetry representing the best poets as well as the versifiers was presented.

Television

With the advent of television, another adjustment had to be made; once more the performers were seen as well as heard. If one had learned his trade as a radio reader or announcer, he had to learn to make a favorable visual appearance just as had performers before the advent of radio. In one respect he had the same problems that faced many radio artists; usually, unless he was on a major national program, he had no live audience before him. This meant that he had to sense his timing for the unseen viewers. In ancient Greece the actor's face was covered with a mask, and his facial expression was of no importance. He was far removed from his audience, and large gestures were necessary. Today's television artist, on the other hand, has the opposite problem; frequently nothing but his face is shown on the screen. His viewer is within a few feet of his visage, and his facial expression must reflect exactly the thought he is trying to convey.

Readers' Theatre

Another term, Readers' Theatre, evolved in the twentieth century, although this form of presentation had been used for a long time. In the Middle Ages the nun, Hroswitha, wrote plays which were presumably read by a group. Again, in the eighteenth century this method of presentation was used. In the first part of the twentieth century this form of presentation was referred to as a library reading; used frequently by club groups, it was very successful for the presentation of literature. When Sir Cedric Hardwicke, Agnes Moorehead, Charles Laughton, and Charles Boyer presented *Don Juan in Hell* in 1951, it brought this form into the realm of professional theatre where it was given enthusiastic acclaim. This was followed by other professional productions, and the term Readers' Theatre gradually came into general use. This form of expression is still used extensively in colleges and universities where it is very popular. There has been great latitude in the definition and in the actual techniques used. Some prefer the use of costumes; others object to such a literal element because it lessens the imaginative activity that should be demanded of the spectator. Some maintain that the entire production, including the "interaction" of the characters, be projected into the realm of the audience, while others do not demand this projection. Physical placements and levels for the various readers are often used. The fluidity of this form of presentation is often regarded as a major asset. Another form which has aroused considerable interest is Chamber Theatre.

Chamber Theatre

It is, of course, impossible to prophesy the nature, practice, and trends in the oral interpretation of literature in future centuries. The fact, however, that it has survived, and thrived, in some form or other for three thousand years gives considerable hope for it in the next comparable space of time.

References

1. Loren LaMont Okey, *A Descriptive Biographical Study of Thomas Clarkson Trueblood* (Unpublished Ph.D. Dissertation, The University of Michigan, 1951), pp. 64-65.

2. Andrew Thomas Weaver, "Experimental Studies in Vocal Expression," *The Quarterly Journal of Speech Education* Vol. 10. No. 3. June, 1924, p. 119.

3. William John Miller, "Motor Control and Ability in Interpretation," *The Quarterly Journal of Speech Education,* Vol. 10, No. 3. June, 1924, p. 119.

4. Elsie Viola Haney, *Incipient Motor Responses in the Oral Interpretation of Literature* (Master's Thesis, Northwestern University, 1927).

5. E. M. Cogswell, *A Description and Application of the Significant Contribution of Psychology to the Problems of Interpretative Reading* (Master's Thesis, University of Southern California, 1931).

6. S. S. Curry, *The Province of Expression* (Boston: Expression Co.), 19th ed., pp. 293-360.

7. Charlotte Stewart, *Brief History of Elocution in the United States* (Master's Thesis, University of Utah, 1909).

8. Eugene Bahn, "Interpretative Reading in Ancient Greece," *Quarterly Journal of Speech,* Vol. 18. No. 3. June, 1932, p. 432.

9. Eugene Bahn, "Interpretative Reading in Classical Rome," *Quarterly Journal of Speech,* Vol. 23. No. 2. April, 1937, p. 202.

10. Mary Margaret Robb, *Oral Interpretation of Literature in American Colleges and Universities* (New York: H. W. Wilson Co., 1941).

11. William J. Farma, *A Study in Comparative Speech Forms of Delivery with Special Reference to Interpretative Reading* (Unpublished Ph.D. Dissertation, University of Wisconsin, 1946).

12. Daniel Vandraegen, *The Natural School of Oral Reading in England, 1748-1828* (Unpublished Ph.D. Dissertation, Northwestern University, 1949).

13. Alethea Smith Mattingly, *The Mechanical School of Oral Reading in England, 1761-1821* (Unpublished Ph.D. Dissertation, Northwestern University, 1954).

14. Patricia M. Evans, *Oral Interpretation in Anglo-Saxon England* (Unpublished Ph.D. Dissertation, Northwestern University, 1957).

15. Evelyn M. Sivier, *A Study of Interpretative Speech in England, 1860-1940* (Unpublished Ph.D. Dissertation, Wayne State University, 1961).

16. James R. L. Linn, *A Historical Study of Oral Interpretation As a Form of Professional Theatre in London, 1951-62* (Unpublished Ph.D. Dissertation, University of Southern California, 1964).

17. Henry J. Jisha, *The Development of Imagery As an Integral Element in Interpretative Reading, 1900-1969* (Unpublished Ph.D. Dissertation, Wayne State University, 1965).

18. Kimball Flaccus, "An Adventure in Poetry," *Quarterly Journal of Speech,* Vol. 28, October, 1942, p. 315.

19. Henry W. Wells, "Literature and the Phonograph," *Quarterly Journal of Speech,* Vol. 29, February, 1943, p. 68.

20. C. C. Cunningham, *Literature As a Fine Art* (New York: Thomas Nelson and Sons, 1941).

INDEX